A PROMISE KEPT

A PROMISE KEPT

The Muscogee (Creek) Nation and *McGirt v. Oklahoma*

Robert J. Miller and Robbie Ethridge

University of Oklahoma Press : Norman

Publication of this book is made possible through the generosity of Edith Kinney Gaylord.

Library of Congress Cataloging-in-Publication Data

Names: Miller, Robert J. (Professor of law), author. | Ethridge, Robbie Franklyn, 1955– author.
Title: A promise kept : the Muscogee (Creek) Nation and McGirt v. Oklahoma / Robert J. Miller and Robbie Ethridge.
Description: Norman : University of Oklahoma Press, [2023] | Includes bibliographical references and index. | Summary: "Examines the *McGirt v. Oklahoma* case from historical and legal perspectives, placing the case within the historical context from which it derived, the legal context that took the case to the Supreme Court, and the legal and political implications of the decision"— Provided by publisher.
Identifiers: LCCN 2022023743 | ISBN 978-0-8061-9171-3 (hardcover) | ISBN 978-0-8061-9172-0 (paperback)
Subjects: LCSH: Land tenure—Law and legislation—Muscogee (Creek) Nation. | Creek Indians—Land tenure. | Creek Indians—Government relations. | Indian reservations—Law and legislation. | Muscogee (Creek) Nation—History.
Classification: LCC E99.C9 M55 2023 | DDC 975.004/97385—dc23/ eng/20220701
LC record available at https://lccn.loc.gov/2022023743

The paper in this book meets the guidelines for permanence and durability of the Committee on Production Guidelines for Book Longevity of the Council on Library Resources, Inc. ∞

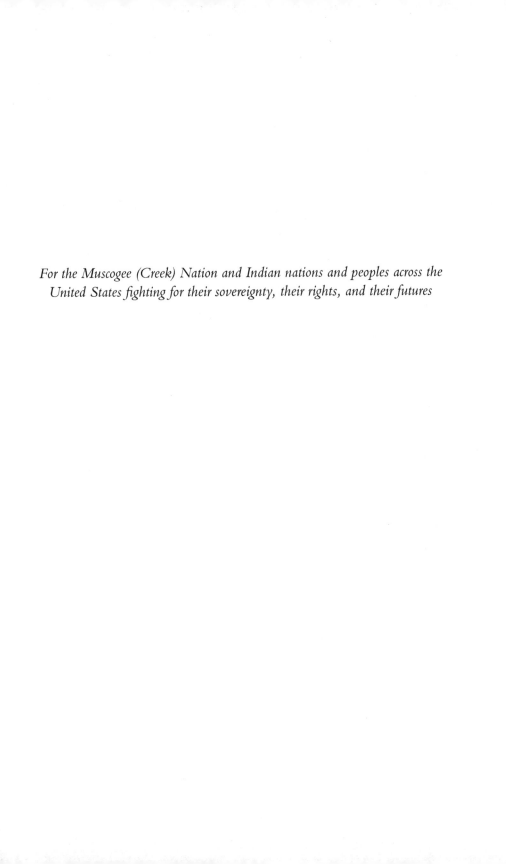

For the Muscogee (Creek) Nation and Indian nations and peoples across the United States fighting for their sovereignty, their rights, and their futures

CONTENTS

MAPS

ACKNOWLEDGMENTS

Bob Miller: On July 9, 2020, my wife, Molly Smith, woke me and said, "I think the tribe won that case [*McGirt*]." I was quite surprised and immediately began reading, analyzing, and writing about the case. Since then, as Molly says, "It's been all *McGirt*, all the time." Thank you, Molly, for your support and love.

Robbie Ethridge: As always, I thank my husband, Denton Marcotte, for his interest, support, love, and kindness. Unbeknownst to Bob, when he asked me to collaborate on this project, he also threw me a lifeline, and I thank him, my colleagues Maureen Meyers, Tony Boudreaux, and Jay Johnson, and my sister, Nonie Dunn, for helping me to steer through rough waters.

We both thank Alessandra Tamulevich for her guidance in getting this book published—from conception to publication, she has been an integral part of the process. Finally, we thank the Muscogee (Creek) Nation for the strength and leadership it has demonstrated in the long years of litigation that were the *McGirt* case.

INTRODUCTION

"On the far end of the trail of tears was a promise." On July 9, 2020, Justice Neil Gorsuch of the United States Supreme Court wrote these words about the Muscogee (Creek) Nation (MCN) and its reservation, which is located in modern-day Oklahoma. On that day, the Court decided *McGirt v. Oklahoma* by a 5 to 4 vote and held that the constitutionally guaranteed treaty promises the United States made to the MCN from 1832 to 1866 were still binding. Consequently, the reservation that was guaranteed to the MCN by those treaties still exists today.[1]

Before the *McGirt* case was decided, the amount of land over which the MCN government exercised sovereignty and governing powers within the state of Oklahoma was about 135,000 acres. Following the Court's ruling in *McGirt* that the MCN Reservation still exists, the area over which the MCN has sovereignty is once again the full 3.25 million acres that were guaranteed to the nation in its 1866 treaty. Oklahoma and Oklahomans will now have to deal with the issues arising from the MCN exercising its jurisdiction and governance over this vastly expanded area. Clearly, the *McGirt* case has enormous ramifications for the MCN, Oklahoma, and the United States, and for other Indian nations and states across the country.[2]

Moreover, in the months following *McGirt*, multiple Oklahoma state courts, applying the same analysis and precedent of that case, held that four other large Indian reservations and three smaller Indian reservations still exist in eastern Oklahoma. Now, approximately 43 percent of Oklahoma, up to nineteen million acres of land in the eastern part of the state, is "Indian Country" under federal law, and 1.8 million Oklahomans, about 90 percent of whom are non-Indians, have discovered that they live on reservations. The *McGirt* decision itself held that almost one million Oklahomans, including four hundred thousand people in Tulsa, live on the MCN Reservation. The subsequent re-recognition of the Cherokee Nation Reservation means that Tulsa, the second-largest city in Oklahoma, is now located entirely in Indian Country, on either the MCN Reservation or the Cherokee Reservation.[3] These court cases have already led to significant changes in the daily life and law of the state and have created major issues and questions about day-to-day life and governmental sovereignty and jurisdiction over these areas and Oklahomans. In fact, *McGirt* has created fear and anxiety for the government of Oklahoma and for some citizens in that state. Governor Kevin Stitt (who is Cherokee) stated on May 17, 2021, "I don't think there's ever been a bigger issue [for Oklahoma]."[4]

Despite its new status, the Oklahoma case is not unique. Other states also have large areas of Indian Country within their borders, and Indian nations and state governments have cooperated for decades. For example, 27 percent of the landmass of Arizona is within a reservation and is thus Indian Country, and Indian nations own 50 percent of the water in that arid state. The twenty-two Indian nations in Arizona have litigated issues with the state in past decades, and today these governments look to have acclimated to this reality: through respectful relationships and negotiations, they have entered into agreements and handled many issues cooperatively. Hopefully, once Oklahoma and the Indian nations in that state adjust to the changes *McGirt* produces, the initial fears raised by Governor Stitt and others will be addressed and ameliorated. In fact, Oklahoma and the thirty-nine Indian nations located within it have for decades worked out governance, taxation, and other issues via negotiations and by entering into more than 650 agreements called compacts.[5]

But *McGirt* and the state cases in Oklahoma that have followed, along with the fact that 43 percent of the state is now Indian Country, raise the possibility of significant, wide-ranging immediate and long-term impacts on Oklahoma and Indian nations. These changes will present obstacles, challenges, and opportunities for all these governments and their citizens and will raise issues that will have to be resolved by either litigation or negotiation. *McGirt* was specifically about state or federal criminal authority over an Indian who had committed a crime on a reservation. Oklahoma argued vigorously to the Supreme Court, and has argued ever since, that the case is crucial because it could lead to thousands of Indian inmates being released from state prisons. The state has continued to be concerned about the civil and tax law implications of *McGirt* as well. In fact, the Oklahoma Tax Commission released a report two months after the case was decided in which it estimated that the state would lose $72.7 million in income tax revenues each year, face an additional $218 million in state income tax refund claims, and see an annual reduction of $132 million in state sales and use taxes. The outcome for the state's finances from *McGirt* is potentially so serious that the credit rating organization Standard & Poor felt it necessary to announce right after the ruling that it would not immediately lower the state and county governments' credit ratings due to the case.[6]

Besides these immediate and critical impacts on the state's criminal jurisdiction and the reduction of state and local tax revenues, the full impact of *McGirt* on Oklahoma, the Indian nations, and all their citizens will play out over the next several decades and beyond. In the chapters to come, we examine the history and law in regard to the Muscogee (Creek) Nation and its reservation, the Indian Territory, Oklahoma, and the *McGirt* decision, as well as the consequences that have already ensued and those that will likely follow.

We have divided the book into two parts. Part 1, "A Brief History of the Muscogee (Creek) Nation," offers an overview of the MCN from its seventeenth-century origins as a political entity into the twenty-first century, with a focus on treaties, legislative acts, and court rulings that are pertinent to the *McGirt* case. Chapter 1 lays out the origins and early history of the Creek Confederacy, as it was known at the time, and its relationships with first the British and then the U.S. government. Chapter 2 takes the reader through the removal of the Creeks from the American South to the Indian Territory, which is now the eastern part of Oklahoma. Chapter 3 explores the history of the MCN Reservation in the Indian Territory. Chapter 4 delves into the history surrounding

Oklahoma's and Oklahomans' encroachments on the MCN, its reservation, and the Creek people, and the presumed disappearance of the MCN Reservation.

Part 2, "The *McGirt* Case," focuses exclusively on *McGirt v. Oklahoma* and the Supreme Court's ruling in the case. Chapter 5 examines the twentieth- and twenty-first-century case law that preceded and set the legal context for the Court's decision. Chapter 6 then closely analyzes the case, which agreed that the MCN Reservation continues to exist today. Chapter 7 presents a detailed analysis of the legal precedents that control the changes and consequences that are taking place on the MCN Reservation and within the other newly re-recognized Indian reservations. We also attempt to foretell some of the unknowns—the issues, yet to be defined, that will control and impact the future of these reservations. We conclude with our thoughts and hopes about what the future decades hold for the MCN, other Indian nations, Oklahoma and the Indian and non-Indian peoples within it, and the United States after *McGirt*.

Fundamental to the *McGirt* case are the definitions of Indian reservations and Indian Country. The tangled history of Native and colonizer relationships, however, makes those definitions not so clear. European countries that attempted to colonize North America were interested in building empires by acquiring land and resources and subjugating Native peoples. After the founding of the United States, Americans embraced the same goals for the new nation. In fact, in a letter dated September 7, 1783, General George Washington reiterated these goals and laid out many of the principles that became federal Indian policy for nearly two hundred years.[7]

Washington was writing in response to a congressional committee request for his opinion on what sort of relationship the new United States should forge with the Indian nations. Washington had eyed Indian territories since he was a young man, and he, along with most Americans, understood that the acquisition of Indian lands would form the national territorial base of the new United States. He was also concerned about waging costly wars with Indians for acquiring their lands. With these things in mind, Washington suggested that the U.S. Congress acquire Indian lands by means of legal purchases through treaties.

To delineate the boundaries between Native landholdings and those of the states, Washington suggested that Congress draw a boundary line between the new American states and Indian Country, but he noted that "care should be taken neither to yield nor to grasp at too much." He also encouraged the United States to engage in trade with Indian peoples to "fix them strongly in our Interest." In his words,

> policy and oeconomy [sic] point very strongly to the expediency of being upon good terms with the Indians, and the propriety of purchasing their Lands in preference to attempting to drive them by force of arms out of their country; which as we have already experienced is like driving the Wild Beasts of the Forest . . . ; when the gradual extension of our Settlements will as certainly cause the Savage as the Wolf to retire; both being beasts of prey tho' they differ in shape. In a word there is nothing to be obtained by an Indian War but the Soil they live on and this can be had by purchase at less expence [sic], and without that bloodshed.[8]

The lethal nature of this advice is obvious. First, Washington expressly compared human Indians to animals: "the Savage as the Wolf . . . both being beasts of prey tho' they differ in shape." Second, he voiced two common opinions among Americans at the time—that Native peoples were like beasts of the wild and that the United States would spread across the continent and acquire all Native lands. Not surprisingly, as we will see, the U.S. from its inception as a nation adopted Indian policies expressly designed to achieve land acquisitions. The policies initially followed Washington's advice for a treaty system dedicated to peaceful land purchases, but when Native peoples resisted and the treaty system faltered, federal policies became more coercive, harsh, and violent.[9]

In 1849, federal Indian policy for lands west of the Mississippi ostensibly moved away from treaties, but in practice, treaties were formulated until 1871 and even thereafter. Called "treaty substitutes," these were negotiated agreements between the United States and Indian nations, enacted by the U.S. Congress as congressional laws. The purpose of many of these congressional laws was to establish a reservation system. The reservation era was relatively short-lived, from 1849 to 1887, but it came to define the land claims of many Native nations. The United

States has long made other federal "reservations" of lands that are unrelated to Indian law. In those situations, the federal government removes a specific plot of land from the "public domain"—the public lands owned by the U.S. for the benefit of American citizens—and reserves that plot as a "federal reservation" for various purposes like military bases and national parks and forests. These lands remain publicly owned in a sense, but they have been reserved or set aside for a specific purpose, and the American public has fewer rights in these reserved areas than they might have in the federal lands of the "public domain."

Indian reservations are somewhat similar, but they differ in significant ways from the federal reservations just mentioned. One difference is that the tribal nation, not the federal government, was "reserving" the specific plot of land from their tribal domain. In other words, under the reservation system, the federal government allowed a tribe to reserve a small area of land for its "reservation" out of a much larger landmass that the tribe already owned and governed and whose ownership may or may not have been recognized by the federal government. The Indian nation would then, usually under some compulsion, agree to sell the remaining territory to the United States through treaties. The tribe retained the reserved plots for their homes, towns, and livelihoods; these reserves became known as "reservations," and the lands were held in common by the indigenous nation and not as individual private properties. In a 1905 landmark case, the U.S. Supreme Court, interpreting tribal treaty fishing rights in the Pacific Northwest, recognized that the lands called reservations, and the rights defined in those treaties, were not gifts from the United States because they were "not a grant of rights to the Indians, but a grant of rights from them—a reservation of those granted." Consequently, in those situations, it was the Indian nation and the Native peoples who reserved specific rights and reservations for themselves out of a greater pool of rights and lands they had previously owned.[10]

In other situations, including that of the MCN, "reservations" of land are different. For one, the removed tribes such as the MCN were not given an opportunity to reserve plots of their original homelands. Rather, the United States coerced them into signing removal treaties, wherein the tribes agreed to sell all of their homelands and move to lands across the Mississippi River that the U.S. had previously claimed and had "reserved" for the removed tribes (the so-called Indian Territory). These removal reserves, then, can be properly characterized as having been established by the U.S. with the agreement of the removed Indian nations. So, while one might be technically correct to say that the United States did the "reserving," the Creek Nation and other removed tribes had agreed by treaty to sell their lands in the East to the U.S., and to remove and accept lands in modern-day Oklahoma and elsewhere.

The term "Indian Country" includes all Indian reservations, and it is within these areas that tribal governments primarily exercise their sovereignty, jurisdiction, governance, and authority. State governments and state jurisdiction are largely excluded from Indian Country. Consequently, the definition and existence of Indian reservations are crucial to tribal sovereignty, jurisdiction, and governance. The sovereignty and governmental powers of Indian nations are at their strongest in Indian Country, and state sovereignty and jurisdiction are at their weakest. In addition, federal power, sovereignty, and jurisdiction are also increased when land, peoples, and events are within Indian Country, because this increases the application of various federal laws in this area, and it is where the majority of federal laws regarding Indian affairs apply. Today, there are over 330 Indian reservations in the lower forty-eight states.

In 1948, Congress used a variety of U.S. Supreme Court cases to draft a statute, 18 United States Code, section 1151 (18 U.S.C. § 1151), to specifically define "Indian Country" for purposes of federal criminal laws. The Court has applied this same definition to civil law issues.[11] Under section 1151, "Indian Country" includes (a) all lands within reservation borders even if some of it is owned in fee simple title by non-Indians and even if it includes, for example, easements or rights-of-way for highways, railroad lines, pipelines, and telephone lines; (b) dependent Indian communities (a complex subject that we need not address); and (c) all Indian allotments when the land is still held in trust, that is, when the legal owner is the United States and the land is held in trust for an Indian nation or an individual Indian. It is noteworthy that until the *McGirt* case was decided, most people assumed there were no reservations in Oklahoma and that the only "Indian Country" in the state consisted of small allotments of land that were still owned by Indian nations or individual Indians and held in trust by the United States. Now that the Supreme

Court and several state courts have re-recognized five large reservations and, to date, at least three smaller ones in eastern Oklahoma, there is a lot more "Indian Country" in the state under 18 U.S.C. § 1151(a).

The dissent from the *McGirt* ruling argues that the MCN Reservation was disestablished through the General Allotment Act of 1887. We devote much of chapter 3 to the Allotment Act. In sum, the act was intended to fragment the tribally owned land base by moving all Native lands from communal ownership to individual private ownership. It retained the sole right of the U.S. Congress to treat with tribal nations, and it also was explicit that part of the allotment agenda was to dismantle tribal governments and to bring the tribes wholly under federal jurisdiction. When allotment ended in 1934, many Indians in Oklahoma Indian Country had lost their lands in unethical land swindles, which resulted in a checkerboard pattern of ownership by Indians and non-Indians. However, one thing is clear: although the intention of allotment was to limit tribal and Indian ownership of the lands within reservations, it did not, in fact, disestablish the boundaries of the MCN Reservation. Lands owned by Creek people, as well as Creek township lands and other public Creek lands, were still within the MCN Reservation. That reservation can only be disestablished through an act of Congress.

The United States Supreme Court decides major cases impacting American law and life every year. Some decisions reverberate for decades, like the abortion case of *Roe v. Wade* in 1973 and the school desegregation case of *Brown v. Board of Education* in 1954. The Court also decides several Indian law cases every year. Some of these decisions might alter federal Indian law or have a major impact on a particular Indian nation. But sometimes an Indian law case drops like a bombshell and creates impacts that take decades to reveal themselves and to be dealt with. *McGirt v. Oklahoma* is that kind of case. On July 9, 2020, the Muscogee (Creek) Nation Reservation was re-recognized as encompassing 3.25 million acres in eastern Oklahoma. This entire area is "Indian Country" under 18 U.S.C. § 1151(a). In addition, Oklahoma state courts subsequently re-recognized four other reservations, for the Cherokee, Seminole, Choctaw, and Chickasaw nations, and three smaller reservations. Oklahoma now has approximately nineteen million acres of re-recognized Indian

Country in the eastern part of the state, and the renewal of tribal and federal jurisdiction and sovereignty over those enormous areas. *McGirt* poses crucial challenges for Oklahoma, the Indian nations, and the United States. These governments will have to address and settle a multitude of issues in future negotiations, litigations, and perhaps legislative efforts in tribal, state, and federal legislatures. There is no question that *McGirt* has already impacted, and will continue to impact, daily life and governance in Oklahoma for all peoples and all governments, and for decades to come.

Part I

History of the Muscogee (Creek) Nation

1

THE ORIGINS AND EARLY HISTORY OF THE MUSCOGEE (CREEK) NATION

Although *McGirt v. Oklahoma* explicitly involves contemporary Creek Indians in the present-day state of Oklahoma, to fully understand the import and impact of the case, and the promise made and kept, one must begin the story with the origins and consolidation of the Muscogee (Creek) Nation (MCN) in the sixteenth, seventeenth, and eighteenth centuries. The MCN originated in the present-day states of Alabama and Georgia when the precolonial Native South was fundamentally transformed during the crucible of contact between Natives and Europeans. Scholars have identified some of the forces for this transformation—things such as military losses and cultural exchanges with early explorers and Spanish colonizers in present-day Florida, the introduction of Old World diseases, and the consequences of political and economic incorporation into the modern world economy through a trade in Indian slaves, animal skins, and guns.

Across the Native South, people had myriad responses to these historical forces, from violence and resistance to accommodation and negotiation. Natives' lives changed from living in a purely Indian world to living in a multicultural, multiracial, globally situated colonial world. A region-wide political restructuring of the Native South ensued, and the precolonial Native polities of the American South transformed into the large Indian nations of the eighteenth and nineteenth centuries—the Creeks, Cherokees, Chickasaws, Choctaws, Catawbas, and others. Scholars call these early emergent tribal nations "coalescent soci-eties," so named because they were all, to varying degrees, coalescences of people from various fallen precolonial polities of various languages and kin groups, from multiple regions, and so on. The MCN, known as the Creek Confederacy in the eighteenth and nineteenth centuries, was one such coalescent society, and its origins lie in the deep history of the Native presence in North America.[1]

This is not to say that Creek history unfolded only when Europeans arrived on the scene. In fact, North American Indian life has undergone many transformations since the initial peopling of America some fif-teen thousand or more years ago, and contact with Europeans was but one of many historic events that initiated profound changes in Native life. Discussions of Indian origins usually begin with Native origin tales. The Muscogean origin narratives tell of the original Muscogeans emerg-ing from an opening in the earth and a subsequent migration from the west to the east. The point of departure is vague in the narratives—an unnamed place, although usually located west of the Mississippi River. The group was forced to flee when the earth, for unspecified reasons, grew angry with them and began swallowing their children. Thus began their epic journey to find a new home.[2]

Although there are several variations of the journey, the basics are that the original group traveled east for years, enduring many hardships and difficulties, searching for good lands upon which to settle. The narratives also point to the coalescence of the Creek Confederacy. Along the way, the original group met many other groups, most notably the Alabamas, Abihkas, and Tuckabatchees, all of whom joined the migration. Deep into their journey, the group discovered a white path, and they followed it to the Coosa, Tallapoosa, and Chattahoochee rivers in present-day Alabama and Georgia. Here they found a hospitable and rich environ-ment. They built their communities along these rivers, prospered, and continued to admit various peoples from throughout the Native South, including the Coushattas, Yuchis, and Shawnees.[3]

What does the ethnohistory and archaeology reveal about the ori-gins of the Muscogee (Creek) Nation? This narrative, too, begins in the ancient past, during the Ice Age, and involves a west-to-east migration when peoples from present-day Siberia, northern China, and northern

Japan traversed the Bering Strait or traveled down the northwestern coastline to settle in the Americas. Archaeologists call this the Paleo Period, and it lasted from about twelve thousand years (or longer) ago to about ten thousand years ago. At the time, the climate in the American South was much cooler than it is today. The vegetation of the American South also looked quite different—instead of pine, oak, and hickory, the forest cover was more like that of modern-day New England, with broadleaf trees such as maples, birches, oaks, and evergreens. The animals, too, were different. Although some species resembling modern-day deer, rabbits, bears, and wild cats were around, undoubtedly the royalty of the animal kingdom during the Ice Age were the magnificent mammals such as the mammoths and mastodons and other so-called "megafauna." Paleo peoples did not build permanent towns; rather, they lived in small groups, connected by kinship and marriage, with an informal egalitarian political structure, and they made seasonal migrations from camp to camp. They also hunted the megafauna. We know this because we find their large stone spear points designed to bring down such large animals. These are known as Clovis and Folsom points, but only a handful have been found in central Alabama and western Georgia, which suggests either a low population density at the time or sparse hunting of megafauna, or both. Paleo people in the American South probably relied more on smaller game, fish, shellfish, and any number of plant resources, all of which would have been quite abundant.[4]

About ten thousand years ago, the Ice Age began to end, and with its closing the vegetative and animal regimes also changed, to more closely resemble those of today. The megafauna became extinct, and people settled into localized, regional ways of life. This is known as the Archaic Period, and it was a highly successful way of life that lasted seven thousand years. Like their Paleo ancestors, Archaic people continued to hunt and gather wild foods and other resources. They also invented new tools for exploiting the new resources. In addition to making stone tools through a process of chipping, they began grinding stone into a variety of shapes, such as celts, axes, weights for fishing nets, pipes, bowls, beads, and pendants. Many lived in small egalitarian bands, migrating seasonally from camp to camp, but people living along the rivers and coast built permanent towns where they could exploit the plentiful year-round resources from the rivers and sea. In fact, along the Gulf Coast, people also adopted a new technology coming from the Atlantic coast—ceramic pottery, which revolutionized both cooking and storage.[5]

During the latter part of the Archaic, around 3,700 years ago, hunters and gatherers built the great center that is known today as Poverty Point in present-day Louisiana and that was recently designated a UNESCO World Heritage Site. Here Archaic peoples constructed some of the first earthworks in the American South. The mounds at Poverty Point are remarkable, but so are the artifacts recovered from the site. Poverty Point artisans fashioned fine-grade stones and minerals imported from as far away as the Great Lakes and Atlantic coast into pipes, beads, figurines, and plummets, among other things. These items then made their way north, south, east, and west, along wide-ranging trade routes connecting Archaic peoples across a vast space. The number of artifacts, the long-distance trade network, and the earthen mounds indicate that Poverty Point was the social, trade, and perhaps religious hub of the Archaic world.[6]

Toward the end of the Archaic Period, around three thousand years ago, people began to supplement their wild foodstuffs by domesticating wild plants such as squashes, starchy seed plants such as sunflowers, and leafy greens such as chenopodium. They also grew gourds for containers. About six hundred years later, they added corn and beans from Mesoamerica to their diet to form the noted "Three Sisters" of Indian agriculture—corn, beans, and squash. This era is known as the Woodland Period, and it lasted from about three thousand to one thousand years ago. Although they still hunted and gathered wild plants, people throughout the Native South became predominantly farmers. They had no domesticated animals, save the dog, and meat proteins still came from wild game such as turkey, deer, fish, and shellfish. In order to tend to their crops, people established permanent settlements along river bottoms to take advantage of the good agricultural soils. However, there was little political integration of these towns. Although people from different towns knew of and interacted with each other, the archaeological evidence indicates that the farming towns remained politically independent. In addition, their trade became localized, and the long-distance trade networks of the Archaic Period fell into disuse.[7]

People also began to bury some of their dead in conical earthen mounds with elaborate funerary objects, or grave goods. This development originated in the Ohio River Valley with what is known as the Hopewell Tradition. Communities singled out particularly prominent men and women for special attention after death, interring them in carefully built burial mounds. Placed with them for use in the afterlife were finely crafted ritual and everyday objects such as mica and copper cutouts, ceramic wares, engraved shells, projectile points, and ground-stone tools. The presence of these distinctive funeral practices for a select few indicates that the egalitarian social organization of the earlier periods was changing: apparently some people now rose as political and religious leaders who gained enough status and influence to warrant special treatment at death. It also represents a new way of thinking about power and influence.[8]

Around 500 C.E. to 1000 C.E., the archaeological record reveals a sharp decline in the construction of Woodland burial mounds. At the same time, there was a disruption of any long-distance trade. Archaeologists have traditionally viewed the late Woodland as a time of cultural decline. Woodland settlements at this time, with the exception of sites along the Florida Gulf Coast, tended to be small in comparison to earlier Woodland communities, and few outstanding works of art can be attributed to this time period. Today, however, archaeologists view the late Woodland as a very dynamic period. New varieties of maize, beans, and squash gained economic importance, and although settlement size was small, there was a marked increase in the number of Woodland sites, indicating a population increase. Additionally, people invented the bow and arrow and began to make smaller, triangular stone projectile points for their arrows—true "arrowheads." Bow-and-arrow technology rapidly swept across the eastern woodlands, increasing hunting efficiency but also as an effective tool of warfare. In fact, during the latter part of the Woodland Period, warfare increased in intensity and frequency. Woodland people at this time also developed new mound traditions and built civic-ceremonial capitals, such as the site known today as Kolomoki, in present-day southern Georgia. These capitals are found in the Gulf coastal plain, along the Gulf Coast, and in the Lower Mississippi Valley, and most are multi-mound complexes containing both platform and burial mounds arranged around plazas and including residential populations. These factors offer a view of the last five hundred years of the Woodland Period as an expansive period, and not one of cultural atrophy.[9]

The rise of ranked societies followed the Woodland Period, in an era that archaeologists call the Mississippi Period. It lasted for almost seven hundred years, from 1000 c.e. to about 1700 c.e. The Mississippian way of life emerged when Woodland peoples living along the middle Mississippi River underwent a dramatic transformation: they built one of the largest cities in the world for its time, the remains of which are today known as Cahokia. The builders of Cahokia adopted a new religious and world order that mandated a restructuring of their political, social, and religious lives as well as their built environments. Over the next hundred or so years, this new way of life spread throughout the American South.[10]

During the Mississippi Period, the Native South was composed of polities that archaeologists call "chiefdoms." With the exception of Cahokia, most Mississippian chiefdoms were so-called "simple chiefdoms," characterized by a two-tiered social ranking of hereditary elites and commoners, a civic and religious capital where the elite lineages lived, and five to ten affiliated farming towns in close proximity up and down a river valley. The capital towns often had one or more flat-topped, pyramidal earthen mounds situated around a large open plaza. The *mico* (chief or chieftainess) and his or her family lived atop the largest mound in the capital, and lesser people of the chiefly lineages lived on the lesser mounds. Elites were buried in the mounds; after a burial, people covered the mound with a new layer, or mantle, indicating the ascendency of a new leader. Commoners lived in houses encircling the mounds and plazas in the capital and in the farming towns and were required to pay tribute to the elites from the surpluses of their mixed economy of hunting, gathering, fishing, trading, and corn agriculture.[11]

The ritual and political gear of the Mississippian people constitutes some of the most important precolonial artwork in America. The chiefly elite, who were also the religious authorities, sponsored traders who maintained far-flung networks through which they exchanged exotic goods such as copper, shell, mica, and high-grade stones like flint. Elite-sponsored artisans then fashioned these materials into a brilliant array of ceremonial and religious items, including headdresses, beads, cups, masks, statues, ceramic wares, ceremonial weaponry, necklaces and earrings, and figurines. Chiefs distributed these prestige items to other elites to garner goodwill, alliances, loyalty, and religious favors. Sumptuary rules prevented the hoi polloi from acquiring such items.[12]

Chiefdoms showed much variability through space and time, and polities ranged from the size and scope of the metropolis Cahokia near present-day St. Louis to small, one-mound simple chiefdoms, and from highly centralized to decentralized. In some cases, ambitious leaders of a chiefdom expanded their domain into what archaeologists call complex and paramount chiefdoms, incorporating several chiefdoms into a single large polity. The life-span of a chiefdom, no matter the size (thus even Cahokia), was around two hundred years, and over the seven-hundred-year history of the Mississippian way of life, many simple, complex, and paramount chiefdoms rose and fell.[13]

Early Spanish explorers encountered the Mississippian world as it existed in the mid-sixteenth century (see map 1). The Hernando de Soto expedition, which traversed much of the American South, spent considerable time in what would later become the heart of Creek country in present-day central Alabama. De Soto encountered dozens of chiefdoms, and most of them were relatively small. However, he also journeyed through several complex and paramount chiefdoms throughout the Native South. When de Soto's army traveled through present-day Alabama, they passed through the paramount chiefdoms of Coosa and Tascalusa as well as the simple chiefdom of Apafalaya. The people of these chiefdoms were some of the ancestors of the Muscogee (Creek) people.

The interactions between the de Soto expedition and the people of present-day Alabama set the wheels in motion for the coalescence of what would become the Muscogee (Creek) Nation. The early eighteenth-century Creek Confederacy was composed of four provinces—Alabama, Abihka, Tallapoosa, and Apalachicola, all of which formed sometime in the seventeenth century. Archaeological evidence shows that Abihka, situated on the upper Coosa River, formed out of the collapse of the paramount chiefdom of Coosa. At the time of the de Soto *entrada*, Coosa was a large paramount chiefdom that spanned about three hundred miles, from eastern Tennessee into central Alabama. It was a multilingual polity

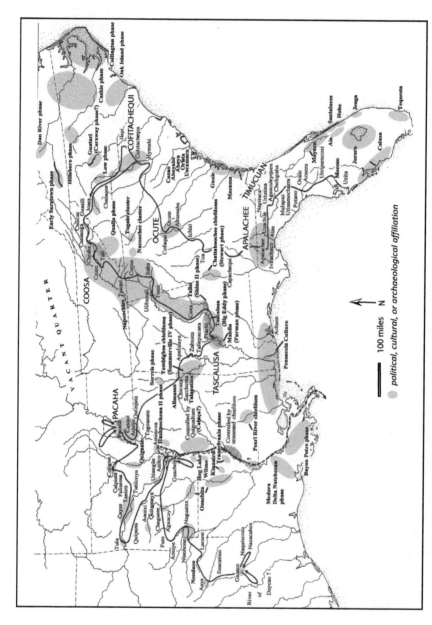

Map 1. The Mississippian world, ca. 1540, showing the route of Hernando de Soto. Map by Robbie Ethridge.

that encompassed the smaller chiefdoms of Coosa (which was the capital of the paramount chiefdom), Tasqui, Itaba, Ulibahali, Napoochie, Talisi, Coste, and Chiaha.[14]

De Soto passed through the entire paramountcy of Coosa in 1540, and Spanish eyewitnesses described it as an expansive, fertile province, with numerous large towns, impressive capital towns, and abundant agricultural fields stretching from town to town. Twenty years later, when a contingent from the Tristán de Luna y Arellano expedition surveyed Coosa, they were disappointed to find only small towns, many abandoned agricultural fields, and a much smaller population. Archaeological research indicates that the chiefdoms that formed Coosa were abandoned by the late sixteenth century. The people of Ulibahali, Coosa, and Itaba began a one-hundred-year sojourn down the Coosa River valley, eventually settling near present-day Gadsden, Alabama. There they congregated into three towns, which would later be collectively known as the province of Abihka (see map 2). The fate of the people in the other chiefdoms of Coosa is less certain, but we do know that as Coosa went into decline, some migrated to the Alabama River, some to the Chattahoochee River, some to the Appalachians, and some perhaps as far as northern Florida.[15]

The Alabama province of the Creek Confederacy formed on the upper Alabama River, just south of its confluence with the Coosa and Tallapoosa rivers (see map 2). At the time of de Soto, this region was home to the chiefdom of Tascalusa, ruled by a chief of the same name (see map 1). By all contemporary accounts, Chief Tascalusa was a powerful, authoritative leader, and he most likely ruled over his own paramountcy, which consisted of the chiefdoms Tascalusa, Piachi, and Mabila. He orchestrated a surprise attack against de Soto at a town in the Mabila chiefdom. The Battle of Mabila was costly to the Indians of Chief Tascalusa's paramountcy, but it did not spell immediate disaster, and people continued to put mantles on the mound at Atahachi, the capital town of Tascalusa, until at least around 1560. We know this because some of the gifts brought by the later de Luna expedition when they visited there were buried in the mound. However, the de Luna reports on Tascalusa are curt; apparently it was no longer the noteworthy paramountcy that de Soto had encountered. In fact, the archaeology suggests

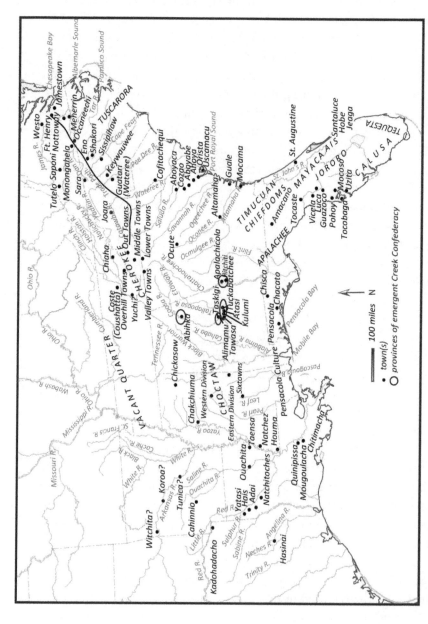

Map 2. The Native South, ca. 1650, showing the four provinces of the emergent Creek Confederacy. Map by Robbie Ethridge.

that the paramountcy, and perhaps the chiefdom of Tascalusa, disintegrated only fifteen years after the de Luna expedition, by 1575 at the latest. Afterward, some people stayed in the vicinity, in small towns, and others moved south, toward Mobile Bay. Some also may have moved east at this time, to the Chattahoochee River. Those who remained near the upper Alabama River would form the core of the later Alabama province of the Creek Confederacy.[16]

The Tallapoosa province formed on the lower Tallapoosa River, where de Soto had encountered three towns of the Talisi chiefdom, a subject of the paramount chief of Coosa yet being courted by Tascalusa (see maps 1 and 2). After de Soto departed central Alabama, the people of the Talisi chiefdom apparently stayed in place on the lower Tallapoosa, becoming an independent polity when both Coosa and Tascalusa fell. The archaeology also shows changes in capital towns, suggesting shifts in hierarchical leadership. These three towns on the Tallapoosa were occupied until removal; their historic names are Kulumi, Atasi, and the famous Tuckabatchee. They and the other towns along the lower Tallapoosa became the province known as Tallapoosa, a major province of the eighteenth-century Creek Confederacy.[17]

The Apalachicola province was centered on the Chattahoochee River (see map 2). De Soto did not travel along the Chattahoochee, but we know that several chiefdoms existed on the river at that time, known only by their archaeological name of Stewart phase sites (1475–1600 C.E.) (see map 1). A significant immigration into the lower Chattahoochee occurred during the Stewart phase and is marked by the replacement of Stewart phase ceramics with Abercrombie phase ceramics (1500–1600 C.E.). On the Chattahoochee, these Abercrombie phase immigrants established a chiefdom with two town sites with mounds, one on either side of the river at present-day Columbus, Georgia. These undoubtedly are the original sites of the two major towns of the eighteenth-century Lower Creeks known historically as Cusseta and Coweta. Although the archaeology is ambiguous as to the origins of these immigrants, it looks as though groups from present-day central Alabama, from either the Talisi or the Tascalusa chiefdom, or perhaps both, migrated to the Chattahoochee River valley sometime around 1585 C.E.[18]

This immigration profoundly affected the local chiefdoms, and archaeologists report a dramatic reduction in the number of Stewart phase sites. They interpret this to mean that Stewart phase people either were incorporated into the two new chiefdoms or suffered some kind of population loss, either from disease or from military confrontations. Even so, the two groups continued to live side by side. By 1630 they would merge into one multilingual polity, known as Apalachicola.[19]

De Soto's expedition came as a hostile army, and in the cases of those chiefdoms that saw intense action, such as Tascalusa, the direct military assault by the Spanish may have precipitated their collapse and reorganization. De Soto also depended on the food stores of Native peoples to feed his army and the livestock in their expedition. The Spaniards commonly ransacked entire regions for food, leading to depletions of local stores, which would have had serious repercussions. Although Native peoples knew much about utilizing wild plant and animal foods, such a shortage of stored cultivated crops would have meant hardship for all and starvation for some. In addition, the leadership of Native polities derived partly from being able to procure and secure stores of food for just such emergencies, and if leaders failed on this count, their polities also would have been subject to political unrest.[20]

Little is known about the lives of all of these peoples after the migrations occurred, except to say that they quit building mounds, moved into smaller towns, and changed some of their pottery designs and the tempering agents for their paste. In the early decades of the seventeenth century, they began acquiring European trade goods from the Spanish who had settled in present-day Florida. The presence of Spanish items in many non-elite burials at this time indicates a challenge to elite authority, a leveling of social statuses, and perhaps the beginning of the end of the Mississippian hierarchical political structures. One can also see the beginnings of the Creek Confederacy when the geopolitical landscape of this region was reconfigured, as towns were destroyed or abandoned, political alliances were reshuffled, and local leadership was strained or usurped.[21]

After a series of colonial failures in the South, including that of de Soto, the Spanish crown settled on maintaining a small garrison on the Atlantic side of the peninsula of present-day Florida from where they could police the shipping lanes of New Spain and ward off English, Dutch, and French pirates raiding in the seas and along the coastlines. This was St. Augustine, and the fort and town housed a small number of military personnel and their families. Instead of conquest, the Spanish sought to colonize this part of North America through the mission system, a colonial strategy wherein Catholic missionaries worked to convert Native inhabitants into Catholic Spanish peasants. The Spanish in what became known as La Florida (present-day Florida and southern Georgia) clearly interacted with viable Mississippian chiefdoms, indicating that some of the Mississippian world, although assuredly shaken after de Soto, was still intact.

Between 1565 and 1704, a handful of Jesuit and then Franciscan missionaries labored to convert thousands of Indians in La Florida to the Catholic faith. They established dozens of missions, proselytizing to the Guale and Mocama chiefdoms on the Georgia coast, the Apalachee paramount chiefdom in northwest Florida, and the thirty-five or so Timucuan-speaking simple chiefdoms spread across northern Florida and southern Georgia (see map 2). The Spanish hoped to assimilate the Indians, not annihilate them, and the mission strategy was devised for using Native inhabitants as colonists. In terms of conversion, the friars focused mostly on those things that conflicted with Catholicism, including polygamy, polytheism, and anything they considered idolatrous behavior, such as playing ball games. In other cases, they sought to work within Native systems; therefore, they did not attempt to revamp everything about Indian life.[22]

For example, the friars and Spanish military officials worked through chiefdom political orders, which helps account for why the chiefdoms in La Florida persisted into the eighteenth century. The friars' method was to first convert a chief, and then, with his or her permission, to establish a mission in the capital town. Here they would then work to convert others. The friars and Spanish officials also worked through the chief's authority to conscript Indian labor for growing corn, building facilities, operating ferries, maintaining the new roadways, and doing other work for the friars, the Spanish military, and colonists in St. Augustine and elsewhere. In addition, the friars and Spanish personnel imported fruits, vegetables, cattle, horses, pigs, iron tools, and many other things typical of Spanish life in the New World, and Indians soon incorporated some of these things into their own lives, as well. The Spanish also brought European diseases, and throughout the mission era, the Native populations of La Florida suffered repeated deadly disease episodes.[23]

Indian life in Spanish Florida became a blend of the old and new. For instance, even though the chiefdom political orders continued in some way, they most likely did not fully resemble their Mississippian antecedents. During the Spanish years, the friars and military officials continually interfered with leadership protocols and practices by placing pro-Spanish micos in office. These machinations inevitably led to suspicions, power struggles within the elite lineages, and general political unrest throughout the chiefdoms. In addition, the conscripted labor system of these missions undermined Indian health and well-being. For example, bioarchaeological studies have revealed that the Indian populations across Spanish Florida suffered from malnutrition and severe and physically damaging labor practices, as well as other associated health risks from displacement into work camps. Native peoples quickly became disaffected with life in the Spanish missions, and violent Native revolts punctuated the entire mission period—evidence that unrest and discontent existed among large numbers of mission Indians.[24]

Spanish officials in St. Augustine had taken an interest in the Indians living further in the interior early on. In the late sixteenth and early seventeenth centuries, they courted the chiefdoms of Ocute and Altamaha, in present-day central Georgia, and even established a mission in Altamaha, which lasted about twenty years. In 1633, just after establishing a permanent mission in Apalachee, the Spanish sought to pacify the hostile relationship that had developed between Apalachee and Apalachicola some time previously, as well as with their closer neighbors such as the Amacano and the Chacato (the latter two groups lived just west of Apalachee, in the panhandle of present-day Florida; see map 2). By 1639, truces had been established, and the Amacano and Chacato in fact moved closer to Spanish Florida, most likely to take advantage of the burgeoning skin and fur trade network.[25]

Following the 1639 truce, the Spanish and the Apalachicolas began to build strong trade and other connections. By 1650, a relatively heavy flow of trade existed between Spanish Florida and the Apalachicola,

Tallapoosa, and Abihka provinces. In fact, Spanish officials were interested enough in Apalachicola to arrange a high-level meeting, and the Spanish governor Damián Vega Castro y Pardo visited there in 1645. Even so, there is no indication that Apalachicola, Tallapoosa, or Abihka ever fell under the rule of Spanish authorities, and no missions were established in any of the provinces.[26]

During the Mississippi Period, Apalachee served as a vigorous trade center, moving valued coastal goods such as shells, pearls, and aquatic resources into the interior. During the mission era, Apalachee and other Indians continued these trade networks, only now they trafficked in Spanish goods as well. Indians from La Florida brought Spanish items such as brass (either in sheets or as ornaments, animal effigies, or bells); various glass beads; iron chisels, celts, and axes; cultigens such as peaches and cowpeas (or black-eyed peas); and perhaps even guns to the interior groups to exchange for deerskins and other furs, which they then transported back to Apalachee. There the skins were sold to Spanish buyers, who shipped them to Havana. Although this trade was ostensibly illegal, friars, soldiers, and some of the governors were involved.[27]

The trade started slowly, but by 1650 it was fairly substantial. The new trade system served to further undermine the tenets of chiefdom hierarchy, as indicated by the widespread ownership of European goods among the Indian populations involved. These goods undoubtedly still served as prestige and status markers, but since the rank and file now had access to them through the new trade network, they could and apparently did challenge, usurp, and rebel against the old leadership. They could also build their own spheres of influence, all of which tended to produce a less centralized political order. Trade with the Floridians also helps explain, in part, why present-day central Alabama and the lower Chattahoochee River became nodes of Native settlement in the seventeenth century. Archaeological sites in Creek country dating to this time period have yielded many Spanish goods, including numerous glass beads, brass discs, brass armbands, copper or brass bells, brass tinkling cones, and even iron celts. Clearly these towns had either direct or indirect connections to this developing trade network.[28]

With increased contact between Natives and newcomers, Old World diseases began to circulate more widely throughout the Native South.

Indian population losses from Old World diseases in the sixteenth and seventeenth centuries are difficult to calculate, and the estimates range from 30 percent to 90 percent. Current interpretations conclude that although population losses could be severe in a particular area, there is no evidence for a catastrophic loss of life across North America before sustained European contact. Rather, epidemics were localized occurrences, albeit with high mortality rates. The epidemics were also serial, occurring with regularity about every seven to ten years, killing off approximately 20 to 30 percent of a local population at a time. Today scholars still accept a 90 percent loss of Native life after contact, but it now appears to have occurred over about two hundred years (from roughly 1550 to 1750) in a gradual, not steep, demographic decline, and only after sustained European contact. In addition, scholars agree that disease was but one factor in the demographic decline, and they now point to contributing factors such as incorporation into the modern world economy, slaving, internecine warfare, dropping fertility rates, violent colonial strategies such as genocide, and general cultural and social malaise from colonial oppression.[29]

By far the strongest force for change was the new capitalist economic system ushered in by the English and Dutch in the seventeenth century—the global market system. It was inaugurated by a trade in dressed deerskins, but even more by a trade in enslaved Indians that enmeshed all of the Native South. Slavery was not unknown to the indigenous peoples of North America, and they practiced a version of it at the time of contact. Once slaves became something to be bought and sold on a commercial market, however, a powerful new dynamic began shaping the lives of the southern Indians.

The Indian slave trade in the South worked like this: European traders would give guns to a group of Indians on credit and ask to be paid in Indian slaves. The armed group would then raid an unarmed rival Indian group for captives, which they would enslave. The unarmed group, now vulnerable to Indian slave raiders, would then need guns and ammunition for protection, because bow-and-arrow Indians, however expert, were at a military disadvantage against slave raiders armed with European-made guns. The Indians could not make their own guns, so they depended on the European trade for guns as well as for shot and powder. At that point, anyone needing guns had to become a slave raider. In this way, a cycle emerged that ensnared all Native peoples who came into contact with it. The process snowballed until virtually all of the Indian groups in the Native South possessed firearms, owed enormous debts to English traders, and paid those debts through the sale of Indian captives.[30]

Indian slave raiders captured Indian slaves by the thousands, mostly women and children, and sold them to English, French, and Dutch slavers, who shipped them to the sugar plantations in the Caribbean, although some were sold to owners of the new coastal plantations in Virginia, South Carolina, and French Louisiana. For most Indian groups, already weakened by losses from disease and political instabilities, slaving was a serious blow. Wherever slaving penetrated, the same processes unfolded: many Indian groups moved to get away from slave raiders; some groups joined others in an effort to bolster their numbers and present a stronger defense; some groups became extinct when their numbers dwindled to nothing because of disease and slave raiding; and those who were left became engaged in the slave trade. The result was the creation of a shatter zone of instability that covered the eastern woodlands. Slaving unleashed chaos and panic because none could be sure that their neighbors would not turn on them as slave catchers. In the American South, some groups moved closer to the English and French coastal colonies, where they became known as "settlement Indians" and "petite nations," respectively. Others joined together in alliance as slave catchers, with agreements that they would not enslave those in the alliance. These were the coalescent societies.[31]

By the mid-seventeenth century, the provinces of Alabama, Tallapoosa, Abihka, and Apalachicola began attracting immigrants and refugees from fractured chiefdoms fleeing slave raiders. People were most likely drawn to this coalescence because of the plural roots of these provinces, because of their relative distance from the colonial disruptions of disease and slaving erupting all along the Atlantic Seaboard and in La Florida, and because of their access to European trade. Coalescence also offered some protection from outside and distant militarized Indian slaving societies such as the Westos and Occaneechis, who had partnered with Virginia and South Carolina slave traders and were raiding far and wide for Indians to sell.[32]

Throughout the seventeenth century, a flood of migrants settled in central Alabama. Between the upper Alabama River and the big bend in the Tallapoosa River, these immigrants established a series of towns so close together that it is difficult to discern archaeologically one from the next. The towns in the Tallapoosa province grew in both size and number from the mid- to late seventeenth century. Tuckabatchee, for instance, which had been a small mound center in 1575 C.E., had expanded into a non-mound town four or five times its former size. People fleeing the Piedmont also migrated down the Coosa River to join the groups coalescing with the Abihka province.[33]

In addition, during the mid-seventeenth century, we see a large migration of Coushatta-speaking people fleeing the lower Piedmont in the wake of Occaneechi, Westo, Iroquois, and perhaps Cherokee slave raiding. When the Spaniard Marcos Delgado visited the nascent Alabama province in 1686, he observed several towns of "Qusate," or Coushatta, speakers. These towns most likely represent Coushatta-speaking peoples from present-day eastern Tennessee who were once part of the Coosa paramount chiefdom.[34]

The number of towns in the Apalachicola province likewise expanded between 1630 and 1690, and a number of these new towns were settled by people moving out of the reach of Westo and Occaneechi slavers, such as the Yuchi and the Coushatta-speaking Chiaha, who originated in eastern Tennessee. People from the former Ocute paramount chiefdom on the Ocmulgee River in present-day central Georgia, who after the fall of Ocute had consolidated with others into the Yamasee Confederacy on the South Carolina coast, settled outposts in Apalachicola in the 1680s. It may have been around this time that another province arose in central Alabama, that of Okfuskee (see map 2). In the eighteenth century, Okfuskee was composed of several towns on the upper Tallapoosa River where the Upper Trade Path crossed the river, and Okfuskee was also the name of their largest town. The Okfuskees' origins, however, are murky, since their settlements have received little archaeological research. Whether or not they were the descendants of Mississippian polities on the upper Tallapoosa or immigrated into this area from regions unknown in later years has yet to be determined.[35]

Throughout the eighteenth century, other groups sought admittance to the Tallapoosa, Abihka, Alabama, Okfuskee, and Apalachicola provinces. Such in-migrations bolstered their numbers and would eventually make the Creeks into one of the largest and most formidable Indian nations in the American South. We can now see that the coalescence of the Creek Confederacy was an imaginative and adaptive response to living in a shatter zone, and we can see that similar processes took place throughout the South with the coalescences of the Cherokees, Choctaws, Catawbas, Chickasaws, and Yamasees.

By the 1680s, South Carolina and French traders were penetrating into the interior South, negotiating trade deals with the Apalachicolas, Tallapoosas, Alabamas, and Abihkas, as well as with other polities that were also beginning to coalesce, such as the Catawbas, Chickasaws, Cherokees, and Choctaws (see map 2). Each coalescent society had certain mechanisms for admitting refugee groups under a political umbrella that, at the very least, required mutual agreements that those in the alliance would not conduct slave raids against each other. The coalescent societies became militarized slave raiders, raiding each other, but mostly attacking the mission Indians of La Florida and the smaller Indian groups in the Atlantic and Gulf coastal regions that had not coalesced.[36]

Around 1689, in a move calculated to place themselves more central to the South Carolina slave trade, the Apalachicolas and their attached groups moved near present-day Macon, Georgia, on the fall line of the Ocmulgee River, near the Early Mississippian site of Ocmulgee in present-day Macon, Georgia. Once there, they divided themselves into two groups—a northerly group composed of the Apalachicola towns of Coweta, Cusseta, Tuskegee, and Kulumi, and a more southerly group composed of the Hitchiti-speaking towns of Ocmulgee, Hitchiti, and Osuchi. The Hitchiti-speaking congregation also attracted more distant peoples such as the Chiaha, who originated in the Appalachians of present-day western North Carolina. There is some evidence that a group of Yuchi, who originated in eastern Tennessee, also settled with the Hitchitis. English traders began to refer to the whole as the Ochese Creeks, an ethnonym that was later shortened to Creeks. At Ocmulgee they built a trading post that has come to be known as the Macon Trading House. It was uncovered by archaeologists along with several of the towns in this vicinity. These investigations show that the Macon Trading House was a thriving trade depot. English items dominate the trade goods, although a small number of Spanish goods are also present.

Although the Apalachicola towns traded heavily in slaves, the archaeology also shows a vigorous trade in deerskins, indicating that the Apalachicolas were already embarking on an enterprise that would become the economic mainstay of the South for most of the eighteenth century.[37]

The slave trade gradually subsided after the Yamasee War of 1715, when the southern Indians, realizing its deleterious effects, allied in armed rebellion against the South Carolina traders. Thereafter, the groups on the Ocmulgee moved back to the Chattahoochee River. The Yamasee War failed to extricate the southern Indians from the global economic system, but it did succeed in diverting English trade interests from Indian slaves to deerskins. By this time it was more profitable to import slaves from Africa. Plus, the armed resistance of the Indians in the Yamasee War made some things very clear to the English. For one, the Indian slave trade could be a dangerous enterprise. Second, despite their dependency on English-made guns, Europeans had to respect the southern Indians as a numerically superior military force. The Yamasee War also succeeded in forcing the South Carolinians to establish a more regulated trade in deerskins, which ultimately gave the southern Indians a measure of political and economic power for most of the eighteenth century.[38]

By 1715, then, the Mississippian world had been transformed into a new Native South, composed of large, powerful coalescent societies and beachheads of European trade. Although each coalescent society was unique, generally speaking, they were organized as collections of towns under loose political affiliations. The basic political unit was the township, which consisted of a capital town and its affiliated satellite towns. Each township was led by a council of ranked warriors, or headmen. One of the deepest and most abiding civic affiliations and loyalties for a Creek, or any southern Indian, lay with his or her township. Unless there was a crisis of international proportions, a member of an Indian nation rarely referred to herself or himself as a Creek, a Cherokee, a Chickasaw, and the like. People usually referred to themselves by their township or province affiliation—as a Yuchi, an Alabama, a Coweta, an Echota, a Yaneka, a Chucafalaya, and so on.[39]

Capital towns still punctuated the landscape, albeit now featuring political and religious spaces in the form of large square grounds rather than earthen mounds. These so-called square-ground towns were laid out around a central public area that consisted of a rotunda, a square ground, and a town plaza. The square ground was the focus of all formal public events. It consisted of three to four open-faced "warrior cabins" situated in a square formation around a yard, with a central fire in the yard area. Important assemblies of the ranked warriors took place there, weather permitting. The rotunda was a round semisubterranean structure that housed public gatherings in inclement weather and also served as sleeping quarters for the elderly, guests, and others. Towns also had a plaza, which was a large area in the center of town adjacent to the square ground and rotunda. The plaza was kept clean and swept and served as the main gathering place for socializing, playing games, and performing ceremonies. The households, which were matrilineal courtyard compounds consisting of three or four homes surrounding an open yard, were tightly clustered around the town center.[40]

If the town was a person's most important civic entity, the clan was the most important social one. "Clan" is an anthropological term used to designate an extended unilineal kinship group, one that unites several extended kin groups, or lineages. People of the same clan have strong prescribed relations and obligations to one another, even to members whom one does not know personally. The southern Indians were matrilineal, reckoning their kinship through the female line, and they were matrilocal, meaning that upon marriage the husband moved into his wife's homestead. The nuclear homestead was typically situated within a cluster of house compounds occupied by the members of a matrilineage. A single household, then, consisted of a woman and her husband and children, but they were surrounded by the wife's relatives, such as her mother, her mother's husband, her unmarried brothers and sisters, her married sisters with their husbands and children, and perhaps even her maternal aunts and their families. Males in the neighborhood fell into two categories— those connected by descent and those connected by marriage. Those connected by descent had authority and represented the matriline and clan in council. A man connected by marriage had an unsanctioned voice in his wife's matrilineal decisions (his clout rested with his own matriline). Matrilineal descent ties were also a person's strongest emotional, social, and obligational connections.[41]

Daily life played out along gender lines. Women's duties included such things as child rearing, cooking, maintaining the household, farming, gathering wild plant foods and medicines, calling men to war, lobbying for the family, and almost all private and domestic affairs. Of course, all the women in the matriline would pool their labor for these chores. Men's duties included hunting, warfare, politics, ball games, public affairs, maintaining public buildings, and taking the lead in the trade. The men of a matriline likewise pooled their labor for these roles.[42]

Some social institutions among the Creeks resembled those of their former chiefdoms, including town councils, blood revenge, the gendered division of labor, reciprocity, and matrilineality, all with set rules governing polite behavior and proper courses of action in most situations. These horizontal social institutions, in fact, proved to be highly adaptable. For example, the southern Indian domestic economy and division of labor was flexible enough to form linkages to the world economic system. The broad structural patterns of southern Indian households show some continuity from the Mississippi Period until the early nineteenth century. Reciprocity and redistribution became formalized in gift giving, a practice wherein European and later American traders and officials lavished gifts on certain Indian men with whom they dealt. The Indian men, in turn, distributed these gifts among various people with whom they had connections.[43]

The hierarchical political institutions of the old chiefdoms, though, could not work when dealing with Europeans, and especially Europeans who held the key to needed guns, ammunition, and other goods. At first, Europeans attempted to work within the framework of the Indian political order, and the French and Spanish actually succeeded for a while. But within the British sphere of influence, any vestiges of a hereditary elite quickly eroded. British traders did not have to persuade an anti-British chief to their side. They would simply ally with another person in that society. Given the origins of the coalescent societies, there were usually several men who could claim influence over a particular town or faction.[44]

The British chose to deal with whoever seemed most inclined to listen to their overtures, which, given the new opportunities for self-gain, could be any number of people. An Indian man who held a modicum of influence over a particular faction could broker good trade deals and rise in prestige and authority. An Indian man's position soon became tied to his access to European trade goods and his political and business savvy. The overall effect was at once a leveling of political power and a check on the rise of any one person to political prominence. Now, instead of hereditary chiefs as in the Mississippi Period, the towns were led by councils of headmen with achieved status, and each town had autonomy to act as it wished and to independently enter into agreements with Europeans. In other words, there was no centralized government.[45]

This nonhierarchical organization worked well in the eighteenth-century colonial South. Europeans courted Indian allies for trade and also for defense. Colonial settlements and their militias were relatively small, and Spain, France, and Britain could not patrol their borders in defense against each other. Therefore, they relied on gaining Indian allies through good trade agreements to help protect their colonies. The towns of a coalescent society, then, could make use of what came to be known as the "playoff system," playing the Europeans off each other in order to garner the most favorable trade deals and alliances. Since coalescent societies such as the Creek Confederacy were made up of various groups and organized under loose political umbrellas in which people's allegiance was with their township rather than the polity as a whole, they were particularly well suited for the playoff system. In turn, men who were adept at dealing with trade and Europeans rose to prominence. And although the eighteenth century was punctuated by strife such as the Choctaw civil war and ongoing conflicts between the Chickasaws, Choctaws, and Creeks, it was a time in which the coalescent societies held the balance of power in the colonial world.[46]

The deerskin trade era, which lasted into the early nineteenth century, was an especially lucrative and opportune time for the Native South. Creek and other southern Indian men and women were integral to the trade system, procuring and dressing deerskins for sale on the European market. Assuredly they still farmed, hunted, fished, and gathered wild plant foods, but they did so within a new economic context. Most of the men had become commercial hunters, and the women now sold their surplus foods on the informal market. Indian men and women also entered into a series of new part-time occupations—guide, translator, mercenary, postal rider, slave catcher, horse thief, and so on. Indian peoples developed good purchasing power and traded skins for European-made items such as guns, ammunition, metal tools, cloth, and alcohol. They also incorporated European foodstuffs, including melons, peaches, potatoes, and black-eyed peas, and European domesticated animals such as the horse.[47]

Non-Natives also began to make their homes on Indian lands. Throughout the eighteenth century, European field traders, working for large corporate trade companies in France and England, settled in Indian towns, married Indian wives, and raised families of mixed descent. Runaway African slaves also sought refuge among Indian groups, and they too married into Indian societies and raised families of mixed descent. Since the southern Indians were matrilineal, tracing their descent through the female line, they understood the progeny of a foreign husband and a Native wife to be fully Muscogee, Chickasaw, Choctaw, and so on. The progeny of European and Indian marriages, the so-called "mixed bloods," would later constitute a rising class of elites as defined by Western conceptions of wealth and property.[48]

The Creeks, whose territory abutted French, Spanish, and English land claims, were geographically well situated to take advantage of the playoff system. In 1714, for example, the Alabamas welcomed the French building of a trading fort, Fort Toulouse, near present-day Montgomery. Yet the Alabamas, as well as the other provinces, continued to trade with British South Carolinians and to openly entertain trade and diplomatic possibilities with Spanish Florida. In 1733, another avenue for trade and alliance opened when General James Oglethorpe established the colony of Georgia and bargained with Creek leaders for various trade alliances. Around this time, the great Coweta headman Emperor Brims formulated the doctrine of neutrality for the Creek provinces, and all in the confederacy agreed that they would parlay and work with all European prospects, but not ally with any single one: the Creeks would remain neutral. Around this time, the Creeks also created the National Council, which was a governing body through which all Creek towns were represented.[49]

The Creeks, using the playoff system and the doctrine of neutrality, had previous trade agreements both with the French and with the colony of South Carolina. South Carolina, founded in 1670, had regained its footing after the costly Yamasee War and was a leader in the southern skin trade. Charleston, or Charles Town as it was called at the time, was a thriving Atlantic trade port and maintained trade alliances with the Catawbas, Cherokees, Chickasaws, and Creeks, as well as the many settlement Indians who had been drawn to the South Carolina coast for trade and protection against slave raiders. Georgia now offered another avenue for trade.

Both Georgia and South Carolina claimed territory from sea to sea, using the doctrine of discovery to legitimate their claims in the eyes of European nations. The doctrine of discovery was a late fifteenth-century Catholic decree that all "non-Christian" territories could be "discovered," or possessed, by Christian people. While it was clearly not recognized by indigenous inhabitants, it became the basis of all European claims in the Americas for the next four hundred years.[50] The Indian population, although diminished by Old World diseases and the slave trade, still vastly outnumbered the colonists. Hence European colonists recognized that, despite their bold land claims, actually acquiring lands had to be done peacefully, through amicable and mutually beneficial trade alliances. The three-way European colonial contest in the American South meant that negotiations often favored Indian partners. It also meant that the colonists could not simply take land; they had to negotiate for it through treaties with Native groups.

When the Apalachicola and Hitchiti towns on the Ocmulgee returned to the Chattahoochee River after the Yamasee War, the move essentially left most of present-day Georgia sparsely inhabited by Native peoples. The territorial boundary lines of the coalescent societies were unformed at this time, although each group seems to have understood certain areas to be under their control. The Creek towns, now clustered on the Coosa, Tallapoosa, Alabama, and Chattahoochee rivers, laid claim to much of present-day Georgia and Alabama. A 1717 treaty between South Carolina and the Creeks formally concluded the Yamasee War, although many in the Indian coalition sporadically attacked colonists until 1728. The treaty also established a negotiated boundary between the colony and the Creeks and confirmed that the land between the colonial boundary and the Creek towns belonged to the Creeks.[51]

When Oglethorpe and his colonists landed at present-day Georgia, they were landing on Creek shores. However, they were not met by Creek leaders from the major Creek provinces. Instead, they were met by a small group of Yamacraw Indians led by Tomochichi and by the Creek mixed-descent woman Mary Musgrove. The Yamacraws had been exiled from Apalachicola after a disagreement over European trade relations, and they had relocated near present-day Savannah, Georgia. Mary Musgrove, or Coosaponakeesa, was a high-ranking Coweta mixed-descent woman from the Wind clan with an English father. She and her English trader husband had relocated to the Savannah River to open a trade house. She also served as an interpreter for the British. Both Musgrove and Tomochichi became fast friends with Oglethorpe, and they eased the way for the Georgians to acquire the land on which to build the town of Savannah and later Augusta in the interior, arguing to the Creek leadership that the colony would open lucrative avenues for trade. In 1733, Oglethorpe and Creek leaders negotiated a treaty confirming a gift from Tomochichi to Oglethorpe of lands for the colonists' use between the Savannah and Altamaha rivers and inland as far as the tide flowed. The treaty is vaguely worded and stipulates that any settlements within those boundaries had to be approved by Creek leaders. Six years later, on August 21, 1739, Creek leaders clarified and formalized the arrangement in the Treaty of Savannah, which guaranteed that a wide section of land along the Atlantic coast belonged to the British colonists, thus establishing a colonial boundary line.[52]

The European rivalry for North America culminated in the French and Indian war of the 1760s, which ended with British victory. The British now claimed much of the land east of the Mississippi River that had formerly been claimed by the French and Spanish. But the region had been occupied by thousands of Native peoples for millennia, and Native peoples naturally contested British claims over their tribal territories. British officials, having spent excessively on the Ohio River Indian uprising known as Pontiac's Rebellion, saw the futility of prolonged Indian wars, and in an effort to peacefully coexist, Britain drew up its Proclamation of 1763 for the colonies. According to the proclamation, the British colonies' western boundary extended to a line that followed the eastern Continental Divide and down the Ocmulgee River in present-day Georgia. West of this line was the "Indian Reserve," or Indian lands claimed and occupied by American Indian groups. The proclamation further stated that Indian Reserve lands could only be acquired through treaty. The Proclamation of 1763 was a diplomatic attempt to ensure that the Indian trade, upon which both the colonies and Indian nations now depended, would flow uninterrupted. Perhaps less intentional, it promised Native sovereignty and territorial rights. It also sowed the seeds of rebellion in the American colonies.[53]

In effect, the proclamation thwarted westward expansion, forcing land-hungry colonists to look instead to the Atlantic and the British trade for economic stability. It also meant that colonial land companies, many of which involved America's founding fathers, including George Washington, could not speculate, capitalize on, and occupy lands in Indian territory. Canvassing colonial American history, one can see that the Proclamation of 1763 exposed and attempted to freeze the frenzied land grabs by land speculators and so-called "land companies," which by the mid-eighteenth century were underwriting many of the colonial economies and enriching many elite colonists. American colonists, both elites and commoners, detested the proclamation's dividing line and flagrantly disobeyed its injunctions. Land companies illegally surveyed Indian land tracts in the Indian Reserve to sell, then sent squatters to illegally settle farmsteads on the tracts. Colonial resentment toward British rule solidified.[54]

Native peoples resented the trespassing as well as Britain's inability to control land speculation and squatters, and they grew increasingly suspicious of British colonists eyeing their lands. In some cases, Indian groups responded with violent altercations, such as the Shawnee wars in present-day Kentucky. The coalescent Creeks, though, responded by inventing the Creek Nation "as a territorially circumscribed legal entity," claiming Creek country as their national landholdings. Creek leaders also agreed on the legal decree that any lands within Creek national territory could only be sold by consent of the nation as a whole. Private land transactions were now unlawful in the Creek Nation.[55]

Furthermore, the boundary lines established by the Proclamation of 1763 had annexed thousands of square miles of Creek territory to the Georgia colony. In 1773, in Augusta, Georgia, Creek leaders confronted

Georgia officials on this point. After deliberations, in exchange for a liquidation of Creek trader debts, the Creeks agreed to cede lands between the Little and Tugaloo rivers in present-day northwest Georgia. Historian John Juricek observes that the 1773 treaty is unique in that it departed from the "Native framework of gift-giving" to one of reciprocal payment, in this case a payment of trade debts. This set the precedent for all subsequent land cessions. Over the next decade, the British superintendent of Indian affairs, John Stuart, convinced the Creeks to cede additional small portions of their land in present-day southern Georgia and northern Florida because illegal settlers continued to establish their farms there. Stuart also argued that these cessions would settle any debts the Creeks owed to British traders. Although the playoff diplomacy and the doctrine of neutrality effectively ended with the conclusion of the French and Indian war, the Creeks now entered into a productive relationship with the British. John Stuart, who respected and admired the Creeks, upheld Creek land rights, enforced trade regulations, and guarded Creek borders against Georgia squatters and other trespassers. The latter proved quite difficult. Land speculators continually interfered with Stuart's agenda, made specious land claims, and sponsored settlers to cross the lines. Although they maintained trust in Stuart and the British authorities, the Creeks grew to hate the Georgians.[56]

The Proclamation of 1763 was but one of many efforts by Britain to control the growth and economies of the American colonies. American colonists of all socioeconomic and philosophical backgrounds grew bitter and angry at their homeland with each new decree from the Crown. The result, as we know, was rebellion and the American Revolution. Most Indian peoples across the eastern woodlands backed the British in the conflict, understandable given the protections that the Proclamation of 1763 afforded them and the wanton violations of it by the colonists. The Creeks, largely sympathetic to the British but also shocked by the devastating retaliation by American troops against Cherokees who aided the British, claimed neutrality and stayed out of the conflict for the most part. When the war ended in 1783, though, the Creeks faced a wholly new, and wholly threatening, geopolitical situation.

2

REMOVAL OF THE
CREEK INDIANS

After the American Revolution, the position of the southern Indians came under threat when land for growing cotton replaced deerskins as the most valuable commodity in the South. Eli Whitney invented the cotton gin in 1793, which reduced the amount of labor needed in cotton production. The gin, combined with new varieties of cotton, also meant that cotton production could expand beyond the wealthy Tidewater planters, who owned hundreds of slaves, to less wealthy interior planters, whose smaller numbers of slaves now could efficiently remove seeds from the cotton bolls. Concurrently with the invention of the cotton gin, a worldwide boom in cotton occurred, raising cotton prices. Cotton became a highly profitable enterprise, despite the investment of labor. Thus, land became the natural resource most in demand throughout the South.

The geopolitical winds also had changed after the revolution. Although Spain, Britain, and France still held territories in the South into the nineteenth century, their positions were considerably weakened, while America was ascending. The playoff system, which had worked so well for the southern Indians during the era of the deerskin trade, came to an end, and now the southern Indians stood toe to toe with the Americans. During the deerskin trade era, the southern Indians had been integral to colonial defense and a necessary part of the global economic machinery. European officials and traders understood the necessity of maintaining decent relations with Native nations; in fact, their fortunes and positions depended on it. With their social, economic, and political prominence in the colonial South, European officials and traders managed to protect their own interests by protecting, to some degree, those of the Indians. However, after the American Revolution, a new kind of American leadership emerged: one based in land speculation, one that had no desire to continue the Indian trade, and one that had little interest in maintaining good relationships with the Creeks or any other Indian group. The Creeks, like all of the southern Indian societies, found not only that they were unnecessary to the southern cotton economy but that they had in fact become impediments to it. For now, instead of deerskins and trade, southern Americans wanted land for cotton production and all of its attendant agriculture, husbandry, and industry, and the Creeks and other Indians possessed much of the land in the lower South—land that they were legendary in their refusal to relinquish.[1]

Indians still occupied and claimed much of the interior South, and the Creeks, in particular, owned a substantial portion of what later became the cotton belt. The exact boundaries have yet to be worked out by historians, but we do have a general idea of how Native boundary lines fell (see map 3). The Choctaws claimed land from present-day southern Louisiana into Mississippi and Alabama. Their northern boundaries, which reached to present-day central Mississippi and west-central Alabama, abutted Chickasaw lands in northern Mississippi and Creek lands in western Alabama. The Chickasaws claimed territory from present-day central Mississippi into western Tennessee and northwest Alabama. The Cherokees lived in present-day western South Carolina, northern Georgia, and most of Tennessee. The Seminoles claimed present-day northern Florida and parts of present-day southern Georgia.[2]

In 1783, in the aftermath of the revolution, Georgia colonists pressured Creek leaders for a substantial land cession. After much acrimonious debate and much Creek dissent, those present at the negotiations signed the 1783 Treaty of Augusta, which ceded the lands between the Savannah and Ogeechee rivers to Georgia, marking the Ogeechee River as the colonial boundary line. The Creek Nation, then, held territory from the Ogeechee River in present-day Georgia to the Tombigbee

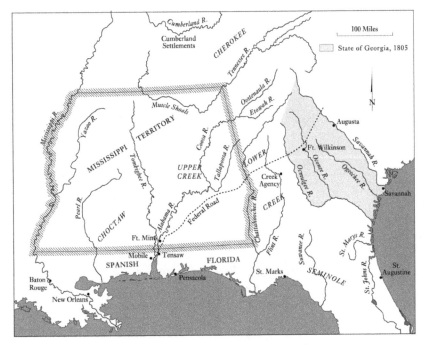

Map 3. The American South, ca. 1800. Map by Robbie Ethridge.

River in western Alabama, and from the Gulf Coast to northern Alabama. The core of the confederacy still consisted of towns on the Coosa, Tallapoosa, Alabama, and Chattahoochee rivers. Muscogean, Hitchiti, and Alabama speakers formed the original four provinces, but the Creek Confederacy, a well-known refuge for dislocated peoples into the nineteenth century, allowed various non-Muscogean speakers to establish their own towns within its territory. In time, the Creeks divided themselves into two divisions—the Upper Creeks (composed of the Tallapoosas, Alabamas, Abihkas, and Okfuskees) and the Lower Creeks (composed of the Apalachicola province). By this time, seventy-one towns, ranging in size from as few as ten or twenty families to over two hundred families, made up the Creek Confederacy—forty-seven Upper Creek towns and twenty-four Lower Creek towns, in total about twenty thousand people (see map 4).[3]

The European and American boundaries in the South are better known. Spain still claimed Florida, which included a strip along the

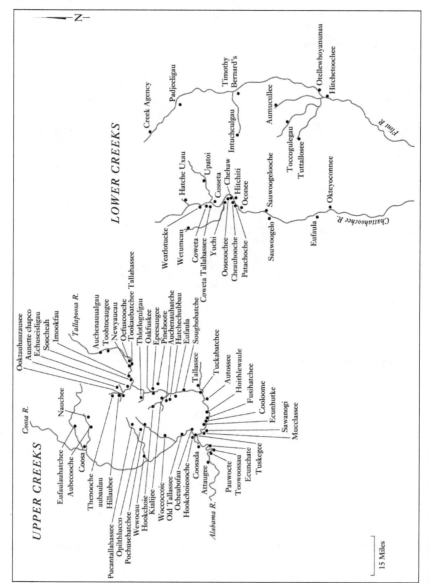

Map 4. The Creek Confederacy, ca. 1800. Map by Robbie Ethridge.

western Gulf Coast to French-held Louisiana. But the Seminoles, who were especially antagonistic to settlers, controlled the interior, and the area was sparsely occupied by Euro-Americans. With the Louisiana Purchase in 1803, the United States acquired from France what became known as the Mississippi Territory, a tract encompassing all of the Choctaw and Chickasaw lands and most of the Creeks' western lands. New Orleans, Mobile, and Pensacola were major port cities. Outlying American settlements on ceded lands, like Baton Rouge, Natchez, Tensaw, and Bigbe, bordered Indian territories upriver from the port cities.[4]

The population of Americans and African Americans in the South also grew substantially after the revolution. Between 1800 and 1810, the white and black population of Georgia increased, from approximately 163,000 to 250,000. After the Mississippi Territory was opened in 1803, the white and black population there rose from less than 10,000 to about 40,000 by 1810. This western growth is also reflected in the addition of states. Between 1792 and 1821, ten states were admitted to the Union—Kentucky in 1792, Tennessee in 1796, Ohio in 1803, Louisiana in 1812, Indiana in 1816, Mississippi in 1817, Illinois in 1818, Alabama in 1819, Maine in 1820, and Missouri in 1821. New American immigrants rushed into the new states and pressed against Indian borders, increasing pressure on state and federal officials to acquire more Indian lands.[5]

Georgians, especially, kept constant pressure on the Creeks for land cessions. The Creek leadership, however, held steady, and over the next three decades, the Creeks made only four land cessions. The 1796 Treaty of Colerain, which confirmed the earlier 1790 Treaty of New York, ceded Creek lands roughly between the Ogeechee and Oconee rivers in Georgia and allowed for the stationing of military posts in Creek territory. The 1802 Treaty of Fort Wilkerson ceded a portion of land between the Oconee and Ocmulgee rivers, and in the Treaty of 1805 (also known as the Treaty of Washington) the Creeks sold the remaining section of land between the two rivers, making the boundary between the Creek Confederacy and Georgia roughly the Ocmulgee River (see map 3).[6]

Federal and state leaders, however, were determined to acquire all Indian lands west of the line demarcated by the Proclamation of 1763, and they openly considered ways to do so. The three solutions debated in the U.S. Congress for how to acquire Indian lands, the so-called

"Indian problem," were assimilation, extermination, and removal. Hoping to avoid costly Indian wars as the price for extermination or removal, George Washington promoted assimilation as the most cost-effective approach. The federal government then instituted an economic and social development program for American Indians throughout the eastern woodlands, called the "plan for civilization." The idea was to settle Indian families on ranches and individual farmsteads and to institutionalize private property, after which the Indian nations would be more willing to sell, and the U.S. could then purchase any remaining lands in private land transactions.[7]

The plan for civilization, as an economic development plan, appealed to some Creeks. The deerskin trade and the era of Indian power in the American South were coming to a close. There were multiple reasons for this. For one, the population of white-tailed deer in the South appears to have seriously declined because of commercial overhunting. For another, the American Revolution disrupted the southern Indian trade. European traders who had lived and worked among the Creeks for decades had close ties with England and took the Loyalists' side in the conflict. Afterward, in defeat, many of them had their property confiscated. Several fled to Europe; some were hanged. In addition, the Treaty of Paris prohibited commercial arrangements between the U.S. and Britain, and transatlantic commerce came to a temporary halt. The British trading houses in the territory now claimed by the U.S. were shuttered. Only one continued to operate—Panton, Leslie, and Company (renamed John Forbes and Company in 1805, after William Panton's death), in the port town of Pensacola in Spanish-held West Florida. It remained the primary trade house in the South until 1830.[8]

In place of the British trade system, the U.S. attempted to gain some control over the Indian trade. The Articles of Confederation and later the U.S. Constitution placed Indian relations, particularly trade, in the hands of the U.S. Congress rather than with local governments, although local interests continued to shape the trade. Congress later instituted a series of commissions and offices in the War Department to manage Indian affairs. These were consolidated in 1806 into the Office of the Superintendent of Indian Trade, commonly known as the Office of Indian Trade, which was headed by Virginia merchant John Mason and later by Thomas McKenney. The Office of Indian Trade issued licenses to American traders and maintained the factory system, or trade houses, throughout Indian territory. These arrangements were designed to temporarily prop up the skin trade while the ranching and farming complex took root, after which the federal and state governments could peacefully acquire Indian lands. Congress dismantled the office in 1822 because of falling trade revenues. A few years later, in 1824, Secretary of War John C. Calhoun created the Bureau of Indian Affairs (BIA) in the War Department, known at the time as the "Indian Office," and appointed McKenney as its first commissioner of Indian affairs. (In 1849, the BIA was moved to the newly formed Department of the Interior. Today it is also known as Indian Affairs.)[9]

As the plan for civilization began to take shape in the late eighteenth century, a major Creek player emerged: Alexander McGillivray, whose mother was a Creek woman from the prestigious Wind clan and whose father was a well-to-do Scottish trader. He positioned himself as a strong and central leader of the Creeks by using the old strategy of playing the Europeans against each other while that was still feasible. McGillivray held an unusual amount of influence and power for a late eighteenth-century Creek headman. He tailored his leadership to the Creek clan-based and consensual form of government, and he cultivated links to the English trading firm of Panton, Leslie, and Company, through which he could bring economic pressure to bear on opponents and through which he could influence Creek politics. He also promoted the National Council as a more centralized authority, which earned him some staunch enemies in several Creek towns who were loath to relinquish their independence.[10]

McGillivray's rise to power among the Creeks is a story full of unusual twists and turns in Creek politics and cannot be fully told here. He died in 1793, leaving a legacy of intrigue, duplicity, and harsh retaliations against the Georgians he had always hated. At the time of his death, the situation between the Creeks and the state of Georgia had become explosive. President Washington knew that the Creeks mistrusted the federal government and that they deplored the Georgia government. The present Indian agent, James Seagrove, was ineffectual and terrified of the Indians, and he could not deal with the situation. In 1796,

Washington appointed Benjamin Hawkins as temporary agent to the southern Indians. Upon entering Creek country, Hawkins initially settled in the Lower Creek town of Coweta Tallahassee. In 1803, when his status was changed from temporary to permanent, he moved to the Flint River, just off the Lower Trading Path, where he built the Creek Agency and lived with his family and numerous African slaves (see map 3). One of Hawkins's primary objectives in Creek country was to implement the plan for civilization.[11]

The plan for civilization was official policy, formulated by George Washington, Henry Knox, Thomas Jefferson, and other statesmen to assimilate Indians into American society. It was the culmination of ideas derived from Enlightenment precepts, certain northern philanthropic groups, the agrarian movement, and the philosophies of Protestant sects such as the Quakers. The idea was to provide American Indians with domesticated animals such as hogs, cows, and sheep and manufactured agricultural implements, especially the plow, and to teach them to become herdsmen and agriculturalists, growing cash crops such as cotton and wheat and driving their herds to seaports or frontier markets. They would also engage in cottage industries such as cloth making and blacksmithing. Through such changes, the thinking went, Indians would no longer need large hunting territories for the skin trade, and they would instead become self-sufficient farmers who could clothe and feed themselves while participating in the market and exchanging agricultural and herd surpluses for manufactured items.[12]

Although the plan for civilization was more benevolent than the other options publicly discussed, it conspicuously ignored the fact that the southern Indians, who had been agriculturalists for millennia, were already more than capable of clothing and feeding themselves. Moreover, they were already experimenting with cash crops, and they had already diversified their market endeavors with cattle and hog ranching when the deerskin trade began to decline, and some even before then. Much of this ignorance derived from eighteenth-century Euro-American ethnocentrism. It also derived from Euro-American ideas on land use and so-called "improvements," a concept that elite agrarians understood to be the hallmark of proper stewardship of the land and of progress and civilization. Appropriate land use meant farmsteads that mimicked Euro-American ones, complete with fences, outbuildings, storage facilities, gendered divisions of labor, and other Eurocentric "improvements."[13]

Ultimately, however, the plan for civilization and Indian economic developments did not matter, because there was a hidden hand at work behind the scenes: U.S. expansion. In the government's reasoning, the plan for civilization, simply put, was a way of promoting expansion so "that the U.S. may be saved the pain and expense of expelling or destroying [the Indians]." According to the propaganda, once the southern Indians had been transformed into herdsmen and commercial farmers, they would no longer rely on the hunt and therefore would not need as much hunting territory. Thus, as Americans needed more land, the Indians would be more willing to sell. The real idea was to assimilate the Indians into American society, undermine their national sovereignty, and appropriate their lands in the process.[14]

By this time, Indian life in the American South already blended with that of many other people and was well integrated into the larger global world. At the turn of the nineteenth century, the people in Creek country were quite diverse and included not only descendants of the original people who had coalesced to form the Creek Confederacy, but also foreign Indians who had married into the group, people from various European countries, Americans, African slaves, and descendants of African slaves who either had run away from slavery or were freedmen who figured that life would be easier among the Indians. The progeny from the genetic mixing of all these people were also part of the new southern Indian citizenry.

Euro-American men who were living among the Indians at this time were usually "Indian countrymen"—traders who had married into Indian families, established farmsteads and ranches, owned slaves, and were living out their lives among their wives' people. Most had started out as traders and had transitioned to ranchers by the early nineteenth century, although many maintained their trading networks. Indian countrymen usually did not live in the towns. Instead, their wives' townships would grant them use rights to a piece of land, on which they established individual farmsteads and ranches with their wives and their unmarried and married children. Neither Indian countrymen nor their Indian relations owned this property, and they would be required to vacate it if and when they were no longer using it and living on it. These ranches and farms had a distinctively American flavor, with log cabins, outbuildings, and fenced fields. The children of these Indian countrymen formed a stratum of métis elites in the late eighteenth and early nineteenth centuries.[15]

The métis elites were men and women of mixed Indian and Euro-American descent who had a foot in both the Indian and the Euro-American worlds. (This category usually does not include those of African Indian descent, although there were many people in Creek country of this mixed parentage as well.) Like Mary Musgrove and Alexander McGillivray, they were usually multilingual and could read and write English, and most blended their Indian and Euro-American lifeways. The children of mixed white and Indian descent had distinct advantages in the larger global world because of their Western educations, English speaking and writing abilities, and Euro-American social, economic, and political connections. At the turn of the nineteenth century, they were growing in power and prestige among Indian groups as well as among Americans. They also adopted a market-oriented mindset and sought to accumulate wealth and status. Although they still could not hold private property, many of the elite established large American-style plantations.[16]

In addition to Euro-American and Creek mixing, Africans and Creeks also blended their lives. Africans had been a part of southern Indian life since they began arriving in North America in the sixteenth century, and by the end of the eighteenth century their place in Creek society was considerable. Some Africans were slaves owned by Creeks or Indian countrymen. However, their status was different from that of slaves in American society. Unlike southern American planters, Creek slave owners gained little from slaves in terms of labor. Consequently, the position of these slaves was more like that of tenant farmers. They lived with or near their owners and tended agricultural fields, and the crops were theirs except for a small payment to their owners. Slaves also took care of ranching and other tasks, but most of the day-to-day work was divided between them and the matrilineage, so, with occasional exceptions, they were not the principal source of labor. Their treatment, however, depended on the nature and temperament of their owners. They were property, and they were bought and sold as such.[17]

The number of African slaves in Creek territory at this time has not been thoroughly studied, but we do know that many Creek families owned at least two slaves, and the emerging wealthy Creeks owned dozens. In addition, there were runaway slaves and former slaves in Creek country, many of whom married into Creek society. Needless to say, such closeness resulted in mixed progeny. Africans and mixed African Creeks occupied an ambiguous social station—some were held in slavery, while others were considered free; some were accepted as full Creek citizens, while others were considered affinal relations only. But after the American Revolution, their status took a menacing turn.[18]

In earlier times, southern Indians had not subscribed to the black and white racial binary of the U.S. South. As scholars have noted, however, around 1800 they began to look on their African Indian citizenry through a racialized lens adopted from southern Americans. Americans had always offered rewards for runaway slaves, and before this time, the Creeks and other southern Indians had been averse to turning over runaways, largely because they did not conceive of them as property. After the revolution, with more and more Creeks acquiring slaves, the danger for runaway slaves and other Africans and even African Creeks of being returned or sold to Americans increased, because many Creeks now advocated chattel slavery and the plantation economy and thought of slaves as property.[19]

The plan for civilization conformed to much of southern Indian life economically. Indian men and women already were engaged in wage labor, and they continued to hire themselves out as guides, translators, spies, and postal riders. Many also now opened their own small businesses and cottage industries, including traveler's lodges, ferries, and blacksmith shops. Once spinning wheels and looms became available through the plan for civilization, Indian women became devoted cloth makers, producing cloth for themselves and their families as well as for sale.[20]

Mostly, though, southern Indians relished ranching. Although some had begun acquiring cows and hogs in the early years of colonization, it was not until after the American Revolution, and with the decline in the deerskin trade, that they began to own them in any number. Ranching was a relatively easy alternative to the deerskin trade. Ranchers free-ranged their cattle, hogs, and horses; thus the new enterprise did not entail additional labor needs. Ranching also functioned to keep the formal trade economy afloat, and switching commodities from deerskins to livestock could be done within the well-established methods of the trade system. The number of cattle and hogs in the American South by the turn of the nineteenth century is not known. However, there is every indication that the numbers were high. Most Indians, men and women, owned some kind of livestock, if nothing more than a horse. Although the Creeks were not wholly accepting of the plan for civilization, on the issue of raising cattle and hogs, Hawkins found the Creeks and other southern Indians well on the road to becoming ranchers at the time of his arrival in the South in 1796. Surveying Creek country two years later, Hawkins listed almost every town in Creek country as having herds of livestock, with the size of some herds ranging from 30 to 150 head, and free-ranging over the whole of Creek country.[21]

While southern Indians raised cattle and hogs in part for their own consumption, Indian ranchers drove their livestock to markets in Mobile, Charleston, Savannah, and Pensacola, where they were sold on the hoof. They used the proceeds to purchase cloth, guns, ammunition, metal goods, and other European-manufactured items, and some purchased African slaves. Some Indian families, especially the métis elites, were more ranchers than commercial hunters and grew quite wealthy. Creeks of lesser means, too, began to establish individual or family farmsteads, albeit on a more modest scale in comparison to the elites, resulting in a dramatic change in settlement patterns. Before, a typical Indian town was located within the alluvial floodplain of a major stream. Most people lived in and around their town, farmed communal fields in the floodplains, and actively participated in community life. By the early nineteenth century, however, people began to move away from the square-ground town centers. Indian ranchers allowed their animals to free-range, and as the natural forage around the major population centers began to show signs of depletion, more and more people fanned out across the country, settling farmsteads on the alluvial floodplains of smaller streams and ranging their livestock in the hinterlands. They did not, however, privately own their farmsteads; the lands remained communal property for which the families were granted use rights only.[22]

One can see that the Indian ranching complex was part of the larger interior economy as also practiced by American small farmers. It should not be surprising, then, that the settlement patterns of the southern Indians were similar to those of American small farmers, as both vied for the exact same resources, in this case good rangelands and floodplain soils. Clearly, American frontier families and Indian families had much in common. Even though there were boundary lines between them marking the legal lines of separation, Americans and southern Indians lived side by side, and Indians, Americans, and Africans routinely penetrated far beyond those lines so that there was, in fact, no real boundary between them.[23]

People passed between the Indian and American territories continuously and quite easily, despite the efforts of federal, state, and territorial officials to control such movements. Southern Indians and frontier Americans forged pervasive economic connections because each depended on the other for various goods that were hard to come by on the frontier. Indian visitors brought wild meats, baskets, agricultural produce, buckskins, and other items to trade for cloth, metal pots and pans, trinkets, ammunition, and difficult-to-find foodstuffs such as coffee, flour, and sugar, as well as any other items that a frontier family could spare. But most frontier homesteaders were not wealthy and did not have large quantities of goods to exchange, and Indian men and women could only afford to barter their surpluses. These sorts of exchanges, then, were small, but they were necessary because of the irregular access to commercial goods on the frontier and because of the risks and unpredictability of subsistence farming and hunting.[24]

Southern frontier farmers adopted Indian agricultural methods and crops. They also learned herbal remedies from the Indians and fused their folklore with Indian mythology and tales. Friendships formed, as did marriages and business partnerships, most notably between gangs of horse thieves composed of Indians, Africans, and Americans. Genetic exchanges took place through intermarriage, which also promoted an exchange of ideas and lifeways. Indian men and women regularly visited American settlers to drink, socialize, and stage competitions such as horse and foot races. American frontier people likewise crossed into Indian territory to visit with friends and family and to barter. Even in the larger port cities, such as Charleston, Savannah, Pensacola, Mobile, and New Orleans, Indian men and women from the interior could be found trading and visiting. Such mingling, exchanges, and interactions between southern Indians and Americans were so routine that they would not necessarily have aroused suspicion and animosity. Despite boundary lines and many distinctions of habit, their world was a single one composed of their interactions and reliance on one another. As each adopted traits from the other, a new world emerged, composed of elements of both. This world, however, was built on the unstable foundation of American westward expansion.

We note that Indian land acquisition was driven not by the needs of the American frontier family, but by the avarice of wealthy southern land speculators. These men, most of them prominent government officials such as William Blount and Andrew Jackson, did not wish to wait to obtain land under the plan for civilization, and they incessantly pushed for land cessions. Furthermore, they clearly understood how to use American frontier families as agents of speculation. They sponsored the illegal settlement of American towns on Indian lands, including places like Muscle Shoals in Tennessee and Wofford's settlement in Georgia. They promoted border jumping and squatting on Indian lands by financing the migration of American settlers and by using their influence with state governments to protect the newcomers' fraudulent land claims.[25]

The towns of the Indian coalescent societies recognized early in their colonial experience that they had to work together in dealing with Europeans and later Americans over land issues. By the nineteenth century, virtually every one of the towns in a coalescent society had agreed that their national territory was held in common and that land could only be ceded by a unanimous agreement made with a full representation of towns from a particular group. For the Creeks, it meant that only a full representation of Creeks could cede Creek lands. However, Creek land tenure was complicated. At the most inclusive level, Creek lands were the national territory held in common by the Creek Confederacy. The fragmented nature of the confederacy, though, meant that the Upper and Lower Creeks had land rights over specific regions, and that the townships had land rights over the watersheds on which they were located and beyond. Thus, there were oftentimes overlapping and competing claims to land rights. Land speculators exploited such ambiguities. Agents of land companies penetrated into Indian territory in order to negotiate land and resource-use deals with anyone they could sway with promises of gifts, money, and shares in their company; and by the turn of the nineteenth century, there were many Indians who could be easily swayed. Consequently, with land speculators involved at every step, the U.S. government pressured southern Indians into making land cessions.[26]

In addition, as war with Britain became imminent in 1812, the federal and state governments demanded that the Indian governments allow roads to be cut through their territories. Such pressure for land cessions and roads, along with the rising number of American immigrants, guaranteed that hostility, suspicion, and distrust would come to characterize relations between southern Indians and the United States. It also meant that those animosities would eventually bleed into the dealings between Indians and frontier Americans. And soon, even within Indian nations, sides began to form around controversies such as land cessions, roads, the plan for civilization, the increasing disparities in wealth, the role of the métis elite, and relations with America.[27]

In 1811, a Shawnee prophet, Tenskwatawa, and his warrior brother Tecumseh would give violent expression to these growing internal tensions, and their reach would penetrate into the Deep South. The Shawnee brothers advocated a return to Native ways, a separation of all Indians from the United States, and a pan-Indian confederacy. Tecumseh hoped that, with supernatural aid against American bullets and cannons and material aid from the British, a war could be won to achieve these goals. With Tenskwatawa he launched a religious revitalization movement that swept across the Ohio country, and began building a pan-Indian alliance to take down America.[28]

Seeking southern Indian allies, Tecumseh traveled into the South to speak with the Chickasaws, Choctaws, and Creeks. He met with little success with the Chickasaws and Choctaws, but when he spoke at the Tuckabatchee square during the Creek National Council, his words drove a wedge into the Creek Confederacy, dividing Creek society. The result was a Creek civil war, known as the Red Stick War after Tecumseh's followers, who were known as Red Sticks because of the red war clubs they carried. Creek fought Creek as the Red Sticks attempted to turn the Creeks away from America. Even towns became divided, and lines were drawn across the Creek Confederacy. In reality, Tecumseh himself did not divide the Creeks. He only gave voice to a growing conviction held by many that the United States aimed to dispossess them of their lands and to undermine their sovereignty as a people. As we have seen, this conviction was, in fact, what the U.S. government had intended all along.[29]

After speaking to the Creeks, Tecumseh returned to the Ohio country, where his Indian coalition joined the British when the War of 1812 broke out. In 1813 he joined with British forces to face the Americans at the Thames River. After three volleys, the British retreated, leaving Tecumseh and his seven hundred Indian warriors to fight the Americans alone. Tecumseh was killed, and his Indian forces were defeated. Earlier that same year, Creek Red Sticks, inflamed by the teachings of Tenskwatawa, had turned their wrath against America and attacked Fort Mims in southern Alabama, where surrounding American and métis families had taken shelter when hostilities broke out. The battle was a ferocious Red Stick victory, and it prompted the southern states to immediate action. Tennessee and Georgia had waited for such an opportunity for years, and the southern states led the call for an invasion of Creek country. The men who headed the U.S. war movement were the same men who had been vying for Indian lands all along, including Andrew Jackson. Georgia, Tennessee, and the Mississippi Territory readied their militias and enlisted aid from the Choctaws, Cherokees, and Lower Creeks. The invasion forces were led by Jackson.[30]

U.S. retribution was swift and merciless. Federal forces invaded Creek territory and engaged the Red Sticks in numerous bloody battles. Hundreds of Red Sticks died. U.S. forces burned many of the Upper Creek towns, drove women and children into the canebrakes and swamps, and forced the Red Sticks to move north to their refugee town, Tohopeka, at Horseshoe Bend on the Tallapoosa River. Jackson's army attacked Tohopeka on March 27, 1814. The Battle of Horseshoe Bend spelled defeat for the core of Red Sticks, and Jackson and his army routed the remaining members of the movement with little difficulty. In the aftermath, Creek country lay in ruins, and thousands of Red Stick women, children, and warriors fled south, into Seminole country, where they would continue the resistance for over two decades.[31]

In August 1815, Jackson forced the leaders of the Creek Confederacy to sign the Treaty of Fort Jackson, which he had personally engineered. Indeed, in a startling show of power, Jackson was the sole U.S. commissioner at the negotiations, and he demanded that the Creek headmen sign the document under threats of renewing the war. The Treaty of Fort Jackson, ostensibly touted as reparation for U.S. expenses incurred in the war, cut away twenty-three million acres, some two-thirds of Creek country.[32]

With millions of acres of Creek lands now available for white settlement, American squatters poured into Georgia and Alabama. They were aided and abetted by wealthy land speculators, who sent their agents into the newly ceded lands to cajole, intimidate, and outright illegally force Creek households into "selling" additional tracts of land. Creek people resented the Treaty of Fort Jackson, and most did not respect it as a legally binding document. They challenged speculator land grabs and confiscated settler properties. Tensions mounted, resulting in increasing outbreaks of hostility. The turmoil in Creek country intensified the call from southern Americans for the expulsion of all southern Indians. By 1820, the push for Indian removal was heightening across the United States and generalized into a blanket call for the removal of all Native peoples east of the Mississippi River.[33]

Although it would take another two decades for removal to be fully realized, both federal and state governments began reducing or ignoring Indian treaty rights and undermining rights to which sovereign nations were commonly entitled. As early as 1790, in an effort to constrain land speculation, Congress had passed a series of statutes, known as the Indian Trade and Intercourse Acts, to regulate Indian land sales. These acts stipulated that only the federal government could obtain Indian lands, and only through treaties, thus slowing the private speculators and state governments that were seeking land. Nevertheless, speculators came to control the federal and state governments and obstructed federal efforts to retain authority over land deals. After Benjamin Hawkins died in 1816, a string of notorious land speculators filled his job as agent to the Creeks. And over the next decade, the U.S., through a series of forced and illegal land cessions, whittled away at the Creek lands in Georgia. By 1825, the Creeks' eastern boundary lay at the Flint River, and their holdings in Alabama now included only the lands in central Alabama between the Chattahoochee and Coosa rivers. The future indeed was bleak for Creek men and women.[34]

Seven years earlier, in 1818, in an effort to stave off land speculators, Creek leaders had experimented with centralizing their government by codifying Creek laws and formalizing the National Council as a representative governing body, complete with elected offices and with true centralized authority, meaning that all Creek adults would be compelled by force of law to comply with any decisions made by the National Council. Arguing that the Creeks must present a unified and centralized government to the United States, the métis Creek William McIntosh drafted a series of Creek legal codes, in writing and in English (since the Creeks had no written language at this time), and pressured the National Council to pass them. With historical hindsight, many scholars understand that McIntosh designed the 1818 codes to undermine traditional Creek legal principles and to protect land speculators and wealthy slave-owning Creeks. These codes outlawed clan-based revenge, enshrined private property, deemed inheritance to proceed from father to son (rather than through the matriline), instituted a slightly milder version of the southern states' black codes governing the treatment and behavior of black slaves, and authorized a Creek constabulary to enforce the laws.[35]

One of the laws, however, confirmed that only the National Council, as representative of the entire nation, could sell Creek lands. Unauthorized land sales would not be tolerated, and any infractions were punishable by death. However, Creek leaders were uncertain how to implement centralized authority outside the international arena. Sure, the National Council served as a representative body when dealing with the Americans, but regulating internal domestic affairs proved difficult. Most Creeks ignored the new laws, and the policing agents, faced with clan retaliations, were reluctant to enforce them. As a coalescent society, the Creek Confederacy had operated as a loosely unified group of independent, self-governing townships. Power was diffuse, more heterarchical than hierarchical. The National Council, then, was ineffective in policing the affairs of individual towns and of self-serving, ambitious Creek men such as William McIntosh.[36]

McIntosh was a wealthy métis elite from Coweta and a member of the Wind clan who rose to political prominence after the Red Stick War. He was also a cousin of Georgia governor George McIntosh Troup. McIntosh had dabbled in Creek politics as a young man; he also had aided Andrew Jackson's forces against the Red Sticks, gaining the trust of Jackson and the Americans. After the war, McIntosh's political ambitions grew, and, being fluent in English, cousin to Troup, and trusted by both the Georgians and the federal authorities, he was instrumental in key land cessions after the Treaty of Fort Jackson. He also most likely enriched himself and his followers through illegal bribes and bonuses with these cessions. In 1818, McIntosh played a heavy role in the Treaty of Fort Mitchell, which shaved off several eastern parcels of Creek country. In 1821, he muscled through the Treaty of Indian Springs, which moved the eastern boundary line from the Ocmulgee to the Flint River, and after which the National Council debated his execution.[37]

McIntosh represented only a fraction of the Lower Creek towns, and he did not hold any elected office. Nor could he speak for the nation. Even so, he stepped forward as a national representative when the U.S., under pressure from the Georgians, opened negotiations with Creek headmen in 1824 for another land cession. This treaty broached the topic of Creek removal. The U.S. commissioners proposed a bargain: if the Creeks would sell all of their lands in Georgia and Alabama and remove to the West, the U.S. would provide them with land, pay all their removal expenses, and reimburse Creek households for the loss of any "improvements." Upper Creek headman Opothle Yoholo, speaking for the National Council, unequivocally rejected the offer. McIntosh, however, secretly convinced the U.S. commissioners that he represented the nation and could sign the treaty, with amendments to include payments to him and his followers. McIntosh signed the Treaty of Indian Springs at his tavern on February 12, 1825; the other Creeks in attendance, including Opothle Yoholo, refused to sign.[38]

Congress ratified the 1825 Treaty of Indian Springs despite written protests from the Creek National Council. The signing also sealed McIntosh's fate. According to Creek law, his actions were illegal and treasonous and constituted a capital offense. The National Council, for perhaps the first time acting in concert and as a true centralized authority, ordered his execution. A few days later, 150 Creek warriors descended on McIntosh's home and killed him and two of his supporters.[39]

Afraid that the killings portended another war with the Creeks, Georgia and federal officials fretted over McIntosh's execution and the 1825 Treaty of Indian Springs. President John Q. Adams sought to resolve the issue by renegotiating the agreement. To appease the Georgians, the new treaty offered to keep the Chattahoochee River as the eastern boundary of Creek territory; and to appease the Creeks, it would allow the Creeks to retain their lands in Alabama and reimburse them $200,000 for the Georgia lands. The new treaty retained the offers related to removal. Both parties signed the Treaty of Washington in 1826. Scholar Michael Green notes that although the revised agreement was not in the best interests of the Creeks, "they had won some important victories." Most notably, the federal and state governments confirmed Creek national sovereignty in the treaty when they recognized the Creek National Council as a representative governing body for the Creeks.[40]

Even so, with the Treaty of Washington (and a subsequent 1827 Treaty of Indian Agency that relinquished two small slivers of land east of the Chattahoochee), the Creeks were left with only a fraction of their former holdings—namely a relatively small portion of land in Alabama, from west of the Chattahoochee to the Coosa River. The towns of the Lower Creeks now lay in Georgia territory. Recall that the Creeks at this time were mostly ranchers and had moved into the hinterlands for cattle grazing and farming. They needed extensive free-range acreage to maintain their herds, but the treaty constricted their lands, and especially the free-range pasturage, to the point where emigration out of the region looked like a good option. Moreover, land speculators and squatters once again flooded into the newly ceded lands and confiscated Creek homes, goods, herds, and even crops, oftentimes not even giving Creek families a chance to evacuate. There were continuous outbreaks of low-level violence throughout the ceded lands. Creek life grew increasingly uncomfortable, difficult, and dangerous.[41]

Many Creeks and African Creeks opted to move to Florida, where they joined the burgeoning group of Creeks, African Creeks, and African Americans who were now known as the Seminoles. The Seminoles would maintain their resistance to American encroachments for the next two decades in the bitter and bloody Seminole Wars. Many Lower Creeks relocated across the Chattahoochee into Upper Creek towns. Most of McIntosh's supporters, as well as many others from the Lower Creek towns, took advantage of the removal offers in the Treaty of Washington and headed west to present-day Oklahoma, where the U.S. government had designated lands along the Arkansas River for Creek immigrants. Three parties, including Creeks, African Creeks, and African slaves owned by Creeks, were dispatched from Alabama over the next three years. In 1827, the total population of Creeks was around 25,000. That year, over 700 Creeks chose to emigrate; in 1828, another 518 Creeks left for present-day Oklahoma; and in 1829, approximately 1,300 Creeks decided that life would be better there than in their homeland. The majority of Creeks, however, resisted and resented anything to do with removal.[42]

For Americans, the Treaty of Washington exacerbated a growing unease and distrust between the southern states and the federal government. Southern states argued that U.S. authorities were obliged to secure Indian lands for them, and they understood the Treaty of Washington to be pro-Indian and to give the federal government too much authority over Indian affairs. A small group of powerful southern politicians, outraged by the Treaty of Washington, conspired to increase pressure on southern Indian opposition by claiming states' jurisdiction over all Indian territories within their borders, in effect abrogating federal treaty rights and Native national sovereignties. The plan also made a clear distinction: Native peoples would be brought into each state as "subjects" and not "citizens," rendering them the equivalent of the slave population, subject to the extreme and oppressive laws of the slave states, and given few rights within those states. Alabama claimed jurisdiction over the Creeks. Since Indians were not allowed to testify in an Alabama court of law, immoral and illegal land speculators had free rein to pressure beleaguered individual Creeks to sell parcels of land, and American emigrants could harass, rob, defraud, abuse, and even kill Creek men, women, and children with impunity.[43]

Amid this deterioration, Andrew Jackson was elected president in 1828. Jackson had supported Indian removal or extermination for years.

Once in office, he led the national push for the removal of all Indian tribes east of the Mississippi River to western lands designated as the "Indian Territory"—lands in present-day Oklahoma, Kansas, Nebraska, and parts of Iowa that the U.S. had forced the indigenous inhabitants to cede. He also condoned and abetted actions by the southern states to intimidate and harass the Indians within their borders. Jackson did not act alone. Recent scholarship reveals the deep pockets of wealthy land speculators and the international network of banking interests that underwrote, promoted, and ultimately financed Indian removal. There are no two ways about it: Indian removal was a land grab by rapacious capitalist speculators eager to make their fortunes.[44]

The scope of Indian removal was one of the largest and most expensive undertakings of its time. The proposal called for the expulsion of eighty thousand people, reimbursement for losses they incurred when leaving their homes, and the reestablishment of homes and towns in new lands. The benefit to the U.S. was the opening of millions of acres of land to speculators for American settlement. With so much money to be made, national and international financiers eagerly guaranteed the fiscal needs for Indian removal, but wider American public approval was not as easily won. To this end, the supporters of removal drew on a deeply ingrained American racism, denigrating Native peoples as "savage," "uncivilized," "dangerous," and "childlike," and claiming that the only hope for their survival was to be far away from Americans and under the protection of the U.S. government. Jackson and other supporters promulgated these stereotypes and lies about Native Americans in a vigorous public relations campaign to generate broad American and international support.[45]

Still, there were many Americans who were vocal opponents of Indian removal. Public intellectuals, politicians, religious leaders, and journalists argued that the new republic had been built on law and order, good governance, and fairness, and that removing the Indians was morally wrong and violated the goodwill and trust necessary for all diplomatic negotiations between sovereign nations. They predicted that Indian removal would be a dark and indelible stain on America's reputation and history and undermine international trust. The opponents of removal were oftentimes also abolitionists, and many lived in the North, contributing to the widening sectional divide that was already evident in the new nation.[46]

Despite such vigorous opposition and after prolonged and vicious debate, the Indian Removal Act narrowly passed in both houses of the U.S. Congress on May 26 and 27, 1830, delivering a stunning victory for Andrew Jackson and his supporters. As is well known, and as the twenty-first-century U.S. Supreme Court would reiterate almost two hundred years later, the Indian Removal Act made a promise: in return for relocating, the U.S. government would give the removed eastern tribes title to lands in the West that the U.S. had set aside for them. The promise is in section 3 of the act, which reads:

> *And be it further enacted,* That in the making of any such exchange or exchanges [of territory], it shall and may be lawful for the President solemnly to assure the tribe or nation with which the exchange is made that the United States will forever secure and guaranty to them, and their heirs or successors, the country so exchanged with them; and if they prefer it that the United States will cause a patent or grant to be made and executed for the same: *Provided always,* That such lands shall revert to the United States, if the Indians become extinct, or abandon the same. (Emphasis in the original)

The U.S. government would also pay for the removal process and reimburse Indian families for properties and improvements left behind. It would support removed families for one year after their arrival in the new territory and offer protection against any hostile parties in the West, Native or otherwise. The act also guaranteed that no existing treaties would be violated, in essence stipulating that no Indian nation would be forcibly removed.[47]

The United States was still a relatively new nation in 1830, and American politicians, businesspeople, and military leaders were among those who were keenly interested in fostering a good international reputation for the fledgling state. It was imperative that the world of nations view the U.S. as a nation under the rule of law. The state-sponsored expulsion of tens of thousands of Indians challenged this perception because of its cruelty and immorality. The Jackson administration and removal supporters, then, needed to ensure that Indian removal followed the letter of the law set forth in the Removal Act. They had no objections, however, to violating the spirit of the law.[48]

The act required the consent of the tribes to be removed, so Jackson immediately appointed commissioners to begin negotiating removal treaties with all of the eastern tribes, with a focus on those occupying valuable cotton lands in the South, which of course included the Creeks. Each of the so-called Five Civilized Tribes—the Creeks, Cherokees, Choctaws, Chickasaws, and Seminoles—resisted removal in their own way, but one by one, the U.S. forced the southern Indian nations to sign treaties agreeing to cede all of their southern lands to the states and to remove to new lands in Oklahoma. The Choctaws signed the Treaty of Dancing Rabbit Creek in 1830; the Chickasaws signed the Treaty of Pontotoc Creek in 1832; one group of Seminoles signed the Treaty of Payne's Landing in 1832, while others fled into the Everglades, where they would continue the Seminole resistance for another decade; the Cherokees signed the Treaty of New Echota in 1835; and the Creeks signed the 1832 Treaty of Washington (also known as the Treaty of 1832 or the 1832 Treaty of Cusseta).

Each removal treaty was different, although the goal was always the same—acquiring Indian lands. For the Creeks, the 1832 Treaty of Washington was by all accounts a desperate attempt by Creek leaders to thwart Indian removal and to stay in their homelands. When Alabama extended the state's jurisdiction into Creek country, the Creek National Council sent delegations, at three different times, to Washington in protest. In 1832, the fourth delegation, led by Opothle Yoholo, presented an agreement devised in Cusseta to Jackson's secretary of war, Lewis Cass, which became part of the final treaty. In it, the Creeks agreed to relinquish all Creek land to the U.S. government. In return, the government would provide lands in the West for those Creeks willing to emigrate, as well as pay for the emigration and one year of supplies once they were in their new homes. The U.S. would also compensate emigrants for any material losses. For those who wished to remain in Alabama, the federal government would survey Creek lands and divide them into family allotments (320 acres to heads of households and orphans, 640 acres to headmen). The National Council then would sell any remaining lands to the U.S.

The promise about the western lands made in the Removal Act was repeated in article XIV of the 1832 Treaty of Washington, which reads:

> The Creek country west of the Mississippi shall be solemnly guarantied [*sic*] to the Creek Indians, nor shall any State or Territory ever have a right to pass laws for the government of such Indians, but they shall be allowed to govern themselves, so far as may be compatible with the general jurisdiction which Congress may think proper to exercise over them.

Cass also agreed to expel any intruders and to regulate land speculators. However, he left to the Alabama legislature the question of Alabama "citizenship" for any Creeks who chose to remain in the state.[49]

The 1832 Treaty of Washington was disastrous for the Creeks. Cass did not uphold his promise to expel intruders and regulate land speculators; compensation was slow, if it came at all; contractors, who doubled as land speculators, were hired to supply the emigrants, and they consistently failed to show or offered only meager food and water when they did; and the Alabama legislature promptly rejected the appeal for citizenship. The treaty disallowed communal ownership of lands, effectively dissolving the territorial base of the Creek Nation. In a foreshadowing of the late nineteenth-century allotment era, lands were now doled out to those who remained in Alabama in allotments with individual titles, or as private property. The result was much suffering for those who removed, both en route and once in their new lands, and a losing battle against frenzied speculation and violent intrusions for those who stayed behind. Intruders, with no legal restraints whatsoever, trespassed onto the now privately owned Creek allotments, sometimes attempting to swindle families out of their holdings, sometimes violently forcing them off their lands.[50]

Many Creeks began to reconsider removal, and two more parties chose to emigrate: 630 Creeks voluntarily relocated to the West in 1834, followed in 1835 by another 511. The option for voluntary removal, however, was about to disappear. In 1835, the young Seminole leader Osceola led a group of warriors in an assault on federal troops who had been deployed to present-day Florida to deport Seminoles. Secretary of War Cass dispatched American troops under General Winfield Scott to Seminole country, this time not as supervisors of voluntary deportations, but as full-fledged military operatives sent to defeat the Seminoles and force them to remove. The conflict spilled into Creek country in May 1836, when a group of Lower Creek men, fed up with the incessant harassments by American intruders and speculators, attacked a party of Georgians who were traveling to Alabama to participate in the looting and mayhem. Cass redirected the Florida troops, who were unable to subdue the Seminoles, and dispatched new troops under General Thomas S. Jesup to Creek country with orders for immediate deportation of all Creeks. The conflict that ensued, known as the Second Creek War, was short-lived, but brutal.[51]

The Second Creek War and the humiliation of American troops at the hands of the Seminoles generated much apprehension among American southerners. Not only were they worried about igniting a widespread Indian war across the South, but they also feared slave revolts, since it was well known that Africans were fighting alongside Indians. The war also made it clear that Native peoples did not want to leave their homelands, and that they would not do so peaceably. For many Americans, removal ideology hardened, from promoting and hoping for a peaceful voluntary departure to supporting forced removal against the will of Native peoples. In the words of historian Claudio Saunt, these conflicts "exposed the dark impulse that underlay federal policy—a mounting desire to eliminate native families."[52]

Federal militia began rounding up Creek families for involuntary deportation. The first group, which left in 1836, consisted mostly of the surviving resistance fighters and their families—2,300 men, women, and children. General Jesup treated them as war criminals, keeping them heavily guarded with shoot-to-kill orders for any disrupters, and marching the men in chains to Montgomery, Alabama. At Montgomery, steamboats waited to transport the group to Mobile and New Orleans, after which they were marched overland to Fort Gibson, in present-day Oklahoma. Over eighty people perished in this forced march alone.[53]

Six more roundups followed. Approximately 19,400 Creek citizens in total were involuntarily deported from their homelands. Federal troops seized families from their households with little notice and marched them to concentration camps to await forced removal. Many Creeks sought refuge with the Seminoles and Cherokees or disappeared into the woods. State militiamen hunted the escapees, stole their belongings, and marched those they captured to the concentration camps. Then, at bayonet point, federal troops forced them all to leave. Some of the refugees traveled on horseback, in wagons, or by steamboat, but most were on foot. They were allowed to take only a few possessions or foodstuffs, so they had to rely on contractors for supplies of food, water, shelter, and transport. The contractors, however, proved as depraved as the speculators and intruders. They consistently cut costs by purchasing inferior foods, tents, boats, horses, wagons, and other supplies, oftentimes denying provisions altogether. The whole enterprise was an unmitigated and shameful disaster.[54]

The Creek people's suffering was immense. The trip from Alabama to the Indian Territory covered 770 miles and took two to three months to complete. Exhausted and with little to no food, medical attention, or shelter, hundreds of people fell ill while on the march, and hundreds more died along the way. Mothers smothered their children rather than subject them to such suffering. Suicides were common. Escapees were frequently shot. One particularly shocking tragedy occurred when the steamboat *Monmouth*, carrying over 600 Creek refugees, collided with another boat on the Mississippi River. At least 415 of the Creeks on board perished. The total number of Creeks who died during removal is difficult to calculate, especially when one factors in the deaths that had already occurred in the months leading up to the forced deportations and during the people's first months once in the Indian Territory.[55]

Historian Christopher Haveman perused contractor claims for financial reimbursement in the involuntary detachments and found that contractors had reported more than seven hundred deaths on the march, or about 4 percent of the total number of involuntary refugees. The number of those who died while en route during the voluntary migrations was not tallied and appears to have been substantially lower than the death rate for the involuntary detachments. The death rates in the Indian Territory, however, soared for both the voluntary and involuntary detachments. Once the removed people were in the Indian Territory, U.S.

troops forced them to stay in squalid immigration camps where disease was rampant. Scores of Creeks died in 1837 when smallpox ravaged Fort Gibson, the first destination for Creek detachments in Oklahoma. Many of their bodies were left unburied, their bones whitening on the ground where they had fallen. Others suffered through long, unfamiliar winters in ragged government-issue tents, with inadequate food and heat. Many succumbed to frostbite, infections, and malnourishment—not to mention despondency, as depression and social malaise took physical expression through suicides, indifference, and neglect. Again, the exact totals of deaths in the Indian Territory in the first twelve months after arrival are elusive, but estimates are that between 1837 and 1840, Creeks lost an additional 23 percent of their population (approximately 5,750 people in total). An 1857 census put the number of Creeks in the Indian Territory at 14,888, meaning that the population had continued to decline, and that between 1837 and 1857, almost 10,000 Creek lives were lost, or 33 percent of the population.

Even so, survivors began to build towns, homes, and farmsteads in the lands reserved for them in the Indian Territory. They soon reconstituted the Muscogee (Creek) Nation.[56]

3

THE MUSCOGEE (CREEK) RESERVATION IN THE INDIAN TERRITORY

"Indian Territory" was the destination for the removed southern Indians. The term deserves explication because the definition goes to the heart of what the Muscogee (Creek) Nation (MCN) Reservation is and was intended to be. The British had introduced a similar term, "Indian Reserves," in the Proclamation of 1763 in order to distinguish between lands ceded or granted to the colonists and the lands claimed and occupied by indigenous groups. At the end of the eighteenth century, when America embarked on its aggressive campaign of westward expansion, the U.S. Congress distinguished between "organized" and "unorganized" territories with regard to lands claimed by the United states—the former having a body of laws, an appointed governor, an elected legislature, and territorial judicial courts. In 1803, Thomas Jefferson negotiated the Louisiana Purchase, and he and other U.S. officials eyed the enormous swath of land, already home to thousands of Native peoples, as a future home for removed eastern Indians as well. A year later, in 1804, Congress administratively divided the purchase into the Territory of Orleans and the Territory of Louisiana. When Louisiana became a state in 1812, the lands not included in it became known as the Missouri Territory, part of which was subsequently organized in preparation for Missouri statehood, which occurred in 1821. At the time, talks for Indian removal were already underway in Washington, and the advocates for removal had argued that the remaining Missouri Territory was the most logical destination for the thousands of people they intended to displace. Removal treaties with the Choctaws and Cherokees carved out of those lands the organized Arkansas Territory. The remainder of the Missouri Territory, still unorganized, became known as the Indian Territory and encompassed present-day Oklahoma, Kansas, Nebraska, and parts of Iowa.[1]

In the Indian Removal Act of 1830, the U.S. government set aside lands in the Indian Territory for removed Indian people, with the provision that "districts," with clear boundaries, were to be established for each tribe or nation. Each of the Five Tribes eventually received a patent title for communal ownership of its lands in fee simple. All of the Five Tribes issued decrees stating that these lands were inalienable, meaning that they could not be sold except with the consent of the tribe. The district boundaries were drawn on a case-by-case basis. For the Creeks, the 1832 Treaty of Washington deemed that the boundaries of Creek lands in the West would be ascertained at an unspecified future date. Once the treaty was signed, the federal government dispatched surveyors to the Indian Territory to mark the Creek boundaries so that deportees could be quickly resettled. In 1833, after a dispute with the Cherokees over which lands in the Indian Territory were Creek and which were Cherokee, an 1833 Treaty with the Creeks clarified in article II the exact boundaries of the Creek lands (see map 5):

> Beginning at the mouth of the north fork of the Canadian river, and run northerly four miles—thence running a straight line so as to meet a line drawn from the south bank of the Arkansas river opposite to the east or lower bank of Grand river, at its junction with the Arkansas, and which runs a course south, 44 deg. west, one mile, to a post placed in the ground—thence along said line to the Arkansas, and up the same and the Verdigris river, to where the old territorial line crosses it—thence along said line north to a point twenty-five miles from the Arkansas river where the old territorial line crosses the same—thence running a line at right angles with the territorial line aforesaid, or west, to the Mexico line—thence along the said line southerly to the Canadian river or to the boundary of the Choctaw country—thence down said river to the place of beginning.

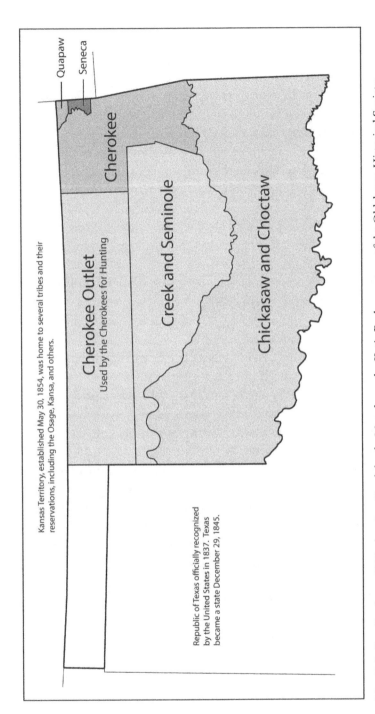

Map 5. Indian Territory, 1833, showing Creek lands. Map drawn by Katie Bush, courtesy of the Oklahoma Historical Society.

In 1852, the Creek Confederacy would receive its land patent title for communal ownership of these lands in fee simple.[2]

For the United States, the Indian Territory was explicitly and exclusively under the jurisdiction of the federal government. When the Cherokees challenged the removal treaty in 1832, the two resultant U.S. Supreme Court cases, *Cherokee Nation v. Georgia* and the landmark case *Worcester v. Georgia*, ruled that Indian tribes were domestic dependent nations and therefore remained distinct political bodies under federal authority. In short, Indian tribes were not under any state laws except where agreed to by the tribes or as determined by an act of Congress.[3]

But what is a "domestic dependent nation," and what sort of relationship does this confer between the U.S. government and Indian nations? This relationship is usually referred to as the "trust doctrine," and defining it is not straightforward. Is it a trust responsibility, a trust obligation, a guardian-ward relationship, a beneficiary-trustee relationship, or what, exactly? Some scholars of Indian law point to the Cherokee cases as mid-nineteenth-century formal enunciations of a relationship between Native groups and colonists that began with the doctrine of discovery and has existed since the meeting of the two worlds in the fifteenth century. Others proclaim that while the trust doctrine may have centuries-old antecedents, it was only vaguely formalized in the twentieth century. Needless to say, there is little agreement on what constitutes the trust doctrine.[4]

Scholars David E. Wilkins and K. Tsianina Lomawaima observe that, at a general level, most scholars and policy experts agree that the trust doctrine implies "federal responsibility to protect or enhance tribal assets (including fiscal, natural, human, and cultural resources) through policy decisions and actions." The exact constraints, flexibility, and mandates of this management, however, vary widely, are subject to multiple interpretations, and are, to date, not systematic or coherent. We cannot here untangle the trust doctrine skein; however, we can document how it has informed U.S. and Indian relations throughout the nineteenth, twentieth, and twenty-first centuries, and, importantly, how it informed the *McGirt v. Oklahoma* ruling.[5]

One federal obligation to the removed Five Tribes was made explicit in the removal treaties and concerned the complication that the Indian

Territory was already occupied. The Comanche, Osage, Kiowa, and other Plains Indians inhabited those lands, and they resented the immigration of eastern tribes, forced or otherwise, into their homelands. Furthermore, both Americans and eastern Indians viewed western Indians as "wild" and eastern Indians as "civilized," thereby setting up a false dichotomy that fueled intra-Indian distrust and prejudices for decades. Inevitably, tensions arose as soon as the eastern deportees began arriving. Section 6 of the Indian Removal Act promised the emigrants U.S. protection against "any other tribe or Indian nation." Consequently the U.S. built a series of military forts, ostensibly to keep peace between the eastern and western tribes, but also to establish a military policing presence in general. In 1835, the eastern and western Indians agreed in the Camp Holmes Treaty to abide by the boundaries set by the U.S. government and to accept federal arbitration of inter-tribal conflicts. That treaty quelled some of the difficulties, but trouble between the tribes always lay just beneath the surface.[6]

On June 30, 1834, Congress passed the last of the Trade and Inter-course Acts. It codified the United States' relationship with Natives living in what the act designated as "Indian Country," which was any part of the United States not within the states of Louisiana and Missouri and the Territory of Arkansas. "Indian Country" should not be confused with the "Indian Territory"—the latter was the reserves of the Five Tribes, and was a subset of "Indian Country." According to the Act of 1834, Indian Country was off-limits to non-Indians, with the exception of federally approved military personnel, Christian religious organizations, traders and businesspeople, and scientific or exploratory expeditions, of which there were many. The act also included provisions banning the sale of alcohol, stipulating punishments for whites who stole from Indians, and applying U.S. criminal law to white-on-Indian crimes committed in Indian Country. It did not, however, extend federal jurisdiction to Indian-on-Indian crimes; these were to be handled by Native judicial systems. Finally, the act attached the Indian Territory to the judicial system of Arkansas Territory. When Arkansas became a state in 1836, the new Arkansas federal district courts became responsible for non-Indian judicial matters in the Indian Territory, such as the trespassing of non-Indians. Despite the guarantees of expulsion in the Act of 1834, illegal intruders and land speculators were a constant menace, creating disturbances throughout the territory and testing the commitment of the Arkansas courts to punish white offenders. Removal treaties and the 1834 act ensured that all non-Natives in the Five Tribes reserves would be removed by the U.S. military at the United States' expense, but enforcement was exceptionally lax. Creeks bitterly scorned the white squatters who attempted to settle on Creek lands and the eastern speculators who traveled to the Indian Territory to swindle families out of parcels of unsold Alabama holdings. The United States' lack of attention to the problem only reinforced the Creeks' and other Five Tribes' distrust of the federal government and judicial system.[7]

Creek deportees who survived the squalid, diseased environment of the initial resettlement camps now faced the monumental task of rebuilding their homes and lives, as well as their nation. By the time of the forced migrations in the late 1830s, the voluntary migrants had managed in the ten years since their departure to reconstitute to some extent their former towns and political order. These voluntary migrants were mostly wealthy, slave-owning, profit-oriented Lower Creeks. They had the resources and economic connections needed to ease their transition into their new lives in the Indian Territory. Within the decade, many had established flourishing farmsteads and ranches on the Arkansas and Verdigris rivers near Fort Gibson and were fully participating in the burgeoning market economy through a commerce in corn, cotton, and livestock. In addition, since the first voluntary migrants were largely from the Lower Creek towns, and many of them were followers of William McIntosh, they had instated William's brother, Roley McIntosh, as their primary leader.[8]

The involuntary migrations of 1836 and 1837 brought almost twenty thousand additional Creeks into the reserve. They were largely from Upper Creek towns and of mostly lesser means. Many also had disdain for the McIntosh pro-removal Creeks and carried a simmering hatred of America and Americans. Their principal leader was Opothle Yoholo, who had led the removal resistance in the homelands. To avoid conflict in the Indian Territory, Opothle Yoholo and Roley McIntosh agreed that the new Upper Creek migrants would settle along the Canadian River. Although there was intermingling between the groups, this geographic separation effectively transferred the distinctions between the Lower and Upper Creek divisions to the Arkansas and Canadian Creek divisions, respectively.[9]

The migrants attempted to replicate in the Indian Territory much about their lives in their homelands. We have seen that prior to removal, most Creeks were subsistence farmers and ranchers, although the métis elites had more substantial agricultural and ranching establishments. The square-ground towns still functioned as political, cultural, and social centers, but most matrilines had moved into the countryside to accommodate their ranching endeavors. Creek families continued this pattern in the Indian Territory. Most Creek families settled on modest individual farmsteads along the river valleys. But even this proved difficult for the involuntary migrants. They had been stripped of most of their belongings during removal, and they were now dependent on the promised U.S. government subsidies and supplies for their new start in the Indian Territory. Exacerbating an already trying situation, the U.S. government delayed annuity payments and reimbursements, unethical contractors absconded with federal monies, and supplies were slow to materialize, if indeed they ever did.[10]

Despite the struggles, townspeople reestablished not only their farmsteads but also their square-ground towns, although at first the latter more closely resembled large campsites. The relative paucity of wood in the Indian Territory, combined with a dearth of building tools, meant that the size and durability of the square-ground facilities, rotundas, and other public buildings were limited. The townspeople of major towns such as Tuckabatchee, however, eventually secured enough wood and supplies to construct impressive public buildings. Creek families had already begun to favor American-style log cabins over Native wattle-and-daub structures before removal, and once they were in the Indian Territory, the log cabin became their predominant domestic structure. Most of the cabins in Creek country were small, with only one or two rooms. The métis elite, however, constructed large clapboard homes with multiple rooms and numerous outbuildings.[11]

Although the square-ground towns were the gathering place for special occasions, most people settled matriline farmsteads and ranches outside of town for access to good grazing and farming lands. The climate and environment in the Indian Territory posed some problems for Creek subsistence farmers and ranchers. The prairies, of course, were a boon to cattle ranching, except that free-ranging on the prairie meant that cattle strayed far distances. Creek families still depended on subsistence and some commercial crops, so many needed arable agricultural lands, and, being unfamiliar with the prairie, most families favored the forested river bottomlands adjacent to the expansive grasslands. Unlike their southern homelands, the bottomlands in the Indian Territory were more readily exhausted through intensive corn agriculture, and Creek subsistence farmers, who were swidden farmers, found that they had to rotate their fields every few years rather than once a decade. Several of the Canadian Creek townships returned to communal farming, and women of the matrilines gathered to cultivate single large plots of land, the proceeds of which were shared by all.[12]

Moreover, unlike the wide floodplains of the deeply cut, meandering southern rivers, the bottomlands in the Indian Territory were narrow strips along the rivers. Additionally, rivers of the plains are relatively shallow and prone to flash flooding, which could easily destroy a season's worth of crops in a single event. Locusts were an occasional but stupefying pest, covering whole fields and wrecking crops in a matter of hours.[13]

Within a few decades, rank-and-file Creek farmers had adapted to their new environment, and their farming and ranching enterprises began to take root, affording a decent, albeit thrifty, lifestyle. Many of the square-ground towns grew from tent camps into bustling rural centers, providing services for the surrounding farm populations as well as wage-labor jobs for Native blacksmiths, tailors, shopkeepers, tanners, and others seeking employment and business opportunities. The métis elites prospered and expanded their plantations, ranches, business enterprises, and professions to include mining, slave trading, merchandising, transportation, law, milling, and the like. The elites increasingly resembled American southern planter elites, while rank-and-file Creek farmers lived much like their American frontier family counterparts. Even so, both retained a strong Creek identity, and all considered the Creek Nation a sovereign and independent nation.[14]

As they had done since their formation as a coalescent society, Creek towns continued to admit other Indians into Creek territory—small contingents of Cherokees, Shawnees, Delawares, Kickapoos, and Piankashaws came to live along the Canadian and Little rivers, settling their own separate towns. When most of the Seminoles began arriving in the Indian Territory in 1839, the U.S. assigned them to settle within the Creek boundaries. However, the protracted Seminole Wars had cleaved the relationship between Seminoles and Creeks. The western Creeks now looked upon their former kinspeople, townspeople, and neighbors with apprehension, and they especially could not reconcile themselves to the equality of Africans among the Seminoles. The Seminoles, likewise, desired an independent polity and feared that the Creeks would attempt to enslave African Seminoles. The two agreed in 1845 that the Seminole settlements would be concentrated on the Little River, and the Seminoles proceeded to establish themselves as a separate people. The tensions remained unabated, however, and in 1855 the U.S. government intervened and led negotiations between the Creeks and Seminoles for a small tract of land on the western edge of the Creek lands to be set aside as Seminole territory, for which the United States paid the Creek Nation $1 million. The agreement, known as the 1856 Treaty with the Creeks, also severed political ties between the Seminoles and Creeks, thus creating the independent Seminole Nation. The treaty was ratified by the U.S. Congress in 1856.[15]

Articles II and III of the treaty specified the boundary lines between the two nations and reiterated that the Seminole lands were appropriated from Creek lands that had been established in the original 1832 and 1833 treaty agreements regarding Creek landholdings in the Indian Territory. After establishing the boundary lines—and of particular interest with respect to the *McGirt* case—the 1856 treaty also promised that "no portion of either of the tracts of country defined in the first and second articles of this agreement shall ever be embraced or included within, or annexed to, any Territory or State" without the authority of the tribe owning the lands. In article XV, the treaty then guaranteed that both the Creeks and the Seminoles were "secured in the unrestricted right of self-government, and full jurisdiction over persons and property" within their boundaries, excepting "all white persons" who were not members of the two nations. In other words, the 1856 treaty confirmed the said territories as the territories of the sovereign Creek and Seminole nations.[16]

The question of African Indians lay at the heart of the Creek and Seminole disagreements, even though African Creeks, freedmen, and black slaves had accompanied the Creeks throughout the removal process. Most of the enslaved were involuntarily deported to the Indian Territory when their owners, whether by choice or by force, migrated west; free African Creeks migrated primarily as part of the mass forced deportations. Estimates of pre-removal African slaves and free African Creeks in Creek country put the number among the Upper Creeks at around five hundred and among the Lower Creeks at around one thousand. The Lower Creeks had owned the majority of black slaves in the pre-removal years, and now, as the Arkansas Creeks, they still were the primary owners of black slaves, and they were wary of emancipated slave populations. The Canadian Creeks (the former Upper Creeks), on the other hand, welcomed emancipated slaves and runaways, many of whom were refugees from the Seminole conflicts in Florida or had been denied citizenship by other removed Indian nations. The Canadian Creeks even allowed a small group to settle a separate town on the Little River.[17]

Referencing the differences in the status of black slaves between the Canadian Creeks and the Arkansas Creeks, past scholars have proposed that the Upper Creeks of the Canadian settlements were more "traditional" in their lifeways, while the Lower Creeks of the Arkansas settlements were more "progressive." Black slaves among the Canadian Creeks, while they were certainly slaves, had more flexibility in their life choices and some economic freedoms. Lower Creek slave owners, on the other hand, had adopted southern white planter racial ideologies and placed firm restrictions on their slaves' choices, movements, and freedoms. Scholars also argue that the Canadian Creeks were more "traditional" because of their communal farmsteads and redistribution of crops, as well as their eschewing of the Christian missionaries who flooded into the Indian Territory soon after the refugees began arriving.[18]

Contemporary Americans at the time noted these differences, but, in fact, the differences between the Arkansas and Canadian Creeks were ones of degree and not of kind. For example, Arkansas Creek leaders were not the only ones to re-create their former landholdings, farms, and ranches using slave labor. Opothle Yoholo, the Canadian Creek leader, settled a large plantation-style homestead on over two thousand acres on the Canadian River, and owned a large number of enslaved Africans to work it. The Arkansas Creeks owned more slaves, but both groups convened in the National Council to pass black codes, although neither group seriously enforced them. The two groups also agreed, at least for a while, to immediately expel Christian missionaries from their territories and to punish any Creeks found practicing the Christian faith. They instead commanded adherence to Creek religious beliefs and practices of the Green Corn Ceremony, the annual renewal ceremony.[19]

Missionaries, however, offered to school Creek children in English and in an American education. Whereas in pre-removal days Creek families had famously been averse to missionizing efforts, the trauma of removal demonstrated the need for knowledge of English, American law, and American values. Every Creek, from the elites to the common folk, knew that these skills were a necessity if they were to establish a successful sovereign state in America. Disregarding their aversion to Christian missionizing in favor of promoting Western educations, Creek leaders submitted a petition to the Creek Indian agent James Logan in 1845 asking that missionaries return to the nation and open schools. Three years later, the National Council approved all missionary and educational activities in both the Arkansas and Canadian towns, and Methodists and Presbyterians opened schools in both districts. In time, Creeks' attendance at church services also grew, and many converted to Christianity.[20]

Creek men and women also recognized that to be a nation among nations, they would need a centralized government. We have seen that Creek leaders had attempted more than once to institutionalize centralized authority, most notably with the efforts of Alexander McGillivray in the late eighteenth century and William McIntosh in the early nineteenth century. However, the deep-rooted, fragmented nature of the confederacy as a coalescent society proved durable and adaptable to most domestic and even international problems, obviating the need for a centralized government. The 1832 Treaty of Washington, and later treaties, guaranteed to the Creeks self-governance once they were in their new homelands, and in 1840 Creek leaders reassembled the National Council in another effort to form a centralized government. They built a large council house halfway between the Canadian and Arkansas settlements, where the council met once a year. Headmen from each town constituted the council, and the Arkansas and Canadian divisions each elected a principal chief. The principal chief of the Arkansas Creeks was Roley McIntosh, who would serve until 1859. The Canadian Creeks, although still counseling with Opothle Yoholo, elected a series of principal chiefs over the next two decades. The National Council drafted a written constitution, but ultimately, Creek leaders were unable to consolidate their government into a centralized authority, and most decisions continued to be made at the town and clan levels.[21]

Three decades into removal, Creek towns and families, with remarkable determination, had reestablished their township governing bodies, had retained their sovereignty and identity, had forged an amicable if wary relationship with the U.S. government, and had adapted to their new environments and the opportunities afforded in the West with numerous economic enterprises. Although there was a widening wealth and social gap between the elites and common folks, these years proved heartening and even prosperous after the trauma and devastation of removal. The intrusion of the American Civil War into the Indian Territory, however, abruptly halted all progress and dimmed future prospects.

The Civil War, as we know, was fought over whether America would continue to be a slave-owning nation. The question of slavery also permeated the Indian Territory. In fact, on the eve of the Civil War, in 1861, the Creek National Council, led by slaveholding elites, drafted another series of laws that severely restricted the movement of African Creeks, both free and enslaved. Still, racialized slavery was not a categorical question because of the confusing and muddied racial classifications in the Indian Territory. Not all slaves were blacks, and not all blacks were slaves. In fact, many formerly enslaved Africans were now full-fledged Indian citizens through marriage, adoption, or emancipation. There was also a rising generation of free African Indians, born of Indian and African parents. Additionally, although the treatment of slaves by Creek owners was increasingly uncertain and cruel, black slaves in the Indian Territory often experienced a measure of independence and self-determination denied to those in the American South.[22]

Thus the question of which side to support when secession occurred was not an easy one, and Native leaders of the removed Five Tribes found themselves considering a morass of factors. Certainly the question of slavery was primary, especially for the métis elite, who owned vast numbers of slaves, had concentrated economic power, and were staunchly opposed to emancipation. Another factor in the decision regarding which side to support was that Indian experiences with the U.S. government had been fraught, to say the least. Not only was the memory of removal seared into the collective consciousness of the Creeks and the other Five Tribes, but they were confronted almost daily with the federal government's negligence in defending against western Indians and American intruders. Also, most of the Indian agents in the Indian Territory were proslavery southerners who used their influence to lobby Indian leaders to the Confederate cause. The Five Tribes also had deep economic connections to the Confederate States: the southern port cities were the points of import and export for their new economic ventures, and the annuities granted through the removal treaties were held in trust by the U.S. government and heavily invested in southern businesses.[23]

There was also the question of land. Throughout the 1850s, Congress contemplated a series of bills to turn the Indian Territory into organized territories and states and open it to American settlement. In fact, in 1854, part of the Indian Territory was organized into the Kansas Territory, which included most of present-day Kansas and Colorado. In 1861, Congress admitted the eastern part of the Kansas Territory into the United States as the free state of Kansas. These maneuvers were not lost on the Five Tribes, and the Creeks and others grew increasingly wary of U.S. intentions for the Indian Territory. The Confederacy, on the other hand, desired the Indian Territory as a strategic stronghold for their western military plans and therefore heavily courted the Five Tribes upon the outbreak of war, offering to respect the boundary lines and to generally rectify all the wrongs done by the U.S. government.[24]

With both rebel and Union troops amassing at the borders of the Indian Territory, in 1861 the Confederacy formally invited the Five Tribes to join the rebellion when they sent Commissioner Albert Pike to convene a meeting of the Five Tribes at North Fork. All but the Cherokees were signatories to the subsequent treaties, and the Cherokees reluctantly joined a few months later. The treaty between the Creeks and the Confederate States of America (CSA), known as the 1861 Treaty with the Creek Nation, allied the Creeks under the CSA, transferred all U.S. treaty obligations to the CSA, and confirmed that Creek slavery was legal, among other stipulations. It also restated the boundary lines delimiting Creek territory and pledged that those lands would remain in Creek hands "as long as grass shall grow and water run."[25]

The treaty was supposedly binding, but in truth, the Creeks, like most of the Five Tribes, were divided over the issue. Those opposed to joining the rebellion stressed that a neutral position was in the best interest of the Five Tribes. After a majority of Creek headmen signed the treaty, Opothle Yoholo and several Canadian Creek leaders who had voiced strong dissent convened likeminded Creeks into an opposition group. Known as the Neutral Creeks, they included about half of the Creek population (mostly Canadian Creeks), along with their slaves and former slaves who had escaped from the Confederate Creeks. This divisiveness between the Confederate and Neutral Creeks largely fell along well-worn intratribal factional lines that had emerged in the removal era.[26]

Confederate Creek troops, along with troops from the other Five Tribes, volunteered for service in the Confederate army in the Indian Territory, under the command of Douglas H. Cooper. Opothle Yoholo and the Neutral Creeks retreated to Kansas, where they hoped to wait out the war under the protection of the Union. Confederate Creeks pursued the refugees, engaging in at least three battles with their countrymen before the Neutral Creeks crossed into Union-held Kansas. Before the war's end, many of the Neutral Creek men joined Union forces (thereafter becoming known as Loyalist Creeks), and the elderly Opothle Yoholo died in a Kansas refugee camp.[27]

The Civil War divided and devastated the Creek Nation and much of the Indian Territory. Both sides burned Loyalist and Confederate Indian towns to the ground. They ransacked crops and livestock, looted shops and mills, damaged and closed mission schools, confiscated tools and implements, and ruined businesses, leading to collapsed economies and the deaths of over a thousand young Indian men. In addition, the National Council was now a Confederate Creek body, meaning that the Loyalist Creeks were effectively disenfranchised from the nation. After the war, when the surviving Loyalist and Confederate Creeks returned to their homelands, there was little left, and they faced the grim prospect of once again rebuilding their lives, homes, towns, and nation. Divided and conquered, the Creeks faced the U.S. federal government as defeated enemies.[28]

Talks with the reunited United States did not reunite the Creek Nation. Instead, the Confederate and Loyalist Creeks vied for dominant positions in the Creek governing bodies. In 1865, representatives from both sides gathered with U.S. diplomats at Fort Smith to discuss the path forward. In an affront to the Loyalist Creeks, U.S. representatives insisted that the United States would treat the two factions as one nation, considering all as part of the Creek Nation, a defeated enemy of the U.S. They then offered terms similar to the terms offered to the Confederate States. The Creeks and the other of the Five Tribes would be granted amnesty and allowed to rejoin the Union as long as they agreed to a U.S. military occupation for a specified amount of time.[29]

A year later, in 1866, Creek representatives from both factions traveled to Washington to sign a treaty with the United States. The Creeks were in a weak position, and although the former Confederate Creeks managed to achieve some small concessions, they had little choice but to submit to U.S. demands. The preamble of the Treaty of 1866 declared that the Creek Nation had voided all previous treaties with the U.S. when it joined the Confederacy, and that this new treaty would reestablish relations between the Creeks and the United States. The Confederate and Loyalist Creeks were to rejoin as one nation; they and the U.S. would now live in "perpetual peace and friendship"; and the Creeks were to emancipate their slaves and grant them full Creek citizenship. The treaty approved a plan to develop federal courts in the Indian Territory, but stated that the U.S. "shall not in any manner interfere with or annul [the Creeks'] present tribal organization, rights, laws, privileges, and customs."[30]

In reparation for their part in the rebellion, article 3 of the treaty forced the Creeks to cede "the west half of their entire domain, to be divided by a line running north and south; the eastern half of said Creek lands, being retained by them, shall, except as herein otherwise stipulated, be forever set apart as a home for said Creek Nation." Article 3 ceded 3,250,560 acres of land to the United States, which the federal government reserved for future Indian resettlements. However, article 3 also guaranteed to the Creek Nation that the unceded eastern lands would "be forever set apart as a home for said Creek Nation." Treaties for the other Five Tribes carried similar cessions, from which millions of acres of the Indian Territory were carved out for the resettlement of eventually thousands of Delawares, Shawnees, Osages, Kansa, Pawnees, Otoes, Missourias, Nez Percés, Tonkawas, Poncas, Sauks, Foxes, Iowas, Potawatomis, and Kickapoos, among others. Mostly, though, the commissioners who engineered the treaty intended for these lands eventually to be opened to non–Native settlement (see map 6).[31]

The U.S. agreed to compensate the Creek Nation thirty cents per acre for the western lands ($975,168 in total). Article 3 specified exactly how the monies were to be spent: $200,000 was designated for restoring Creek farms and businesses, for repairing damages to the mission schools, and to cover per diems for the representatives who had come to Washington; $100,000 was earmarked for distribution among Creek warriors and freedmen who had fought for the Union; and $400,000 was to be distributed among all remaining Creek households, including Creek freedmen. In return, the U.S. would protect the Creeks from hostile Indians, grant amnesty to any Creeks who had participated on the side of the Confederate States, and safeguard the remainder of their annuity payments, which the U.S. Treasury was holding in trust at 5 percent interest per annum.[32]

Portending future encroachments, the treaty also stipulated that the Creek Nation and the other four nations would convene and accept a consolidated territorial government of the Five Tribes under congressional control. When railroad magnates and land speculators put their thumbs on the scale, the treaty included in article 5 a provision forcing the Creeks to grant six-mile-wide rights-of-way to railroad companies seeking to lay lines across the Indian Territory and to sell the resultant strips of land to the parties involved once the lines were completed.[33]

Such provisions should not come as a surprise, since the plan for reconstruction in the Indian Territory was in fact conceived as laying the foundation for opening the region and beyond to American settlement. Creek leaders responded to these pressures by once again attempting to forge a centralized government. In 1867, leaders from

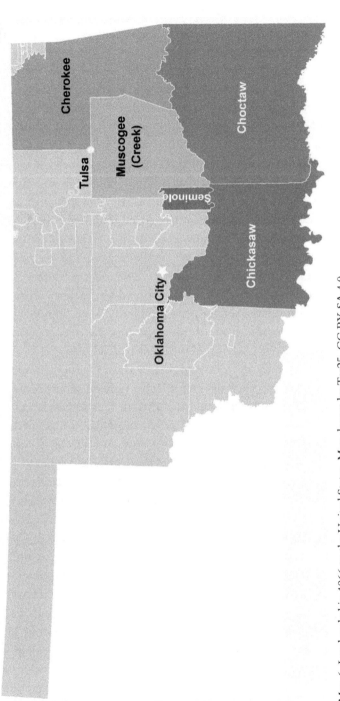

Map 6. Land ceded in 1866 to the United States. Map drawn by Tcr25. CC BY-SA 4.0.
https://commons.wikimedia.org/w/index.php?curid=102457235.

the former Confederate and Loyalist Creeks convened to draw up a national constitution and a code of civil and criminal law. The constitution created a three-branch government, modeled on that of the United States, with legislative, judicial, and executive branches. The National Council, with elected members in the House of Kings and the House of Warriors, constituted the legislative branch. The executive branch included a principal chief and a second chief, both of which would be elected offices. Finally, the judicial branch included six district courts and a Supreme Court of five judges. A year later, the National Council designated Okmulgee as the Creek Nation capital and appropriated monies to build a new council house there.[34]

The implementation of the new constitution created new factions and exacerbated old ones within the Creek Nation, and the next two decades proved politically unstable for the new centralized Creek government. From time to time, those opposed to the new constitution and the new configuration of the National Council and Supreme Court took up arms in sporadic attempts to overthrow the new government, keeping the Creek Nation off balance and its leadership in continual contestation. Not only did political factionalism plague smooth governance, but growing class differences also generated animosity and distrust between Creek families. In addition, Creek slaves had been emancipated, but freedmen were typically marginalized, subject to laws and discriminations similar to the Jim Crow laws of the South, and oftentimes denied Creek citizenship by Creek citizenship boards. Still, freedmen who were deemed Creek citizens had access to lands through the 1866 treaty; many built small but adequate subsistence farms, and some prospered. The place of African Creeks, then, ranged from modest wealth and prestige to poverty and gross mistreatment. Despite such ongoing difficulties, Creek people once again set about rebuilding their nation. They repaired their homes and farms, reestablished their cattle and hog herds, refurbished their towns, and reopened the mission schools. Rail lines soon crisscrossed the Indian Territory and brought prosperity to Indian homes and towns located along the routes.[35]

The pressure on the federal government to open the Indian Territory and other western lands to American settlers continued to mount throughout the decades following the Civil War. After the war,

Americans turned their gaze westward with renewed interest, and the Indians occupying those lands were once again considered an obstacle to the United States' progress, prosperity, and even destiny. The so-called "Indian problem" was more acute than ever in the American public mind. During the mid- to late nineteenth century in the American plains and West, with the California gold rush and other events providing incentives for American settlers to intrude into Indian lands, the western Indian wars heightened. In response, Congress attempted to impose reservations on numerous western Indian groups, most of whom responded with flight and armed resistance. The resultant Indian wars of the American West would continue to the close of the nineteenth century, abating only after the 1890 massacre at Wounded Knee.[36]

Before the Civil War, the American public and politicians had generally agreed that only the physical separation of Indians from America and Americans could resolve the "Indian problem." In the postwar years, the spiraling Indian wars in the West, along with the well-publicized corruption of Indian agents, the dismal failure of military courts in resolving Indian treaty violations, and other mistreatments, gave rise to a group of vocal white activist reformers calling for the reservation system to be dismantled and Native Americans to be assimilated into U.S. society as citizens. The reformers understood themselves to be promoting the best interests of American Indians, and with their untarnished faith in American democracy and equality, they believed that bestowing U.S. citizenship on Indians was a true blessing. They also held racist ideas that Indians were childlike and needed the guiding hand of "civilized" people to help them achieve assimilation and reach their full potential.[37]

Of course, the unspoken correlate of the reformers' position was that Indian lands could then be placed in the hands of Americans. With historical hindsight, we can see that the reformers were naïve, and they were also expansionists. With such calls for reform, American Indian policy took an ominous turn. In 1871, Congress included in an otherwise routine Indian Appropriations Act a clause declaring that Indian people did not belong to independent sovereign nations, and therefore, as of that date, the United States would make no further treaties with them. Treaties concluded prior to 1871, however, were still in effect.[38]

The repercussions for American Indians were weighty. In the treaty system, treaties were made between the U.S. president and Indian nations, and were then ratified by the U.S. Senate. The 1871 act, however, effectively moved Indian relations out of the executive branch and into the legislative branch. Under the treaty system, U.S. and Indian commissioners had gathered to debate and negotiate treaty terms, but with Indian affairs now wholly in the hands of Congress, Indian people, who were not U.S. citizens, had no representation, and therefore "no longer had an equal voice in the process." That also meant that Native objections to congressional legislation would be funneled through the federal court system, leaving the U.S. Supreme Court as the final arbiter. It put into sharp relief the question of Indian national sovereignty.[39]

With Indian affairs now firmly in congressional hands, wealthy American businessmen and speculators with an interest in Indian lands unremittingly lobbied their representatives to open those lands to American development. Much of the greediness for Indian lands in the late nineteenth century was fueled by the furious growth of the railroad industry. American boosters dreamed of a transcontinental railroad system that would alleviate many of the risks and hardships for migrating settlers as well as provide necessary transportation infrastructures for businesses, mineral resource extraction, the meat and leather industries, and agricultural produce. Indians, to their mind, could not contribute to these enterprises, and therefore stood in the way of realizing this dream. Wealthy railroad owners carried much influence in Washington, and Congress passed numerous legislative acts between 1866 and 1900 designed to benefit and protect rail companies. On numerous occasions, several of the Five Tribes disputed the acts relating to the Indian Territory and challenged them in U.S. courts. Many of those cases eventually landed in the U.S. Supreme Court, and the judges typically found in favor of non-Indian interests. Any pro-Indian rulings prompted Congress to pass additional legislation that subsequently disabled those decisions.[40]

The court challenges by Natives centered not so much on whether railroads could traverse the Indian Territory, but on who would reap the benefits. Railroads brought with them the "touch of capital"; railroad towns were boomtowns when businesses central to rail transport flourished, and the railroad connected these towns in an ever-expanding transportation network. Additionally, manufactured goods were more easily transported across long distances by rail and made available to people who otherwise had limited access to them. Competition between non-Indians and Indians over these and other opportunities intensified. The railroads also created lucrative, but uneven, opportunities for extractive economies such as timber, furs, livestock, minerals, and, later, fossil fuels.[41]

One consequence of the railroad's touch of capital was that Americans now had an opportunity to intrude into Indian Country. Under U.S. law, Americans were forbidden to trespass on Indian lands, and, although it was only haphazardly enforced, the federal government promised Indian nations that the U.S. military would expel intruders. Young American men working in Kansas, Missouri, and Arkansas as railroad laborers, however, were in the Indian Territory legally. Under Creek law, individual Creeks did not own private land; nor could they buy or sell Creek lands. Rather, Creek territory was held in common, and the Creek government issued land permits with use rights to individuals and families for farming, ranching, building, mining, and so on. Many of these American men who came in as rail workers harbored hopes of marrying Indian wives through whom they could gain farming, ranching, and mining privileges.[42]

Non-Native settlers also came into Creek country legally under a labor permit system. Access to the railroads gave enterprising Creek farmers and entrepreneurs incentive to expand their commercial endeavors. To do so, however, they required additional labor. In contrast to the American South, where landless freedmen filled the need for labor through tenancy, many Creek freedmen owned land, so there was only a small pool of landless laborers. To meet the demand, the Creek National Council instituted a permit system whereby a Creek farmer or businessperson, after submitting a formal request and paying a tax, could hire non-Creek (mostly white American male) laborers. The other Five Tribes instituted similar permit laws. These unattached American men, like the railroad laborers, embedded themselves in Creek country through marriage to Creek women. The men could not own Creek lands, but marriage gave them use rights to it. The marriages also begat a robust population of American Creeks.[43]

Meanwhile, as late as 1879, much of the western land in the Indian Territory ceded in the 1866 treaties had yet to be designated to newly removed Indian populations. American settlers and speculators eagerly eyed these so-called "unassigned lands," beseeching federal politicians to open them not just to displaced Natives, but to Americans as well. In 1880 a Kansas frontier politician, David L. Payne, formed a land company and, supported by wealthy land speculators and railroad magnates, enticed American settlers to join him in invading the unassigned lands. The squatters, who became known as Boomers, rowdily crossed into the Indian Territory, where they set up camp and defiantly waited for U.S. soldiers to remove them. President Rutherford B. Hayes, most likely angered more by the Boomers' defiance than by any infraction of Indian treaty rights, sent in federal troops to forcibly extricate the squatters. The Boomers were stubborn, however, and they returned, only to again be forcibly removed. This went on for years, until Payne's death in 1884. The Boomer movement stalled out, but not before it had focused public sentiment and political attention on the Indian Territory, American Indian policies, and Indian affairs in general.[44]

Untethered to treaty negotiations and with popular support, reformers spearheaded the passage of numerous legislative acts designed to assimilate Indians into American society, further weaken Indian sovereignty, abrogate treaty rights, and promote American access to Indian lands. One act in particular cemented the oversight of the U.S. government in Indian affairs and directly challenged Native judicial powers. It was passed in response to events on the plains. Reformers had long hoped to disestablish western Indian reservations, and in 1881, events concerning the Brulé Sioux headman Crow Dog opened a door for doing so.

Briefly, Crow Dog had killed Spotted Tail, another Brulé Sioux headman, on the Rosebud Reservation. The Brulé Sioux handled the matter according to their laws and customs. However, the local Indian agent arrested Crow Dog, charged him with murder under U.S. law, and turned him over to the federal courts. The question at stake was who had jurisdiction over crimes committed between Indians and on Indian lands—the Indian nations or the United States? The case (known as *Ex parte Crow Dog*, 109 U.S. 556) made its way to the U.S. Supreme Court, which determined that the Sioux had jurisdictional rights over the crime, thus confirming Indian national sovereignties and reservations as had been promised in numerous treaties.[45]

In response, reformers quickly drafted legislative acts that would void the Court's decision, and in 1885 Congress passed an appropriations act that became known as the Major Crimes Act (MCA). The MCA identified seven major crimes that, if committed by an Indian against "another Indian or other person . . . within any Territory of the United States, and either within or without an Indian reservation," were subject to federal oversight. The crimes were murder, manslaughter, rape, assault with intent to kill, arson, burglary, and larceny. Indian people who committed these crimes were to be tried, "as are all other persons" who commit such crimes, according to U.S. federal laws and in U.S. federal courts. In other words, any Indian committing any of the seven major crimes was to be tried in federal court and under federal law. In two subsequent landmark legal cases—*United States v. Kagama* (1886) and *Lone Wolf v. Hitchcock* (1903)—the Supreme Court expanded the interpretation of the MCA to give Congress, and only Congress, "plenary power," or absolute authority, over Indians living on reservations, and stated that Congress, and only Congress, had the right to violate treaties with Indian nations. In short, Congress, not the states, had supreme authority over Indian affairs and Indian reservations. The MCA and subsequent cases limited Native jurisdiction to lesser crimes and civil affairs.[46]

Between Indian removal and the passage of the MCA, Congress had placed the Indian Territory under U.S. jurisdiction despite the fact that the federal courts were outside the Indian Territory—the court at Fort Smith was in the Western District of Arkansas, the court at Fort Scott was in the District of Kansas, and the court at Paris was in the Eastern District of Texas. The MCA was followed by two bills that gave these federal courts jurisdiction over all criminal offenses committed in the Indian Territory. These three pieces of legislation were the precursor to the federal government's wholesale attempt to extend U.S. jurisdiction into Indian lands, and thereby to incorporate Indian peoples and lands into the U.S. system and disestablish Native reservations. In the words of legal scholar Susan Work, this expansion of federal judicial authority into Indian Country was "a focal point in the mounting onslaught of federal legislation that eventually forced allotment of the Five Tribes land."[47]

This wholesale effort was allotment, and it came in the person of Massachusetts senator Henry L. Dawes and his allies. As reformers, they wrote the General Allotment Act, more commonly known as the Dawes Act, which Congress passed on February 8, 1887. The lawmakers focused on three issues: Indian landholdings, education, and citizenship. The act transferred education from Native and missionary schools to Indian boarding schools, which would prove to be cruel beyond words and ultimately calamitous for all involved. The questions of landholdings and citizenship were intertwined. Indians across America, including the Creeks, famously held their lands in common. Indian tribal members had use rights, but individuals could not hold land as private property, which meant that they could not sell land. In addition, tribal landholdings represented and underwrote tribal organization and sovereignty. For reformers such as Dawes, communal ownership blocked the path to assimilation, which they understood to require both private ownership of land and the dismantling of Indian sovereignties. The corollary, of course, was that communal ownership and Indian sovereignty also blocked westward expansion. The Dawes Act, then, attempted to engineer a poorly conceived transition from Native communal ownership of land to individual private ownership.[48]

At the center of the Dawes Act was severalty—individual private ownership of land. To that end, it enacted the division of Indian nations' communal lands into parcels of 160 acres that would be allotted to heads of households, 80-acre lots for orphans and unmarried adults, and 40-acre lots for anyone under eighteen years of age. The 160-acre lots were divided into two types—homestead and "surplus." The size of the homestead lot was typically about 40 acres, or enough to support the allottee, and the remaining 120 acres were considered the allottee's "surplus." Allottees held title to both their homestead and surplus acreage. This land was allotted in severalty, meaning that the allottees were granted patents and owned the land in fee. In other words, they held it as private property. When allottees died, their allotments would pass to their heirs. After all allotments had been made, any unallotted lands (also called "surplus" and herein referred to as "communal surplus" to distinguish them from the 120-acre fee simple "surplus" given to an allottee) were still tribal lands, but subject to federal oversight. However, the Dawes Act, in a supposed effort to protect new Indian landowners from intruders and speculators, stipulated that for the first twenty-five years, the United States would act as trustee of the allotted lands and that they could not be sold. These lands are sometimes referred to as "restricted" lands. Inherited allotments had fewer restrictions of alienation because, theoretically, the heirs would not be dependent on these lands for their living. The federal government, with tribal consent, had the right to sell any communal surplus lands to non-Indians. The act further stated that an allotment would be given at the U.S. president's discretion, when he deemed an Indian group sufficiently assimilated or an individual sufficiently competent to take on the responsibilities of private landownership. Those who were deemed incompetent were assigned a "guardian," typically a white American, to oversee their property. The act also granted citizenship to allottees, but only after they had received their allotments.[49]

Scholars have long noted that the Dawes Act was an expansive and "remarkably plastic" piece of legislation. Written in general tones, it was more a commitment to Indian citizenship and the disestablishment of reservations than a directive, and it did not specify a timetable for either. In fact, the Dawes Act has few actionable items and allows administrators a great deal of discretionary power, which also means that it has been open to interpretation by both federal and state judicial and legislative branches over the years.[50]

The original Dawes Act excluded the Five Tribes of the Indian Territory and the New York Indians, in part because those nations' reservations were quite large. In addition, western Indian reservation lands were held in trust by the United States, which in turn had granted rights of occupancy to the Indian inhabitants. The Five Tribes, however, owned their lands communally and in fee, which complicated the allotment process. The allotment of their reservations therefore required a special commission, which Congress created in 1893 when it extended the Dawes Act to the Five Tribes. The new commission became known as the Dawes Commission.[51]

A few months after its formation, the men on the Dawes Commission left for the Indian Territory to confer with tribal officials. They were met with intransigent resistance from all of the Five Tribes. Most Creek leaders, as well as other Native leaders, immediately recognized the threat that allotment posed to their national sovereignty, territorial base, and economic progress. The métis elites who controlled the Creek governing bodies had appropriated vast amounts of land for their businesses, ranching, and commercial agriculture. Under allotment, they stood to have their holdings reduced from thousands of acres to merely hundreds. But even the rank-and-file Creeks resented allotment and rallied behind their métis leaders. Especially alarming, the Dawes Commission proceeded to compile citizenship rolls for the Five Tribes, thereby claiming the right to determine who belonged to each nation and undermining one of the basic rights of sovereign nations. Creek and other Five Tribes leaders feared that corrupt federal officials would not hesitate to allot lands to both whites and freedmen.[52]

Exacerbating the anxieties over allotment, a few years earlier, in 1889, Congress had opened the "unassigned lands" in the western part of the Indian Territory to American settlement. The highly publicized land rushes became a notorious symbol of American grit and greed. The number of American settlers soon outstripped the number of Indians in the region by almost three to one, and American settlements sprang up literally overnight. To protect American intruders and settlers, the United States at the same time established the first federal court within the Indian Territory, in Muskogee, with authority over U.S. citizens in both civil and criminal offenses. Although the 1889 act preserved Indian jurisdiction over cases involving only Indians, the Muskogee court's presence was the latest in a series of legislative moves by Congress to protect Americans by preempting Indian law enforcement in the Indian Territory. A year later, Congress passed the Organic Act of Oklahoma of 1890, which created the Oklahoma Territory by organizing the western lands into a territorial government under U.S. protection and jurisdiction. While still honoring Indian jurisdiction over Indian minor offenses and civil cases, the Organic Act expanded the authority of the Muskogee court in both criminal and civil affairs concerning conflicts between non-Indians and Indians. The upshot was that Indian men and women had few legal protections against offenses committed against them by non-Indians. Native leaders, wary of the incessant chipping away of their autonomy, judicial authority, and national rights, stood firm in opposition to allotment, which they understood to be the latest assault on their sovereignty and their territories.[53]

The Dawes Commission spent considerable time in the Indian Territory over the next several years attempting to persuade the leaders of the Five Tribes that allotment was beneficial. In response, the Creek National Council passed a series of resolutions opposing allotment; the debates in Congress, on the other hand, grew strident in support of it. Between 1887 and 1897, as a means of forcing allotment, Congress passed a flurry of acts designed to disable the tribal court system, and hence Indian self-governance, even further. In a last hope to preserve tribal judicial authority, the Seminoles, under Principal Chief John F. Brown, were the first to enter into an allotment agreement in 1897.[54]

The rest of the Five Tribes, however, continued their resistance. In response, in June 1898, an increasingly frustrated U.S. Congress passed "An act for the protection of the people of the Indian Territory," more commonly known as the Curtis Act. As its benign title suggests, American sentiment toward Indians still slanted toward assimilation, but, buttressed by the now-discredited scientific racism and racist anthropology of the late nineteenth century, reformers had difficulty granting Indians and other non-whites equality. Non-white people, according to popular white opinion, no longer required mere guardianship—they required white control. The Curtis Act was grounded in this racist ideology, implying that the Indian Territory could thrive only under the watchful eye of the United States. In truth, it was a thinly veiled strong-arm tactic designed to force allotment by placing all of the Indian Territory under the jurisdiction of the United States, extinguishing all tribal courts, and ending enforcement of tribal laws. It also mandated allotment for the Chickasaws, Choctaws, Cherokees, and Creeks, preferably with, but if necessary without, tribal consent. Legislators also rectified some of the ambiguities in the Dawes Act with an eight-year deadline (1906) to accomplish allotment. Finally, the Curtis Act demanded that all tribal governments be dissolved within the eight-year time frame as well. The act essentially gutted the Five Tribes' legislative, executive, and judicial power; and with plenary power in the hands of the U.S. Congress, the Five Tribes were out of options.[55]

Three years later, following the Cherokees, Choctaws, and Chickasaws, Creek leaders, under Principal Chief Pleasant Porter, signed an allotment agreement with the United States. By cooperating, Porter and other métis elites on the National Council hoped to gain some control over the process and retain some self-governance. The 1901 Creek Allotment Act echoed the General Allotment Act (the Dawes Act), providing 160-acre plots for each Creek family (divided into 40-acre homestead lots and 120-acre surplus lots), 80-acre lots for orphans and unmarried adults, and 40-acre lots for anyone under eighteen years of age. The U.S. would oversee the dispersal of any unallotted communal surplus lands. It also provided provisions specific to the Creeks for their towns, schools, citizenship rolls, and so on. The agreement guaranteed the continuation of the Creek government, but in a much-diluted form, as directed by the Curtis Act. Finally, all Creek allottees would also become U.S. citizens. Congress quickly passed the act, and the United States wasted no time in surveying the Indian Territory, completing the Dawes Rolls, expediting judiciary administration throughout the region, and implementing allotment.[56]

Creek reaction to the allotment agreement was mixed. Many Creeks, seeing little utility in resisting any further, unenthusiastically submitted to the Dawes Commission, signed onto the Dawes Rolls, and received their land lots. Others, however, remained adamantly opposed to allotment, and they boycotted the rolls in protest. One group organized a protest campaign and chose as their speaker Chitto Harjo, or "recklessly brave snake." This group, known as the Snake Indians, went so far as to form a separate Creek government and to pass legislation prohibiting allotment and eliminating the permit system through which white Americans laborers entered Creek territory. Principal Chief Porter, aided by U.S. marshals, raided their stronghold at Hickory Ground and arrested dozens of Snake Indians. They were later released under an agreement that they would cooperate with the commissioners; still, most refused to add their names to the Dawes Rolls.[57]

The Dawes citizenship rolls were the foundation for allotment, in that only enrolled citizens of an Indian nation were eligible for parcels of land. Determining who was and who was not a Creek citizen had been a serious point of interest for the Creek National Council since the Civil War, emancipation, and the cession of the western lands. All of the Five Tribes assembled citizenship committees, which were responsible for sorting out who was or was not a citizen of their nations. This was not an easy task for the Creeks and others. Not only were many Creek citizens now of various mixed descent, but many wealthy former slave owners resented being required to bring their former slaves into Creek society as full citizens. Second, there was a financial incentive to be on the rolls, because only citizens were entitled to the land lots, as well as to the annuity payments from the 1866 cession. Consequently, the National Council initiated censuses and citizenship rolls that were periodically updated and purged, usually amid much contention.[58]

The Curtis Act, however, preempted the Creeks' authority to conduct a census and determine citizenship and handed both to the Dawes Commission. The Dawes Rolls, though, are notoriously flawed. For one, both they and the practice of allotment were founded on racist ideologies that conceived of Native peoples as naïve and childlike and thus requiring white assistance and protection against unscrupulous whites as they progressed along the road to "civilization." To that end, the commissioners decided, much to the dismay of the Five Tribes, that a white person married to an Indian partner could be considered a citizen of that partner's Indian nation and enrolled as "intermarried." The thinking was that intermarried white males were better stewards of property than their Native wives and their extended families. Additionally, the rolls were conceived around the racist ideas of "blood," rather than genetics or personal life histories with a tribe. African Creeks and freedmen fell under the so-called "one-drop rule," which meant that they were now categorized as "black" rather than Indian. Native peoples were evaluated according to a bizarre scale of blood quantum, with "full bloods" requiring the most supervision and protection and those with less than "half Indian blood" requiring the least amount. Those in between, with three-quarters or more than half Indian blood, needed intermediate supervision. The underlying racism in all the categories is obvious—the more "white blood" an Indian person had, the more he or she was capable of handling his or her own affairs.[59]

White census takers were inconsistent in their application of blood quantum and the one-drop rule, often simply designating a person as "full-blood, "half-breed," or black solely on the basis of appearance and skin tone. The Treaty of 1866 guaranteed Creek citizenship to freed African slaves, but the blurred racial lines in Creek country also blurred citizenship status. With allotment on the line, many of the métis elites, with now fully racialized ideologies about black people, sought to limit the number of African Creeks and freedmen on the citizenship rolls. In addition, white intruders, through chicanery, bribery, fraud, and forgery, found various ways onto the rolls. Consequently, the commissioners' efforts to determine who was a Creek citizen became so chaotic that members of a single family sometimes ended up on all three rolls—the "by blood" roll, the freedman roll, and the intermarriage roll. In addition, census takers deemed many Creek citizens, both Indian and African Indian, not to be full-fledged citizens and kept them off the rolls altogether. Any Creeks who boycotted the rolls, of course, were not listed. The commission closed the Dawes Rolls in 1907, at which time there were approximately 6,800 freedmen, 12,000 "by-blood" Creeks, and apparently not any whites through intermarriage on the rolls. We may never know the number of Creek citizens left off the rolls or how extensively the rolls were inflated with non-Indian entries except to say that hundreds if not thousands of Creeks, African Creeks, and Creek freedmen were denied Creek citizenship. Over three million acres of Creek country were divided into nineteen thousand allotment tracts.[60]

Allotment was as traumatizing and disruptive to Creek life as Indian removal. From conception to implementation, greed, corruption, racism, and fraud were the hallmarks of the era. The stakes were high: Indian lands were no longer simply farmland; the remaining individual surplus and communal surplus holdings had significant deposits of timber, oil, coal, asphalt, and grazing lands. Americans convinced themselves that only Americans—not Indians or any people of color—could and should control these resources. The settler population in the Oklahoma Territory increased daily, and by 1900, more than 350,000 non-Indians, both white and freedmen, were living there. Over the next two decades, the federal government steadily opened Indian communal surplus lands for purchase or lease, creating yet another feverish land grab in the Indian Territory, and speculators and intruders laid siege to it in order to swindle new allottees out of their landholdings.[61]

4

OKLAHOMA ENCROACHMENT

With allotment underway, American settlers throughout the region campaigned ferociously for binding the Indian Territory and the Oklahoma Territory into a single U.S. state—Oklahoma. Americans were exhilarated by the prospect of statehood. Native people, on the other hand, were divided over the proposed designation. Some Native leaders were optimistic that statehood would bring opportunities to Native peoples; others were less sanguine. All, however, understood that statehood entailed challenges to Indian Country because it would put Natives' lands at stake, their sovereignty in jeopardy, and their very identity as Indians in question. Of course, these troubles had plagued Creeks and other Indian peoples for decades, but until statehood, the Creeks and the other Five Tribes had retained a modicum of authority, judicial and legislative power, and self-determination. Allotment and statehood would erode the last vestiges of influence they had over American designs on the Indian Territory for the next seven decades.

Native leaders, skeptical about being absorbed into a single state with the Americans, in 1905 convened the Five Tribes to draft a constitution for an alternate all-Indian state. To be named Sequoyah, after the famed Cherokee intellectual who had invented the Cherokee syllabary, it would have encompassed all of the Indian Territory. Under the Curtis Act, of course, all government actions by Natives had to be approved by the U.S. Congress, and Congress ignored the proposal. Instead, the petition for Oklahoma statehood was approved, and the Indian and Oklahoma territories were combined into the single state of Oklahoma in 1907. The result, as far as the United States was concerned, was the end of self-governance for the Creek Nation and the other Indians in the new state.[1]

Proponents of statehood pushed for the completion of allotment so that Indian lands could be freely bought and sold by non-Indians. Embedded in the General Allotment Act, though, were protections for new Indian landowners against thieves, speculators, and grafters, including the prohibition against individuals selling land for the first twenty-five years of ownership. By 1900, however, American attitudes had turned from protecting Indian lands for Native communities to perceiving Indian lands as part of the American public domain. Historian Fred E. Hoxie observes that the Indian land policies formed during these decades drifted from a basis of assimilation and inclusion of Native Americans to one of exclusion. The policies of allotment left "Indians on the outskirts of American life and promised them a limited future as junior partners in the national enterprise." This new perspective, combined with the clamor by American promoters and developers for a loosening of the restrictions on Indian severalty, led to a series of congressional acts designed to upend the protections for Five Tribes landholders.[2]

In truth, these protections had run into problems from the beginning. For one, the allotment surveys did not consider natural boundaries and lands already being used by Creek families. Under Creek allotment, any Creek citizen could select his or her acreage provided that no one had already "improved" that parcel or already claimed it. Improvements included farm fields, outbuildings, pasturage, and fencing. Allotment, then, reopened old land and lease disputes and led to new ones. Families quarreled amongst themselves and with others over land boundaries, equipment, livestock, and improvements, with many taking their disputes to the Creek courts, to the Dawes Commission, and, after the Curtis Act was passed, to the federal court system. Because both Americans and many Creeks held racist ideologies regarding blacks, African Creeks were at a distinct disadvantage in any such dispute, and many lost their allotments altogether.[3]

The prohibition against individual land sales also collided with Creek inheritance rules and complicated the division of lands upon the death of

an original allottee. If they were to be American citizens and landowners, many Creeks insisted, then the twenty-five-year oversight should be
eliminated and they should be able to buy, sell, inherit, and own land just
as any other American could. These demands, of course, squared with
the U.S. Congress's assimilation plans for the Indian Territory, and in
1902 Congress drafted a supplement to the Creek Allotment Act allowing adult heirs to sell their lands. Many of these parcels were later sold to
non-Indians. Additionally, many American men who had entered Creek
country under the labor permit system had sought and received lease
rights for farmlands. By 1900, there were thousands of Americans living
on these contract farms, and they, with good reason, were confident that
the Dawes Commission and other federal agencies would recognize their
land claims and improvements and thus deed the land to them. When
the Dawes Rolls were compiled, the commission accommodated some
of these white men by enrolling them as Indian citizens by marriage.[4]

Allotment proved especially problematic for the land leasing program in the Indian Territory. For decades intruders had been stealing
timber, illegally grazing cattle herds, sponsoring illegal mining, and
squatting on Indian farmlands. Native leaders across America recognized early on that selling lease rights for these resources could regulate
such intrusions and provide a lucrative revenue stream for their citizens.
In an effort to do so, the Creek National Council, like the other Five
Tribes, passed several lease laws regarding timber, farmlands, pastures,
coal, and oil. Leasing subsequently became rampant in Creek country,
especially by certain wealthy Creeks.[5]

In 1889, for example, Principal Chief L. C. Perryman persuaded the
Creek National Council to pass the first contract pasture laws, and many
Creeks, especially the wealthier ones, leased expansive prairie pastures
to Texas cattle companies. Creek lands also held valuable coal and oil
deposits, and since at least 1878 the National Council had required Creek
citizens to pay royalties on all coal sales. Then, throughout the 1880s, the
National Council under Perryman passed a series of coal and oil laws,
including lease laws. In 1901, American oil prospectors struck the Red
Fork and Glen Pool deposits near the city of Tulsa, and Creek leaders,
seeing the potential for profits from oil pools, insisted that their allotment
agreement be amended to allow mineral rights to be privately owned

and to provide for lease rights. Although revenues from the coal and oil deposits would not start gushing until the early twentieth century, Chicago oil capitalists immediately sought lease rights in Creek country and began drilling operations. A few select Creek families fortunate enough to have oil reserves under their allotments became instantly and fabulously wealthy.[6]

The authors of the Dawes Act and later allotment acts for the Five Tribes were ambivalent about lease rights, presciently fearing an onslaught of corruption, bribery, and general skullduggery if leasing were to be allowed to continue after allotment. The original allotment acts nullified all leases and contained no provisions for the continuation of leasing. But as early as 1891, Congress amended the Dawes Act to include leasing privileges for any Indians who were unable, for whatever reason, to work their allotted land. This was followed by a series of legislative acts designed to open Indian land sales and lands to American development, including relaxing the lease laws.[7]

The most sweeping of these legislative acts, and the one with the longest-lasting effects, was the Five Tribes Act of 1906. It was implemented in response to a provision in the 1898 Curtis Act stipulating that Indian governments were to be dismantled by 1906, or as soon as the allotment distributions were completed. However, when 1906 dawned, the land dispositions were only about half complete, forcing Congress to pass another act acknowledging the continued existence of the Five Tribes' governments. Signed by Congress on April 26, 1906, the legislation rescinded the separate status that the five nations had been granted in the allotment agreements and instead grouped them into one entity. The act assumed that the Five Tribes governments would eventually be dissolved, but stated that the governments of the Chickasaw, Choctaw, Cherokee, Seminole, and Creek people were "in full force and effect for all purposes authorized by law until otherwise provided by law." The act reiterated the Curtis Act in limiting council sessions and requiring that all Native legislation and property issues be approved by the U.S. president.[8]

Since under the Dawes Act Indian lands could only be allotted with the permission of the nation that owned them, the principal chief of each of the Five Tribes was responsible for executing the land deeds.

To ensure that the U.S. kept control over the process, section 6 of the Five Tribes Act authorized the U.S. president to appoint and dismiss principal chiefs. (In 1951, an executive order shifted this authority to the secretary of the interior.) For the next six decades, the U.S. gestured to section 6 to deny the Five Tribes the right to elect their principal chiefs by popular vote.[9]

The Five Tribes Act, however, was mostly concerned with Native properties, allotment, and lease rights. It required blood quantum rolls for determining Native competency, mandated federal oversight, and set a deadline for being added to the Dawes Rolls—March 4, 1907. The act clarified sale and lease restrictions according to blood quantum and undermined land sale prohibitions by giving the secretary of the interior the authority to grant the right of alienation to any Indian landowner, regardless of blood quantum, whom the secretary deemed competent to manage his or her affairs.[10]

The act furthermore stipulated that the U.S. government would hold, in trust, all unallotted lands for the Five Tribes until the dissolution of tribal governments. In addition, all records of the Indian Territory land offices were to be transferred to federal court clerks' offices, and all tribal revenues were to be submitted to the Office of the Secretary of the Interior in trust and for payment of any lawful claims. This provision alone enabled much graft and corruption when scurrilous developers and speculators bribed and lobbied federal clerks and politicians for favors.[11]

The act also gave the secretary of the interior oversight of the Five Tribes' communal surplus holdings—over six million acres containing valuable timber, grazing land, coal, and oil—and in fact required the office to sell or lease these lands on behalf of the tribal nations. This clause gave the secretary of the interior, acting as trustee of the Indian lands, the right to sell or lease unlimited amounts of this acreage to corporations as well as individuals. Over the next decades, the revenues from these land sales and leases added substantially to Native coffers, monies that were ostensibly reserved in trust for the tribes. But since the Office of the Secretary retained oversight and distribution privileges, these funds, too, were subject to corruption.[12]

The oil, coal, timber, railroad, and cattle industries had been hovering in and around the Indian Territory for decades, their greed abated only by Native leaders' efforts to regulate lease rights and expel intruders. Allotment and the Five Tribes Act now flung the door wide open to them. Coal and asphalt, in particular, figured prominently in the debates around the Five Tribes Act. Prior to Oklahoma statehood, the federal government had sponsored a prospecting survey in the Indian Territory by the U.S. Geological Survey, which determined that there were 437,734 acres of coal deposits there, worth approximately $4.3 billion. Only a fraction of this acreage had been leased by 1906. The Five Tribes Act declared that any leased lands could be sold once the leases expired, and that any communal surplus lands could be sold or leased by the secretary of the interior. Leasing accelerated rapidly throughout the Indian Territory, and the ensuing debates over the resulting revenues drew public and corporate attention to the rich deposits of natural resources there.[13]

The Five Tribes Act left the Creeks' and the other Five Tribes' legal and property rights in chaos and subject to a myriad of bewildering and contradictory interpretations by Congress, legal professionals, and federal agencies and offices. Federal officials misappropriated trust funds, creating resentment and suspicion among the peoples of the Five Tribes, who argued for their right to administer their own funds. Legal contestations and Native claims against the U.S. landed in outwardly biased federal courts, where attorneys and judges exploited the confusion. The twentieth century would carry the weight of the Five Tribes Act for over eighty years, resulting in a tangle of legislative and judicial proceedings, acts, and rulings regarding Indian affairs that still today confound the Five Tribes, state, and federal legislative and judicial systems.[14]

White Americans combined their greed with patriotism in the push for Oklahoma statehood—they viewed themselves as selfless frontiersmen and women who were building a new and glorious state for the Union. African Americans, many hoping to flee the Jim Crow South, also saw opportunities there that were denied them everywhere else. White and black migrants poured into the region. On the eve of statehood, the white population in the Oklahoma and Indian territories had increased fivefold, to almost 540,000. The African American and American Indian populations also grew, but by much less. The African American population stood at over 80,000, while the Native population was around

60,000. The Muscogee population was just over 25,000. Outnumbered and overpowered, Native leaders attempted to control the allotment process and development, but the Five Tribes Act undercut any such efforts. The coup de grâce would come in 1907, with the official proclamation of the state of Oklahoma.[15]

Less than two months after passing the Five Tribes Act, Congress approved the Oklahoma Enabling Act. It was signed into law by President Roosevelt on June 16, 1906. Noting in particular the abundant resources in the Indian Territory, the act set out the conditions for Oklahoma statehood, stipulating that the Oklahoma Territory and the Indian Territory would be combined into the single state of Oklahoma. It also called for a constitutional convention and the drafting of a constitution for the new state. A few months later, delegates convened to do so.

One of the objectives of statehood, oftentimes explicitly stated in public, was to secure and develop the Indian Territory for and by white Americans. At the Oklahoma Constitutional Convention in 1906, for example, the delegates, who represented mostly white Americans and métis elites, had assumed that the document should enshrine the removal of severalty and lease restrictions on Indian lands and the placement of all Indian affairs under state control. The métis at the convention had welcomed the move because it would effectively nullify any authority that the commissioner of Indian affairs and the secretary of the interior had over Indian land issues and bestow on Native peoples the right to buy, sell, and lease their lands as they saw fit. Staying within the confines of racist ideologies, "full-blood" homestead allotments would still be subject to competency determinations by the Bureau of Indian Affairs (BIA). Despite much opposition among Native people, a large majority of Oklahomans, both Native and non-Native, voted to approve the constitution on September 17, 1907. That same day, Charles N. Haskell was inaugurated as governor. Two months later, on November 16, 1907, Oklahoma became the Union's forty-sixth state. Subsequently, representatives to the U.S. Congress were elected, including Native politicians. One of the senators was the Cherokee métis Robert L. Owen, and two of the representatives, Chickasaw Charles D. Carter and James S. Davenport, who was married to a Cherokee woman, were from the former Indian Territory, now commonly referred to as "the East Side."[16]

Combining the Oklahoma Territory and the Indian Territory resulted in a lopsided demographic. White Americans and African Americans constituted almost 95 percent of the population in the new state, and Natives just over 5 percent. Provisions in the Enabling Act and later included in the Oklahoma state constitution prohibited the sale of alcohol in the former Indian Territory and provided for future taxation of Native citizens (who under the allotment agreement were exempt from property taxes for a number of years) and for Native representation in the state and federal legislative bodies. The constitution also fixed the American biracial categories of "black" and "white." It lumped all Native peoples into the racial category of "white persons"; all persons of African descent were categorized as "colored" or "negro."[17]

Statehood also instantly created a state court system and gave the new state civic and criminal jurisdiction over Americans residing there. The Enabling Act subsumed the Indian Territory into the state but held out some protections for the Indian nations. It instructed that the state constitution was not to infringe on the rights or property of the states' Indian people or limit the authority of the federal government's jurisdiction over Indian land, property, and legal rights. Furthermore, the state of Oklahoma could not claim any unappropriated public lands or any lands owned by Indian individuals or nations.[18]

Despite these protections, the new state leaders set about implementing their agenda of opening the former Indian Territory to American settlement through various state and federal legislative acts, gubernatorial executive orders, and court rulings. Much of their agenda revolved around Indian severalty and taxation, but they also were intent on truncating, if not eliminating altogether, federal jurisdiction over all Indian affairs in Oklahoma. Senator Owen presented a plan to put a court-appointed "curator" in place to oversee the management and leasing of full-blood estates. Although the plan was never implemented, the suggestion was that such an office would interfere with and preempt the authority of the secretary of the interior to oversee Five Tribes land issues. Owen went so far as to publicly dedicate the whole of Oklahoma's U.S. congressional delegation to the task of "compelling the Interior Department to give up jurisdiction over all Indian lands in Oklahoma."[19]

The Five Tribes were divided over these issues. The wealthy elites and even many rank-and-file Indians had accepted the inevitability of allotment and the consequences of Oklahoma statehood and now demanded full decision-making control over their lands and economic interests. Others, particularly Creek leaders, stubbornly insisted that federal protections, however imperfect, must remain in place as a bulwark against speculators, land thieves, and the inexorable corporate pressure for resource leases.[20]

On May 27, 1908, the Oklahoma congressional representatives won the day in regard to severalty when Congress passed the Act of 1908. It lifted all restrictions on both the 120-acre individual surplus lots and the 40-acre homestead lots for intermarried whites, freedmen, and Natives with less than half "Indian blood," including minors. Allottees with more than half but less than three-quarters Indian blood also were free to sell their surplus lots, but not their homestead lots. The act continued the restrictions for both "full bloods" and those with "three-quarters Indian blood," whose competency for alienation still required evaluation by the secretary of the interior. Restrictions on all inherited lands were also lifted. The new unrestricted lands were now subject to state taxation; still, the act required the secretary of the interior to supervise long-term resource leases. The act further insinuated Oklahoma state courts into federal jurisdiction by proclaiming that all minor-aged allottees were subject to Oklahoma probate courts, although the secretary of the interior retained the right to oversee the guardianship program. The probate courts also had oversight of all sales and leases by full-blood heirs and were now the vehicle for any allottees wishing to bring suit against illegal land conveyances. The act set a date of 1931 for the lifting of all restrictions and for the expiration of the trust period. (In 1928, Congress extended the deadline to 1956.) Historian Angie Debo summarizes the Act of 1908 as having opened over twelve million acres to sales and taxation, restored the leasing system, and given probate courts "almost complete control of Indian administration."[21]

Within a few years of statehood and the Act of 1908, most Indian lands in Oklahoma were allotted, amounting to over 250,000 land patents. Five Tribes communal landholdings were effectively a thing of the past. Legal scholar L. Susan Work notes, "This transfer of tribal

ownership to individual ownership set the stage for non-Indian intruders to acquire the lands—intruders who had prevailed in convincing
Congress to ignore the Five Tribes treaty guarantees of self-government
and absolute tribal ownership of tribal lands."[22]

Speculators and developers swarmed the former Indian Territory,
stripping allotments and leases from the citizens of Creek country by
an assortment of devious, evil, and criminal stratagems. Since most
Creeks could not read or speak English, they were easily duped by
grafters into signing deeds for land sales that they were led to believe
were lease rights or receipts for the sale of agricultural produce. Representatives from cattle companies secretly persuaded trusting Creek
allottees to select acreage coinciding with the companies' pastures, with
an agreement that the allottees would then lease grazing rights to the
company and sell the plot to them after the twenty-five-year prohibition expired. Oil and gas teams, as well as lone strikers, thickly dot-
ted the Indian Territory with oil wells in what Debo described as "a
free-for-all scramble" and "unrestricted rivalry." Lumber dealers would
negotiate with unsuspecting Indian owners for a timber lease, clear-cut
the stand, and move on, leaving the leased land unrecoverable and use-
less. Guardians exploited their positions to steal the lands and revenues
of their wards. Many times, aggressive Americans leveled threats of
physical violence to force Creek men, women, and even children to
sign over their allotments and lease rights. Murder, too, was not out
of the question. American men married to Indian women killed their
wives and the wives' kin in order to inherit their land grants. Guardians
murdered their wards to take possession of their lands and leases. And
in some cases, Indians killed Indians in order to obtain possession of
an allotment. Not only did the U.S. government, federal courts, and
the Bureau of Indian Affairs turn a blind eye to the criminals and their
crimes, but federal officials and politicians publicly applauded the mass
transfer of properties to Americans.[23]

The Creeks and other Five Tribes peoples were particularly concerned about the guardianship program, which was now overseen by
Oklahoma probate courts. Unscrupulous guardians had been extorting
huge sums of money and stealing large parcels of land from their minor
wards, mostly orphans, since the allotment program began. Corrupt

probate judges, in partnership with crooked land speculators and oil-men, went so far as to declare fully functioning adults to be incompetent and then handed subsequent guardianships to their cronies. In one case in 1909, Kate Barnard, the reformist Oklahoma commissioner of charities and corrections, reported that three small children were living, destitute, in the woods. The children, it turned out, owned Glen Pool allotments and were in fact quite rich. Their guardian, who was also the guardian of fifty-one other children, had been living off their oil royalties, with no concern whatsoever for his young wards' health and well-being.[24]

In 1912, an attorney for the Creeks, M. L. Mott, submitted to Congress a report detailing widespread abuses of the guardianship program, including exorbitant sums paid to guardians for their services, "loans" that guardians had taken from their wards, and land sales and leases made by guardians who then acquisitioned the proceeds. Mott documented that Native claims against guardians went to state courts, which were ill prepared for and overrun by the number of claims registered, and which rarely decided in favor of a Native complainant. The more corrupt judges, as we have seen, rewarded their supporters and friends with guardianships. Kate Barnard and her successors in the Department of Charities and Corrections persistently attempted to expose and correct the abuses of the guardianship program, and they had some successes. Generally, though, Oklahoma state legislators thwarted their efforts, instead passing a series of both major and minor bills to support American settlers, businesses, and land speculators and to strengthen the role of state courts in Indian affairs. The Office of the Secretary of the Interior, which had final authority, was indifferent if not downright complicit in the desultory administration and enforcement of the program.[25]

In fact, historians conclude that one of the most significant results of the Act of 1908 was "the enormous increase in opportunities for exploitation through the [state] courts." Coupled with the oil boom of the early twentieth century, well-heeled and rival speculators and developers inundated the state courts with claims against Native allottees and contestations over land titles. They jockeyed for influence over the secretary of the interior's Indian Office as well as over state politicians. The Act of 1908 had continued, at least in name, Interior Department

jurisdiction over Indian allotments by dividing the former Indian Territory into districts with politically appointed Indian agents in each. The
agents, though, were subject to the flattery and payoffs of speculators,
prioritized removing the lingering severalty and lease restrictions, and
had little interest in overseeing probate issues, thus leaving guardianship
complaints to the state courts. On a few occasions, the Department of
Justice intervened by challenging state court rulings, but these challenges only created more confusion. Individual cases ran through the
state court system, oftentimes ending in state legislative bills tailored to
a specific infraction, creating a quagmire of laws. Many of these cases
went on to the U.S. Supreme Court, whose ultimate rulings alternately
and confusingly favored first Indian land rights and then non-Indian
appropriations of Indian lands and leases.[26]

The allotment acts and the Five Tribes Act also attempted to dismantle tribal governments. The Creek National Council, as well as
town councils, continued to meet on a limited basis, but the federal and
state governments only recognized the principal chief as the legitimate
governing office. However, shadow governments emerged among each
of the Five Tribes when citizens revitalized old tribal organizations and
formed altogether new ones, such as the Ketowahs (Nighthawks) among
the Cherokees, the Snakes among the Creeks, and the conventions of the
Cherokees, Choctaws, and Creeks, among others. Through these organizations, Indian citizens prepared petitions for land rights, challenged
fraud cases in court, kept a vigilant eye on their citizenship rolls, and
consulted, informally, with district agents about pending leases and sales
of any unallotted and communal surplus tribal lands and mineral rights
by the secretary of the interior.[27]

Allotment, by all accounts, was an absolute catastrophe for Native
peoples across America. Certainly, new Native wealth exploded for
some across Oklahoma through the extractive coal, timber, cattle, and
oil industries, but that wealth was concentrated in the hands of only
a few Indians with experience in commercial enterprises. Most of the
money flowed to white Americans and corporate headquarters outside
of Indian domains. Towns, with separate allotment provisions favoring
intruders, prospered for American, but also some Indian, businesses and
services. But many Creeks, like others in the Five Tribes and no matter

their "blood quantum," lost both their 40-acre homestead lots and their 120-acre surplus lots. Corporate swindlers and complicit courts stole the revenues, leases, and titles of those whose lots had oil, coal, asphalt, timber, or pasturage resources. The Bureau of Indian Affairs, the district agencies, and even the Office of the Secretary of the Interior skimmed heavily off the proceeds from the sales and leases of unallotted communal surplus lands. Most Creeks were now penniless, and many were landless. While allotment was intended to assimilate Native peoples and their properties into American society, it ultimately robbed them of their lands and reduced the majority of them, in the words of Creek historian Michael D. Green, "to a state of utter poverty."[28]

Creek people had shown great determination and grit in rebuilding their lives and their nation after removal and again after the Civil War. The allotment era, however, created unprecedented uncertainty and ambivalence about the future, and especially about Natives' place in the U.S. economic, political, social, and cultural systems. Despondency followed, and many Creeks simply lost heart. All Creeks, even those who had garnered much wealth, suffered financial losses to varying degrees, and in the worst cases, scores of families lost everything. Those many unfortunate citizens who did not make it onto the Dawes Rolls were now homeless and destitute, without a way to make a living and without a country. In the words of Eufaula Harjo—speaking for the Snake Creeks, who in protest refused to be enrolled—"they don't know what to do or where to go." Hopelessness crushed spirits. Creek leaders could not fathom solutions, and they distractedly accepted that many Creeks would simply perish.[29]

Meanwhile, the so-called Progressive Era in America rapidly unfolded as the twentieth century got underway, and modern technologies spread into the new state. Rail, telegraph, gas, and electric lines sliced through Oklahoma, bringing goods and utilities to the urban centers, and even to some of the rural areas. Counties and towns constructed water and sewage systems for businesses and homes. Automobiles made their appearance on city streets, and the first planes flew overhead. Those Creek people who could took full advantage of the innovations, although many also succumbed to the associated American ideology that "civilization" belonged to the "white man," and Indian peoples were on

the verge of extinction. Despite the legal contestations and public outcry from African Americans and African Indians, Oklahoma legislators
passed Jim Crow laws to keep the African American and African Indian
populations subjugated and disenfranchised.[30]

By 1920, the evils, greed, shame, and perils of allotment were clear
to anyone who was paying attention, and a spirit of reform for Indian
policy swept through the federal and state government agencies. The
admirable performances of Native men and women in World War I had
suggested to white Americans that Indian stereotypes might be wrong
and that Native Americans were not only patriotic, but also capable and
complex people, not simple and childlike. Military veterans returned
with novel skills and new ambitions, and they demanded respect and
resented the patronizing and authoritative supervision of the secretary
of the interior and the Bureau of Indian Affairs.[31]

In addition, young Native peoples educated in the boarding schools
were returning home and animating a spirit of reform. Many students
had suffered tremendously in those institutions, and they came home
hotly critical of Indian policies and grew into strong and articulate advocates for Native social and economic justice. Those trained in law and
with degrees in higher education used the American legal and education systems to fight for Indian rights and against Native stereotypes.
They formed numerous local-level Indian organizations advocating
for Native interests, and they reached a wide Indian and non-Indian
audience through intellectual and artistic endeavors such as publishing
journals and hosting art exhibits and public engagements, all of which
challenged common stereotypes of Indian degradation and extinction.
In short, Native peoples across America were pushing back, and hard.[32]

Concurrently, a large subset of white Americans were agitating for
reforms across a number of domains. Social movements proliferated, her-
alding causes such as eliminating poverty, protecting the environment,
implementing social reforms, combating racism, improving conditions
for industrial and agricultural laborers, and rooting out corruption at all
government levels. Some of these white Americans turned their attention to Indian policy and swore to right the wrongs of the allotment
era. As a result of their efforts, in 1924 the U.S. Congress finally granted
American citizenship to all Indians. (The Creeks, of course, had been

awarded citizenship in 1901 with the Creek Allotment Act.) Reform soon seeped into the Bureau of Indian Affairs, and in 1926 the Office of the Interior sponsored a wide-ranging study of Native American life. Lewis Meriam, working with Ho-chunk educator Henry Roe Cloud, directed the project. They published their findings in a report that was officially titled *The Problem of Indian Administration*, but is more generally known as the Meriam Report. In it they directed attention to the utter failings of allotment, the boarding schools, and the assimilation program altogether. Most Indian peoples were now impoverished, discontented, in poor health, and generally suffering. In no uncertain terms, the study pointed directly to the assimilation program as the cause for these ills.[33]

The Meriam Report, along with subsequent surveys, inspired discussions of a complete overhaul of American Indian policy, and although plans for such were interrupted by the Great Depression, the economic crash softened many American hearts toward helping the poor and struggling. This combination of factors created an atmosphere that was ripe for reforms. When Franklin D. Roosevelt was elected president in 1932, he appointed reformer Harold Ickes as secretary of the interior. Ickes, in turn, appointed fellow reformer and Indian sympathizer John Collier as commissioner of Indian affairs. At the time of his appointment, Collier was well experienced in Indian activism and had already embarked on Indian policy reforms through his position as executive secretary of the American Indian Defense Association, which he had founded in order to challenge congressional legislation designed to impinge on Pueblo Indian land and cultural rights.[34]

Collier was strident in his protection of Native rights. He did not believe the answer to the "Indian problem" to be full-scale assimilation, and he embraced the diversity and beauty of Native arts, crafts, religions, and social conventions. He also clearly saw, firsthand, the disasters across Native America that had resulted from allotment and the breaking up of tribal governments. Supported by Ickes and Roosevelt, and with sharp deliberation, he determined to overturn the allotment and assimilation programs. Collier was also a man of science, and his first action was to collect solid data on the health and welfare of Natives across the United States. He initiated censuses, surveys, and field-based research, and used this evidence to formulate new policies. After successfully pushing through a number of reforms to the Indian trust programs and county court procedures as well as integrating Indian recipients into the Depression-era Works Progress Administration and the Civilian Conservation Corps, Collier and Ickes lobbied Congress to pass the Wheeler-Howard Act of June 18, 1934, more commonly known as the Indian Reorganization Act (IRA) or the Indian New Deal.[35]

The IRA extended the protections afforded by the severalty restrictions indefinitely, appropriated $2 million for the purchase of additional lands for reservations, allocated funds for Native education, credit, and resource conservation, and restored communal surplus lands to the tribes, among other things. It also lifted the civil service requirements that had prevented Native men and women from holding federal jobs, opening the way for Native employees to be hired at the Bureau of Indian Affairs. Arguably the most important provisions were the prohibition against any further allotment of Indian lands and the strengthening of tribal governments. In fact, section 6 of the IRA promoted self-government and encouraged tribes to adopt tribal constitutions.[36]

The Oklahoma representatives to Congress, the Oklahoma press, some wealthy and outspoken métis Natives, and non-Native Oklahomans generally loathed the IRA and fought its application in their state. While several tribes outside of Oklahoma objected to the act, most Five Tribes Natives in Oklahoma supported it, although some "venomously hostile" newspapers reported otherwise. Nevertheless, Oklahoma's congressional representatives managed to pass some alterations to the bill and reconstituted it in 1936 as the Oklahoma Indian Welfare Act (OIWA). The OIWA was a compromise bill. It maintained the jurisdiction of state courts over the guardianship program and probate matters, but the provisions for the end of allotment, the land trusts, and self-governance remained, much to the anger of non-Natives in Oklahoma. The Five Tribes wasted no time in transitioning their shadow governments into fully recognized tribal governments. The following year, for example, several Creek towns reestablished their governing bodies, and after restoring their National Council House in Okmulgee, a constitutional committee of Creek leaders met there to draft a Muscogee Nation Constitution. The principal chief, however, was still to be appointed by the U.S. president.[37]

Improvements in the former Indian Territory were almost immediate. Depression-era relief funds and aid workers flowed into Oklahoma, and the Five Tribes certainly benefited from the money and expertise. But now, with access to tribal funds and federal relief funds, Native leaders earmarked these monies for building hospitals and other medical facilities, initiating (with the help of the Red Cross) aid programs for their indigent, opening training programs in business, agriculture, and wage-labor trades, and improving their schools. Oil-rich Native families contributed generous funds to the efforts, and for the third time in less than a hundred years, the Creeks and the other Five Tribes set a course for rebuilding their nations.[38]

But the Creeks still struggled to institute a centralized government, and until the 1950s, governing authority mostly resided with the centuries-old structure of the townships. The National Council still convened from time to time, but neither the body of Creek citizens nor the secretary of the interior gave it any authority. The constitution drafted in 1939 was never ratified by the Muscogee Nation, and another constitutional effort failed in 1944 when the secretary of the interior declined to recognize the draft as legitimate. By recognizing the Office of the Principal Chief as the sole governing body of the Creeks, the secretary of the interior invested it with more power and fiscal responsibility than most Creeks accepted. Mostly rank-and-file Creeks ignored or tolerated the appointed chief, and on occasion they unsuccessfully challenged his authority in state courts.[39]

Despite the improvements in Creek country subsequent to the passing of the IRA and OIWA, the Depression wore on, and the Creek rank and file and even some elites faced the same difficulties as other working-class folks across America—unemployment, falling farm prices, drought, uncertainty, and hunger. Relief programs designed by the Roosevelt administration, Collier, and Native townships proved inadequate in the face of the duration and amount of suffering. The prolonged drought of the dust bowl years saw farms become unproductive and pasturage scarce. The wanton cutting of large tracts of forest by timber and rail companies resulted in irreparable environmental damage and left whole swaths of land devoid of vegetation. Many allottees whose homesteads and surplus acreage were now unrestricted sold both in desperation, and were left homeless and landless. Those who managed to hold on to their homestead lots barely made ends meet because of the decline in farm prices. Oil and coal prices also dropped, temporarily slowing the leasing program and the accruing of tribal revenues. With the exception of the wealthiest Creeks, tribal annuities from mineral leases dwindled from paltry to nothing.[40]

With the outbreak of World War II, American industrial and agricultural production revved up, bringing some relief from the Depression. It also gave Native men and women, as well as other Americans, a new path to employment and training for high-skill jobs. Over twenty-five thousand Native Americans served in uniform during the war, and nearly fifty thousand left their homes to work in the war industries. Although the exact number of Creek men and women who were involved in the war effort has yet to be tabulated, records indicate that those in the military served with honor and distinction. Dozens of Muscogee soldiers received Purple Hearts and other awards. In fact, a young Muscogee man, Lieutenant Ernest Childers of the army's famed Thunderbird Division, earned the second Congressional Medal of Honor ever awarded to a Native American for his daring exploits that broke a German stronghold in Italy.[41]

Scholars agree that World War II transformed Native American life. After the war, scores of young people who had left their homes to work in the war industries permanently relocated to urban centers. This demographic shift aided those at home by relieving local economic pressures caused by the Depression. For young people, life in Native communities was drab in comparison to the excitement and appeal of life in the big cities, which offered ample job opportunities, higher wages, and abundant social activities. The wartime service of these young Native men and women, both military and civilian, had taken them far away from their Native homes and thrust them into white American society, where they worked and fought side by side with young white Americans. Many of these young Natives had attended boarding school, spoke English, and had a Western education, which helped them take advantage of the unprecedented and numerous opportunities that came with military service and living in a large city. They grew comfortable in an urban setting. The war also inspired pride for Native communities, and

Native peoples everywhere celebrated and commemorated their war heroes as well as the achievements and contributions of Native civilians. Both Natives and non-Natives could now conceive of Native peoples as modern peoples in a modern world, but that realization did not mean they were no longer Native. Indeed, a new pan-Indian awareness gestated in the urban centers where young Natives from across the United States congregated, bonded in common cause, and became politicized and sometimes radicalized.[42]

Obstacles to their progress abounded, however, especially in Oklahoma. Between 1940 and the 1970s, the state and non-Native Oklahomans worked strategically and illegally through the court system to diminish the size of the Creek Nation and other Five Tribes reservations, to appropriate their resources, to curb the influence of the Creeks and the other Five Tribes, and to extend state jurisdiction over all of the tribes in the state. Furthermore, the U.S. did not fulfill its legally mandated trust responsibility to protect the Creek Nation and others from these efforts by the state; in fact, it even helped the state to actively destroy Indian governments and their sovereign rights into the 1970s. The Oklahoma Indian Welfare Act, for example, continued the jurisdiction of Oklahoma state probate courts over Indian land and mineral claims. Collier and Ickes had strenuously objected to state court authority over Five Tribes restricted lands and had testified before Congress during the debates over the IRA and OIWA about the many abuses resulting from that system. Collier, Ickes, and others advocated that the sole responsibility for Indian land issues be placed under federal jurisdiction with the Department of the Interior. Oklahoma politicians and developers prevailed, however, and the provision was struck from the final OIWA.[43]

The OIWA also ended in a confusing two-plan system for the state of Oklahoma. Native people in the western half of the state (the former Oklahoma Territory) fell under the IRA, and their restricted allotments were fully protected by the secretary of the interior. The Five Tribes, all located in the eastern half of the state (the former Indian Territory), fell under the OIWA, and their restricted lands were under the jurisdiction of Oklahoma probate courts. Oklahoma's efforts to assert jurisdictional authority over the Five Tribes were in direct violation of the disclaimer clause in the Oklahoma Enabling Act and the Oklahoma state constitution, which said that Indian rights were not to be impaired by the state, the federal government retained exclusive authority over Indian policy, and Indian lands remained subject to U.S. jurisdiction. Furthermore, the disclaimer reiterated the *Worcester v. Georgia* case of 1832, in which the Supreme Court declared that tribes were distinct, independent political bodies subject only to federal, not state, laws. Nevertheless, a decade after passing the OIWA, Congress passed the Act of August 4, 1947, commonly known as the Stigler Act, decreeing in no uncertain terms that findings by the Oklahoma state courts concerning Five Tribes guardianship and probate matters were binding.[44]

Congress went on to make a handful of laws favoring state jurisdiction over Native lands regarding the partition of allotments, strengthening the guardianship program, inheritance, and oil and gas rights, among others. But in none of the many legislative acts passed regarding Five Tribes and other Indian policies between the 1950s and 1970s did Congress ever grant states complete legislative or judicial authority over Five Tribes or other Indian lands. State courts, therefore, did not have supreme authority and were to act only as an instrument of the federal government. The Department of the Interior, however, proved derelict in its duty to enforce this policy and oversee state probate courts. Federal attorneys appointed to represent Indian clients were susceptible to the bribes offered by big oil companies; the field office in Tulsa was inadequate to manage the multitude of claims filed by allottees; and the Department of the Interior was inconsistent in its execution of the cases.[45]

Native probate issues were not the only legal cases under assault by the state of Oklahoma in the mid-twentieth century. The state intensified its efforts to subsume both civil and criminal cases under its own authority, rather than federal or tribal authority. Beginning with the Major Crimes Act in 1885, U.S. politicians and developers had promoted the end of a Native independent judiciary, and of Native governments in general, for decades. The MCA and the subsequent Curtis Act, Creek Allotment Act, Five Tribes Act, Stigler Act, and other legislation were designed with these goals in mind. In fact, as early as 1895, in preparation for statehood, Congress had transferred authority from the three federal courts outside the Indian Territory (Fort Smith, Fort Scott, and Paris) to four court districts within the Indian Territory—the Northern District, the Western District (which was the former Muskogee court), the Central District, and the Southern District. The Creek Nation fell under the jurisdiction of the Western District court.[46]

Soon after their founding, the four federal courts were choked with cases. Of the 6,045 criminal cases in 1903, for example, less than half were settled that year. Of the over 5,500 civil cases, only 2,500 were settled. To relieve the courts, President Roosevelt agreed to add one more judge to each district, bringing the total number of judges to eight. Still, the courts could not keep pace with their mounting dockets. Federal legislators were uninterested in rectifying the situation because they hoped eventually to abolish the Indian Territory courts altogether, and subsequent congressional acts only further undermined the tribal court system. By 1907, only a "miscellany of tribal courts" survived. With statehood, Congress consolidated the four federal court districts in the former Indian Territory into one—the Eastern District of Oklahoma. The district of the former Oklahoma Territory then became the Western District of Oklahoma, giving the entire state two federal districts. In 1925 that number expanded to three when part of the Eastern District became the Northern District.[47]

In the first half of the twentieth century, Congress made some half-hearted attempts to offset the state's efforts to hijack federal judicial authority. The Tenth Circuit, in 1911, and the U.S. Supreme Court, in 1913, 1916, and 1918, held that despite statehood, the former Indian Territory was still under federal jurisdiction. Then, in 1948, to clarify the implementation of the Major Crimes Act, Congress passed legislation that further codified "Indian Country" to be restricted to trust allotments, bounded reservations, and dependent Indian communities, thereby expanding the definition of an "Indian Reservation" to include the Five Tribes. The three federal courts in Oklahoma, though, were once again clogged with cases, which opened a gateway for the state of Oklahoma to bypass Indian federal law and realize its goal of civil and criminal jurisdiction over the whole of the state. The federal courts, drowning in their caseloads, happily turned a blind eye when the state blatantly intruded into federal jurisdictions. In the words of Choctaw attorney and scholar Susan Work, "somewhere along the way, a general belief that the state had acquired jurisdiction over Five Tribes members' activities on restricted lands became the prevailing view of federal and state officials."[48]

The trend toward state jurisdiction over Indian lands, civil and criminal acts, and sovereignty continued through various state court findings that went unchallenged for over four decades. A general perception developed among non-Natives that the Five Tribes were not "reservation Indians"—a view that undermined efforts by any of the Five Tribes to exert judicial and legislative authority over a geographic area and to maintain a functioning government. This misperception, however, also allowed them to escape one of the more draconian Indian laws of the mid-twentieth century. The termination era of the 1950s saw attempts to solidify state power over Indian Country. Termination policy was enacted on August 1, 1953, in House Concurrent Resolution (HCR) No. 108, which resolved to terminate federal supervision over Indian nations and subject all Indians to the same laws that applied to any other U.S. citizen. HCR 108 intended the end result to be a dissolution of tribal courts, jurisdictions, and ultimately sovereignty, although it also meant that Congress had to pass additional acts to actually terminate any tribes. Two weeks after passing HCR 108, Congress passed Public Law 280, giving state jurisdictions over tribes in California, Minnesota, Nebraska, Oregon, Wisconsin, and, after statehood, Alaska, with a provision that other states could opt into the policy. Oklahoma's governor and legislators, though, were confident that the state already had jurisdiction over Indian lands, and they declined to exercise the option. A later amendment to Public Law 280 ruled that termination could occur only with the consent of the tribes. The Termination Act was enormously unpopular with Natives and their allies, and in the face of much public outcry and organized Native resistance, the Kennedy, Johnson, and Nixon administrations had no interest in enforcing it. Congress overturned it in 1975. Nevertheless, termination policy emboldened state governments with Native populations to intercede in federal authority over Indian issues.[49]

After World War II, the Five Tribes had begun to reconstitute their central governments, and in the process they marshaled the strength to challenge the overreaches by the state of Oklahoma. The Creeks, like most Five Tribes communities, had seen large numbers of young people migrate to urban centers after World War II, rendering the centuries-old Creek town governing bodies difficult to sustain. By the 1950s, Creek political power shifted to the national capital at Okmulgee and was centralized in the hands of the Office of the Principal Chief. At this time the president still appointed the principal chief, which lessened his authority over Creek affairs. However, as the 1960s and 1970s unfolded and the political and ideological winds blowing through America shifted from Cold War conservatism to progressive liberalism, and as Native activists became increasingly vocal, federal Indian policy began to emphasize tribal self-government and self-determination over the paternalistic Indian policies of old. An act of Congress in 1970 rescinded the mandate that the president appoint principal chiefs and restored the popular vote to the Five Tribes and other nations. Creek people immediately voted Claude Cox into office; he would remain principal chief into the 1990s.[50]

The Major Crimes Act was also amended and clarified during these years. It was expanded to include more than thirty crimes (18 U.S. Code § 1153), and the 1968 Indian Civil Rights Act returned some concurrent jurisdiction over the MCA crimes to the tribes, allowing tribal courts to prosecute people for the same crimes but at the misdemeanor level. Finally, 18 U.S. Code § 1153 limits the MCA to crimes committed in Indian Country as defined in the statute.[51]

In 1975, Congress not only repealed the now-moribund termination policy, it enacted the Indian Self-Determination and Education Assistance Act. Native peoples across America embraced the new legislation, known as Public Law 638. Rather than federal agencies such as the BIA dominating Indian services and programs, Native peoples were now to become fully participating partners with the agency in the planning, implementation, and administration of those services and programs. The law required contracts that would ensure cooperation between the Department of the Interior and the Department of Health and Human Services and Native nations in federal social services, including education and child welfare. The act also initiated a grant program whereby tribes could apply for funds to assist them with their resource management, schools, construction projects, health services, housing, and the like. In the process of taking on these duties, many tribespeople became experienced administrators and able project directors.[52]

Under Principal Chief Cox, for example, the Creeks built a modern capital complex in Okmulgee, increased health care services, constructed low-cost housing, created educational and employment opportunities, established tribal legal counsel, and opened a bingo parlor in Tulsa. They also adopted a new constitution in 1975 to replace the 1867 instrument. The 1975 constitution mirrored the three branches of government set out in the 1867 constitution, but added a controversial change in National Council representation. Instead of representatives from the townships, representatives were now elected from eight districts. The new constitution thereby attempted to sideline the town councils, if not bypass them altogether. Even so, towns with town councils, now referred to as "ceremonial towns," continued to function at the local level and exert influence within the National Council.[53]

Since the passage of the Self-Determination Act, Creek people, like many Native peoples across the United States, have become resolute in defining and exercising their sovereignty. With organized and fully modern governments and drawing on a talented cohort of Western-educated Native and non-Native attorneys, Five Tribes governments leveled financial claims and jurisprudence challenges against federal and state agencies. And despite their many losses, their victories were of great import with respect to questions of tribal sovereignty. In 1985, for example, the Creeks led a fight to legitimate tribal courts in both criminal and civil cases and to allocate BIA annuity funds to support the MCN courts. In 1988, the federal government recognized the judicial authority of the remaining Five Tribes tribal courts. With the Creek court system reconstituted, the MCN could now oversee both law enforcement and judicial processes. Concurrently, the MCN Supreme Court's decisions increasingly trended toward independence from the American courts and toward self-determination.[54]

By the end of the twentieth century, the Five Tribes were managing their governments, monies, and goals. They had leveraged their tax-exempt status to cultivate business enterprises centered on tax-heavy commodities such as tobacco and gasoline. Because they were separate and sovereign political entities apart from regulations issued by the state of Oklahoma, many opened high-stakes bingo parlors and later casinos. The U.S. Supreme Court struck down state judicial challenges to the

Five Tribes and other Native nations concerning their relationship to the state and their tax status. The Indian Gaming Regulatory Act of 1988 attempted to strike a balance between states and tribes in regard to gaming; it restored some state prerogatives in gaming, but kept intact much of the tribal controls. Today, tribal gaming generates tens of billions of dollars for over two hundred tribes.[55]

The U.S. Congress, the district courts, and the U.S. Supreme Court supported these efforts into the twenty-first century through a series of legislative acts and court decisions that strengthened tribal self-governance and weakened, but did not wholly abolish, the paternalism of the federal government. Five Tribes legal counsels, for example, challenged the BIA's involvement in Native elections and governing actions. The federal courts typically declared that tribal political issues did not fall under federal jurisdiction, and although the rulings retained BIA oversight of tribal constitutions and the distribution of federal funds, the courts generally agreed that Native politics and governance should be controlled by the tribes. Through a quick succession of cases, federal courts strenuously and consistently reiterated that only the federal government, and not state courts, had the authority to prosecute an Indian defendant for criminal acts committed on Indian lands, even Oklahoma.

Federal attorneys, who previously had ceded to Oklahoma most of the Five Tribes' criminal and civil cases, now began vigorously prosecuting crimes under the MCA. These developments also affected civil cases. Despite setbacks, throughout the last decades of the twentieth century, federal courts at all levels and even the Oklahoma Supreme Court enumerated restrictions on state jurisdiction in cases involving Native mineral rights, water rights, fishing and wildlife rights, housing, personal injury, and so on.[56]

One upshot of these cases for the Creeks and the other Five Tribes, and the one that led to *McGirt v. Oklahoma*, was the question of whether the Five Tribes' restricted and tribal trust lands were "Indian Country" and if those lands constituted a reservation. It should go without saying that the snarled history of Creek landholdings, sovereignty, and jurisprudence has contributed to the argument on both sides of the debate. The next section of this book sorts through the complicated legal threads and knots that led to the bombshell decision in *McGirt v. Oklahoma*. Whichever side of the debate one takes, however, one thing is clear: the Muscogee removal treaty did indeed make a promise. The treaty promised, in perpetuity, Creek self-governance and Creek landholdings in present-day Oklahoma, and that promise has been restated numerous times in the almost two hundred years since the original agreement. Those two hundred years have also seen attempts by many to break, to undermine, to change, and to limit that promise. The victory represented by *McGirt v. Oklahoma*, however, underscores an immutable fact about American Indian policy: American Indian rights exist at the pleasure of the U.S. Congress. Congress still has plenary power over Native nations, and how Congress exercises its authority, as we have seen in this brief history, shifts with the prevailing cultural, political, and ideological winds. For now, though, the promise holds.

PART II

THE *McGIRT* CASE

5

THE CASE LAW PRECEDING
McGIRT v. OKLAHOMA

The *McGirt v. Oklahoma* case did not appear out of thin air. In part 1 we presented the historical background of the case and the establishment of and subsequent state and federal infringements on the Muscogee (Creek) Nation (MCN) Reservation in present-day Oklahoma. In this chapter we take a closer look at the centuries of jurisprudence and case law that undergird the *McGirt* case. Because constitutionally binding treaty promises were absolutely crucial to the U.S. Supreme Court's decision in *McGirt*, we begin with treaty rights.

One should not look at Indian treaties as only being of historical interest. As *McGirt* starkly demonstrates, these treaties have modern-day effects, and sometimes dramatic effects. Additionally, the mere existence of Indian treaties continues to reinforce that Indian nations are governments recognized under the U.S. Constitution and that Indian nations and peoples still possess a wide array of treaty rights today. The treaty rights of Indian nations are often misunderstood and misperceived as giving Indians "special rights," when in fact they are constitutionally backed guarantees that were given to Indian nations and indigenous governments. Indians were not "given" rights or "given" land by the United States in these treaties. Instead, through federally sanctioned diplomatic contract negotiations, tribal leaders reserved lands and rights their nations already owned, and then sold and traded other lands and rights to the U.S. In 1905, the U.S. Supreme Court demonstrated its correct understanding of the true nature of treaties when it wrote: "the treaty was not a grant of rights to the Indians, but a *grant of right from them*—a *reservation* of those not granted" (emphasis added). During treaty-making, tribes relinquished rights they owned in lands, resources, assets, and sovereignty in exchange for payments, promises, protection, and sometimes other lands to be granted from the United States. Thus, Indian nations typically agreed to sell some of their property rights while preserving other lands and assets they already owned and wanted to retain. The lands they retained are now called "reservations" or, in the case of the First Nations in Canada, "reserves."[1]

The treaties the MCN signed with the United States conform to the above description. During the removal era, for example, the MCN accepted the United States' promise that if the tribe removed, it would be provided new lands in the West in exchange for Creek lands in the East. In these treaties, the U.S. promised that the MCN would continue to govern itself in the West, would retain its sovereignty, economy, and culture, and would remain free from state and federal territorial laws.

Long before Europeans arrived in North America, Indian nations dealt politically and diplomatically with other Native nations through negotiations and consensual agreements that were in essence treaties. European countries also developed a nascent treaty system when nation-states began emerging in the sixteenth and seventeenth centuries. Once European countries began establishing trade and colonies in North America, they conjoined their own treaty system with the customs of tribal nations and worked through Native and European governmental and diplomatic means of negotiations, agreements, and treaty-making. The early treaties were treaties of friendship, cemented with an exchange of gifts, sometimes including parcels of land for new colonists. In time, treaties became negotiated and transactional and usually involved a transfer of landownership or at least use rights from Native groups to colonists. In exchange, Native peoples would receive goods, protection, debt relief, and so on. Spain, England, France, Holland, and their colonies entered into hundreds of treaties with Indian nations, and once the United States was created, it naturally adopted this accepted practice. Ultimately, the U.S. entered into 375 treaties with multiple Indian nations between 1778 and 1871.[2]

In 1778, during the Revolutionary War, the Continental Congress negotiated the first U.S. Indian treaty. Congress requested a treaty with the Delaware Indian Nation because it was seeking permission for U.S. forces to cross Delaware territory to attack the British at Fort Detroit. In this treaty, the U.S. even asked the Delaware Nation to consider joining with other tribes and perhaps enter the Union of the thirteen states as a state. After the war, the U.S. Congress, under the Articles of Confederation, continued political and diplomatic relationships and treaty-making with Indian nations, signing eight treaties between 1784 and 1789 with different tribes.[3]

Once the current U.S. government commenced operating under the new Constitution in the spring of 1789, President George Washington and his administration dealt with Indian treaties in the same manner as international treaties. Congress ended treaty-making with Native nations in an 1871 act; however, the act stipulated that all preexisting treaties were still binding. The act of 1871 is still law today and contains promises that the U.S. must honor. In fact, under the Constitution, treaties are "the supreme Law of the Land."[4]

Prior to 1871, federal commissioners appointed by the executive branch and funded by Congress negotiated Indian treaties. The treaties usually involved purchasing land, controlling the Indian trade, enlisting military aid, keeping peace, and settling various grievances of the Indian nations. The U.S. regularly engaged, however, in practices that raise questions about the interpretation and fairness of these treaties. First, questions arise about whether the "chief" or "tribe" that signed a particular treaty possessed the authority to engage in treaty negotiations, much less act as the sole signatory. Historians and tribal citizens have documented on numerous occasions that federal commissioners selected the "chiefs" they wanted to negotiate with or picked a specific group or faction to speak for others. One case in point that we examine in part 1 is the machinations of William McIntosh during the Creek removal era. The Creeks later executed McIntosh because he was not, in fact, authorized to sign the 1825 Treaty of Indian Springs. Even so, President Andrew Jackson and the U.S. Congress upheld the treaty as valid and binding.[5]

In addition, all Indian treaties, although typically negotiated with the help of translators, were written in English. Consequently, Indian negotiators had to trust that the federal commissioners and their interpreters were being truthful about the language in a treaty and its meaning. Moreover, Native leaders were expected to understand the legal significance of the English words used in the treaties. And when the power dynamics shifted in the early nineteenth century, federal negotiators, as we have seen, oftentimes coerced and threatened Native leaders into signing treaties. All of these points call into question the legitimacy of many of the treaties the United States signed with Indian nations. Despite these difficulties, after the American Revolution, Indian nations and Native political leaders had little choice but to treat with the expanding and aggressive United States, and many became adroit and hard negotiators, leveraging whenever possible what powers they retained for the best outcomes.[6]

The significance of Indian treaty-making cannot be overstated. The U.S. Supreme Court has declared: "A treaty, including one between the United States and an Indian tribe, is essentially a contract between two sovereign nations." And one federal judge has written: "Indian treaties stand on essentially the same footing as treaties with foreign nations." These statements are correct as a matter of law and fact. They are factual because from the beginning of the office of the president, George Washington established many of the U.S. and Indian treaty procedures and understood Indian treaties in the same fashion as international treaties. Furthermore, the United States has continued for more than two hundred years to relate politically on a government-to-government basis with tribal nations, and the existence of binding treaties is an important component of federal Indian law today.[7]

The status of Indian nations as governments that interact with the U.S. is expressly recognized in the Constitution. In the Interstate and Indian Commerce Clause, the Constitution states that "Congress shall have Power . . . To regulate Commerce with foreign Nations, and among the several States, and with the Indian Tribes." This provision acknowledges Indian nations as governmental entities on a par with the American states and foreign nations. It also delegates to Congress the authority to regulate American commerce with tribes. In addition, Indian nations and Indian treaties are included by implication in the so-called Treaty Clause of the Constitution. Article VI states that "all Treaties made, or which shall be made, under the Authority of the United States, shall be the supreme Law of the Land." This provision includes Indian treaties, because by the time the new U.S. government began operating under the Constitution, it had already entered into nine treaties with tribal nations and twenty-three treaties with foreign countries. And the express language of the Treaty Clause, "all Treaties *made*, or *which shall be made*" (emphasis added), is a clear constitutional ratification of those previous thirty-two treaties as "Treaties made," which included the nine with Indian nations. The language "which shall be made" was another recognition that all U.S. treaties, including tribal treaties, that would be made in the future would also be constitutionally recognized treaties. Furthermore, the Treaty Clause of the Constitution is also called the Supremacy Clause because it states that all U.S. treaties, federal laws, and the Constitution are "the supreme Law of the Land."[8]

In addition, the drafters of the Constitution of 1789 and later of the Fourteenth Amendment of 1868 recognized individual Indians as being citizens of their own political entities, their tribal governments. In 1789, the Constitution provided that Indians were not to be counted in the census as state or federal citizens unless they paid taxes. In 1868, when the Fourteenth Amendment was ratified and African Americans were granted citizenship rights after the Civil War, individual Indians were still expressly excluded from being counted as state or federal citizens unless they paid taxes. These exclusions demonstrate that the Constitution and the Fourteenth Amendment recognize that Indians are citizens of their own separate nations.[9]

The U.S. Supreme Court has also recognized the constitutional significance of treaty-making with tribal nations, and treaties are express evidence that the United States has always recognized Indian nations as sovereign governments. In 1831, for example, in *Cherokee Nation v. Georgia*, the Court stated that Indian nations are governments and distinct political entities that manage their own territories and affairs. The next year, the Court emphasized even more strongly the significance of the U.S. and Indian treaty relationship: "The words 'treaty' and 'nation' are words of our own language, selected in our diplomatic and legislative proceedings. . . . We have applied them to Indians, as we have applied them to the other nations of the earth. They are applied to all in the same sense." In sum, the Constitution and the executive, legislative, and judicial branches of the federal government have all recognized Indian nations as separate governmental entities, with a separate citizenship, and as nations that could engage in political interactions and treaty-making with the United States.[10]

Over the past two centuries, the U.S. Supreme Court has developed fairly liberal rules to interpret and enforce Indian treaties in ways that favor Indian nations. These rules, called the "canons of treaty construction," prescribe liberal interpretations of Indian treaties in favor of the tribes through a mixture of principles borrowed from contract law and the interpretation of international treaties. In 1832, for example, the Court stated one of the rules for interpreting Indian treaties:

> The language used in treaties with the Indians should never be construed to their prejudice. If words be made use of which are susceptible of a more extended meaning than their plain import, as connected with the tenor of their treaty, they should be considered as used only in the latter sense ... How the words of the treaty were understood by this unlettered people, rather than their critical meaning, should form the rule of construction.[11]

In more recent times, the Supreme Court has clarified this general statement. First, courts are to resolve any ambiguous statements in a treaty in favor of the tribe. This seems fair, since the United States drafted the treaties and they were written in English, and if there are any ambiguities it is the fault of the United States. Moreover, basic contract law states that the party who introduced an ambiguity into a contract will have that term interpreted against them. Second, the Supreme Court interprets treaties as the tribal peoples would have understood them, at the time they were written. The Court repeated this principle in 1999 and again in 2019 when it stated that "Indian treaties 'must be interpreted in light of the parties' intentions, with any ambiguities resolved in favor of the Indian'" and must "give effect to the terms [of a treaty] as the Indians themselves would have understood them." Third, courts consider the facts and circumstances surrounding treaty negotiations when interpreting their provisions. In light of these rules, the Supreme Court has directed that treaties should never be interpreted to a tribe's prejudice; instead, they should be read liberally in favor of tribal nations to accomplish the protective purposes they were intended to serve.[12]

Because treaties are also contracts between nations, as the Supreme Court stated in 1979, it is not surprising that the principles of contract law also are used to interpret Indian treaties. In fact, many of the rules of interpretation listed above are no more than the general rules for interpreting contracts. First, in interpreting any contract, courts look to enforce the actual agreement that the parties negotiated. This is called the "meeting of the minds" principle. If a court can determine from the language of a contract what the parties intended to do, and that both parties intended to do the same thing, then a court will enforce that agreement. Similarly, courts interpret treaties to understand the intent of the parties and to ensure that, for example, the U.S. and an Indian nation had a meeting of the minds and were discussing and agreeing to the same things. Second, in interpreting contracts, courts read any ambiguous expressions against the party that wrote the contract. In other words, if one party caused a problem by writing a confusing, ambiguous contract, it should injure that party and not the innocent one. Third, the idea behind liberally interpreting Indian treaties in the tribes' favor is similar to the way courts handle what are called "adhesion contracts." Such a contract is one that was not fairly bargained because one party was in a much weaker position than the other. In these situations, courts will not interpret a contract against the interests of the weaker party. Under contract law, contracts negotiated in this manner should not be enforceable due to undue influence, an unequal bargaining position, and the lack of arms-length bargaining. Because a majority of Indian treaties were negotiated in such situations, they are analogous to adhesion contracts, and thus they are to be interpreted under the liberal rules of Indian treaty interpretation.

Finally, though, it is important to note that, as with any other U.S. treaty, Congress has the authority to abrogate or alter an Indian treaty. However, the Fifth Amendment of the Constitution and numerous Supreme Court cases mandate that Congress must compensate a tribal nation for any property rights that were created by or recognized in a treaty and that are subsequently taken away with the repeal of the treaty. As with any contract, parties to a treaty must fulfill the terms and their obligations or suffer legal consequences. In cases where the U.S. has violated a treaty or its actions would take or adversely affect the property rights a tribe possesses under treaties, the Supreme Court has stated that the U.S. is subject to lawsuits for monetary damages for the taking or destruction of property rights. There seems to be little doubt that this legal principle would also apply if the U.S. were now to attempt to disestablish or take the re-recognized MCN Reservation after the *McGirt* decision.[13]

The question of reservation diminishment is fundamental to the *McGirt* case. Diminishment through an act of Congress entails two scenarios: a congressional act that renders a preexisting Indian reservation smaller or a congressional act that completely disestablishes or erases a preexisting Indian reservation, making it no longer in existence. Both situations are obviously anathema to tribal governments, their sovereignty, and their citizens. Often these cases are raised by criminal defendants who are trying to avoid state jurisdiction and prosecution, or by states, counties, or cities that are attacking tribal sovereignty and jurisdiction. The Supreme Court decided eight diminishment and disestablishment cases between 1962 and 2016. Below we briefly examine each of these eight cases, followed by an analysis of the 2017 *Sharp v. Murphy* case, which the Court left undecided, that set the stage for *McGirt*.

SEYMOUR V. SUPERINTENDENT (1962)

In 1962, the Supreme Court apparently considered for the first time the issue of the disestablishment of an Indian reservation. In *Seymour v. Superintendent*, Paul Seymour, of the Colville Indian Tribe, pled guilty in a Washington state court to attempted burglary. But he also filed a petition for a writ of habeas corpus, arguing that the conviction was void because the state did not have jurisdiction over him since he was a citizen of the Colville Indian Tribe and his crime had occurred on the Colville Indian Reservation (in Indian Country). The state court system rejected his claim because it concluded that the land where the burglary occurred, even though it had once been within the reservation, had been disestablished from reservation status and restored to the U.S.

public domain. The Supreme Court, however, unanimously disagreed, 9 to 0, and reversed the Washington state court decisions.[14]

In reaching its ruling, the Supreme Court analyzed the factual and legal history of the Colville Reservation. The reservation was created in 1872 by an executive order issued by President Grant; it was then diminished by half its size in 1892, when Congress "vacated and *restored* [that part] *to the public domain*" (emphasis added). However, in that 1892 act, Congress reaffirmed that the remaining half of the reservation was "still reserved by the Government for [the Colville Indians'] use and occupancy." In the *Seymour* case, in contrast, the Washington state courts relied on a 1906 congressional act concerning the Colville Reservation. The 1906 act provided for the sale of some specific lands of the Colville Reservation and allotted some other lands to tribal citizens. It also allowed non-Indians to move onto the reservation. Although the act said nothing about disestablishing the reservation, the state's lawyers argued that this kind of allotment and sales disestablished the reservation.[15]

The Supreme Court disagreed with the state courts on the meaning of the 1906 act. The Court noted that Congress used crucially different language in the 1906 act than it did in the 1892 act that everyone agreed had diminished the reservation by half. In the 1892 act, Congress had the clear intent to diminish the Colville Reservation because it took half of it and placed it within the U.S. "public domain." In contrast, the 1906 act did not use any such diminishing language, and in fact used language that indicated that the remaining half of the Colville Reservation, where Seymour's crime occurred, was to continue as a reservation. Consequently, the 1906 act did not diminish or disestablish the remaining part of the reservation. The Supreme Court held that the Colville Indian Reservation still existed and the state did not possess criminal jurisdiction to prosecute Seymour for his conduct on the reservation.

MATTZ V. ARNETT (1973)

In 1973, in *Mattz v. Arnett*, the Supreme Court once again voted 9 to 0 that an Indian reservation had not been diminished or disestablished. Raymond Mattz was a Yurok Indian who since childhood had fished with dip and gill nets on the Klamath River within his tribe's reservation in northern California. In 1969, however, the State Department of Fish and Game seized his nets and filed a lawsuit to forfeit them to the state. The California courts held that the reservation had been disestablished and ordered the forfeiture of his nets. The U.S. Supreme Court unanimously disagreed and held that the Klamath River Indian Reservation had not been disestablished.[16]

In this case, the Court stated one of its established rules, that it was "not inclined to infer an intent to terminate the reservation [in the absence of] clear termination language." This was not a new rule because the *Mattz* Court cited *Seymour* from 1962 and quoted another case from 1909 in which the Court had held that "when Congress has once established a reservation all tracts included within it remain a part of the reservation until separated therefrom by Congress." The Court then applied these rules and engaged in over ten pages of historical and legal analysis, looking for any congressional language or intent to terminate or disestablish the Klamath River Indian Reservation. The Court noted that California members of the U.S. House of Representatives had often been hostile toward the reservation, and the House had produced several committee reports and proposed bills that would have terminated the reservation, but they had never been enacted into law. Granted, on June 17, 1892, Congress passed an act to allot the Klamath River Reservation, but as the Court had already stated in 1962 in *Seymour*, and now repeated in *Mattz*, when Congress merely allots a reservation, that does not diminish or disestablish it.[17]

In light of these facts, the Court pointed out that Congress did not use the kind of specific and exact language in the 1892 act that would diminish or disestablish a reservation. Instead, Congress merely allotted the Klamath River Reservation, and consequently it continued to exist, and California had no jurisdiction to regulate Mattz's fishing or to seize his nets.

DeCoteau v. District County Court (1975)

In 1975, in *DeCoteau v. District County Court*, the Supreme Court consolidated two appeals that both raised the question whether the Lake Traverse Indian Reservation had been disestablished by Congress. In the first case, a mother brought suit alleging that South Dakota did not have jurisdiction over her and her children, all of whom lived within the reservation, to decide whether to terminate her parental rights. The second appeal was by an Indian who was convicted in state court for a crime committed on the reservation. The Lake Traverse Indian Reservation had been established by Congress in 1867, but the *DeCoteau* Court held by a vote of 6 to 3 that the reservation had been disestablished by Congress and that the majority of its more than nine hundred thousand acres had been returned to the public domain.[18]

The majority opinion closely considered the analysis of *Seymour* and *Mattz* discussed above and examined the relevant federal statutes and facts in those cases. The *DeCoteau* Court claimed that it was "not departing from, but following and reaffirming, the guiding principles of *Mattz* and *Seymour*." In contrast to those cases, however, the *DeCoteau* Court held that an 1891 act that Congress enacted regarding the Lake Traverse Reservation, and the circumstances surrounding that legislation, unambiguously indicated that Congress had intended to disestablish the reservation.[19]

According to the *DeCoteau* Court, specific language in the 1891 act and the facts distinguished this case from *Seymour* and *Mattz*. The key point to the Supreme Court was that in 1889, in preparation for allotment of the reservation, the secretary of the interior dispatched a commission to negotiate with the Sisseton and Wahpeton Indians for the sale of unallotted lands that remained after the allotment of individual tracts to tribal members. The federal officials reported that during these 1889 negotiations, the Indian negotiators expressed their desire to sell all of their reservation lands that had not been allotted to tribal citizens. An agreement to do just that was signed by the requisite number of adult male tribal citizens, as required by the tribe's treaty. Crucially, this 1889 agreement and its specific language were incorporated into the 1891 act of Congress regarding the Lake Traverse Reservation. The Supreme Court emphasized that Congress "recited and ratified the 1889 Agreement with the tribe and appropriated $2,203,000 to pay the tribe for the ceded land." This language, according to the Court, was enough to demonstrate that the tribe and Congress intended to disestablish the reservation. The 1889 agreement and the 1891 act stated: "the Indians cede, sell, relinquish, and convey to the United States all the unallotted land within the reservation remaining after the allotments and . . . the United States will pay to the Indians $2.50 per acre for the lands ceded." Years later, in the 1984 case *Solem v. Bartlett*, the Court asserted that language such as this—which entails a total sale of all a tribe's rights and interests in its land, and for a certain amount of money to be paid by the United States—creates a nearly insurmountable presumption that the intent of Congress was to diminish or disestablish the reservation. After analyzing "'the face of the Act,' and its 'surrounding circumstances' and 'legislative history,'" the Court held that there was unmistakable congressional intent to disestablish the Lake Traverse Reservation.[20]

The Supreme Court, though, almost seemed to apologize for its decision:

> This Court does not lightly conclude that an Indian reservation has been terminated. "[W]hen Congress has once established a reservation all tracts included within it remain a part of the reservation until separated therefrom by Congress." The congressional intent must be clear, to overcome "the general rule that '[d]oubtful expressions are to be resolved in favor of the weak and defenseless people who are the wards of the nation, dependent upon its protection and good faith.'" Accordingly, the Court requires that the "congressional determination to terminate . . . be expressed on the face of the Act or be clear from the surrounding circumstances and legislative history."[21]

ROSEBUD SIOUX TRIBE V. KNEIP (1977)

Two years after the *DeCoteau* ruling, the Supreme Court again faced the question of reservation diminishment. In *Rosebud Sioux Tribe v. Kneip*, the Court held in a 6 to 3 vote that the Rosebud Sioux Reservation was diminished.[22]

The majority opinion in *Kneip* relied to a large extent on a 1901 agreement that was never ratified into law by Congress. The Court then used this unratified agreement to interpret what Congress must have meant to do in three subsequent laws about the Rosebud Sioux Reservation that were enacted in 1904, 1907, and 1910. The majority held that these three laws "clearly evidence congressional intent to diminish the boundaries of the Rosebud Sioux Reservation." Clearly, if that 1901 agreement had been enacted into law by Congress, it would have been highly relevant to this appeal. The 1901 agreement was negotiated between a Bureau of Indian Affairs official and leaders of the Rosebud Sioux Tribe. Tribal citizens had apparently voted to sell the unallotted lands on their reservation to the United States for a specific amount of money.[23]

The majority opinion also relied on congressional testimonies and statements as well as historical and legal events that occurred in the sixty years after the 1904, 1907, and 1910 acts were enacted. But inexplicably, the majority also claimed that the 1901 unratified agreement and its language would have been conclusive evidence that the reservation had been diminished. It is crucial to repeat that the 1901 agreement was rejected by Congress and never enacted into law. The dissenting opinion objected to the majority relying on the rejected 1901 agreement, and it is odd that the Supreme Court relied on a proposal that Congress rejected.[24]

SOLEM V. BARTLETT (1984)

In 1984, in *Solem v. Bartlett*, the U.S. Supreme Court rendered a unanimous decision that the Cheyenne River Sioux Tribe's reservation borders had not been diminished even though Congress did open the reservation in 1908 for non-Indians to homestead. The *Solem* Court claimed that earlier cases had "established a fairly clean analytical structure" for addressing diminishment and disestablishment cases and that it would now set out the definitive test.[25]

Solem v. Bartlett is, or at least was before *McGirt*, the most significant diminishment or disestablishment case, because the *Solem* Court explicitly restated two established principles that still guide judicial inquiries into whether a reservation was diminished. First, only Congress can diminish or disestablish a reservation. Second, such an action by Congress "will not be lightly inferred." Thus, the Court requires that Congress use fairly clear language. The Supreme Court then set out its "analytical structure" to determine whether an act of Congress was intended to limit or erase a reservation's borders. This analysis appeared to everyone to be a three-step test.[26]

In the first step, judges are required to examine whether "Congress clearly evince[d] an 'intent to change [reservation] boundaries' before diminishment will be found." The Court expressly mandated an inquiry into the specific "statutory language" used by Congress in the relevant law, and if that language made "[e]xplicit reference to cession [sale] or other language evidencing the present and total surrender of all tribal interests[,] [then it] strongly suggests that Congress meant to" diminish or disestablish a reservation. In addition, if Congress used this kind of express language and coupled it with a statutory requirement that showed "an unconditional commitment from Congress to compensate the tribe for its opened lands, there is an almost *insurmountable presumption* that Congress meant for the tribe's reservation to be diminished" (emphasis added). Consequently, a court is to commence its analysis with a search for the clear and explicit intent of Congress as stated in laws enacted by Congress.[27]

Even though the *Solem* Court stated that "[t]he most probative evidence of congressional intent is the statutory language," the Court also said that "explicit language of cession and unconditional compensation are not prerequisites for a finding of diminishment." Thus, in what was assumed to be step two of the *Solem* test, courts are to examine

> events surrounding the passage of a surplus land act . . . [and if the events] unequivocally reveal a widely-held, contemporaneous understanding that the affected reservation would shrink as a result of the proposed legislation, we have been *willing to infer that Congress shared the understanding that its action would diminish the reservation*, notwithstanding the presence of statutory language that would otherwise suggest reservation boundaries remained unchanged. (Emphasis added)[28]

In explaining how courts should apply this second step, the Court made a statement that is illustrative of what the *McGirt* Court did in 2020. *Solem* stated that part of the evidence for determining the "contemporaneous understanding" about whether Congress did or did not intend to diminish a particular reservation would be the contemporaneous congressional debates, and "particularly the manner in which the transaction was negotiated with the tribes involved and the tenor of legislative reports presented to Congress." As is discussed more fully in chapter 7, between 1893 and 1901, during the allotment era, the Creek Nation repeatedly refused Congress's request to sell any land from its 1866 reservation, and Congress expressly understood that fact. Thus, Congress's contemporaneous intent regarding the MCN Reservation could not have been to diminish or disestablish its boundaries.[29]

Finally, in the third step of *Solem*, courts can consider subsequent history and later events, even decades later, to assess whether Congress intended to diminish a reservation at the time it enacted the law in question. The Supreme Court cautions courts, however, to only use this kind of evidence to "a lesser extent." Such evidence can include how Congress and the Bureau of Indian Affairs, for example, treated the reservation lands thereafter, as well as "who actually moved onto opened reservation lands" and "the subsequent demographic history of opened lands."[30]

Legal scholars, the federal courts, and the Supreme Court have considered *Solem* to have set out a three-step test, and these entities have applied it consistently since 1984. Some argue that the *McGirt* Court appears to have modified or ignored that three-step test. At the very least, *McGirt* made it abundantly clear that *Solem* did not create a mandatory three-step test that courts must apply in every situation. We will discuss that point further in the next chapter.[31]

HAGEN V. UTAH (1994)

After initially pleading guilty to a crime in Utah state court, Robert Hagen moved to withdraw his plea, claiming that the state court lacked jurisdiction over him because he was an Indian and his crime was committed in Indian Country on the Uintah Indian Reservation. The Utah Supreme Court ruled against him, and he appealed to the U.S. Supreme Court. In 1994, in *Hagen v. Utah*, the Court held that the Uintah Indian Reservation had been diminished by Congress and that the location where Hagen committed his crime was no longer in Indian Country, and thus state jurisdiction was appropriate.

The *Hagen* Court stated that it was applying its "traditional approach" as set out in *Solem* and the other cases we have discussed above. It then applied the three steps of *Solem*. First, the Court examined the statutory language Congress used to allot and then to open the unallotted lands of the Uintah Indian Reservation. Second, it looked to the contemporaneous understanding of Congress, the tribe, and the federal and state governments about the intent of Congress. Third, it took into consideration subsequent historical events and how Congress, the BIA, and the state had treated the lands and peoples, and the Indian and non-Indian demographics of the area in question.[32]

Under step one, the Supreme Court's majority held that language in the 1902 and 1905 acts of Congress demonstrated congressional intent to diminish the Uintah Reservation. For example, the Court quoted language from the 1902 act, which states that "all the unallotted lands within said reservation shall be *restored to the public domain*" (emphasis added). The majority and the dissenting two justices disagreed about the significance of the words "public domain," but the majority held that it meant that those portions of the reservation had been restored to full federal ownership and could be sold, distributed, or dealt with at the whim of the United States. In addition, the Court interpreted the 1905 act, in conjunction with the 1902 act, to mean that Congress's intent was to alter the reservation borders.[33]

Using step two of the *Solem* test, the majority examined the historical evidence contemporaneous to the enactments of the 1902 and 1905 acts. The Court referenced letters and statements by Department of Interior officials, congressional bills and statements by House and Senate members, and a 1905 presidential proclamation about the Uintah Reservation. It held that all this evidence indicated that the contemporaneous understanding about the 1902 and 1905 acts was that the reservation borders were diminished.[34]

Applying step three of *Solem*, the Court found inconsistent references in the historical record after the 1902 and 1905 acts were enacted. Congress and others referred to the Uintah Indian Reservation in both the past and present tenses. The Court concluded that little could be gained from this evidence. However, to gauge the common understanding of the 1902 and 1905 acts, the Court relied on another aspect of *Solem*'s step three and considered the modern-day demographics of the part of the reservation that had allegedly been diminished. The Court noted that the population in the Uintah Valley was approximately 85 percent non-Indian and the area's largest city was 93 percent non-Indian. The Court also relied on the fact that Utah had assumed jurisdiction over the opened reservation lands from 1905 onward to gauge what the common understanding was as to the effect of the 1902 and 1905 acts. After considering all these factors, the Court held that the reservation had been diminished.[35]

SOUTH DAKOTA V. YANKTON SIOUX TRIBE (1998)

In the late 1990s, the Yankton Sioux Tribe attempted to enforce its sovereignty and federal environmental laws over South Dakota's attempt to site and regulate a landfill within the original boundaries of the Yankton Sioux Reservation. South Dakota claimed that the reservation had been diminished by an 1892 allotment act with the Yankton Sioux, and that the tribe consequently did not possess jurisdiction over the land in question. The lower federal courts ruled in favor of the tribe, but when *South Dakota v. Yankton Sioux Tribe* went to the U.S. Supreme Court in 1998, the Court ruled 9 to 0 that the Yankton Sioux Reservation had been diminished. The decision appears to have been relatively straightforward under the *Solem* test.

The 1892 agreement, negotiated between the federal executive branch and the Yankton Sioux Tribe, used language that the Supreme Court has stated creates "a nearly insurmountable presumption" that a reservation has been diminished or disestablished. The agreement provided that the Yankton Sioux would "cede, sell, relinquish, and convey to the United States" all of the unallotted lands on the reservation, and the government agreed to pay the tribe an exact amount, a "sum certain," of $600,000 for the land. Congress then enacted this agreement into law in an 1894 act, which restated that the tribe did "cede, sell, relinquish, and convey to the United States all their claim, right, title, and interest in and to all the unallotted lands within the limits of the reservation," and the United States pledged to pay a fixed sum of $600,000 for the lands. The *Yankton Sioux* Court cited the *DeCoteau* case discussed above, and stated that this "cession [and] sum certain [language is] precisely suited" to terminate a reservation.[36]

The *Yankton Sioux* Court, however, proceeded to analyze evidence as outlined in *Solem* steps two and three. The Court found that the step two evidence was unclear about whether there was a contemporaneous understanding that the reservation was to be diminished in the 1894 act. It also found that the step three evidence—a common understanding of diminishment in the years after the enactment of the 1894 act—was uncertain. Thus, the Court relied solely on *Solem* step one, the statutory language, to hold that the reservation had been diminished. In the Court's words, "The 1894 Act contains the most certain statutory language, evincing Congress' intent to diminish the Yankton Sioux Reservation by providing for total cession and fixed compensation."[37]

We will see in the next chapter that the majority opinion of the Supreme Court in *McGirt v. Oklahoma* followed the lead of *Yankton Sioux* and that the *McGirt* decision similarly relied almost exclusively on the first step of the *Solem* test.

NEBRASKA V. PARKER (2016)

In the 2016 case of *Nebraska v. Parker*, the Supreme Court once again was faced with the issue of diminishment and disestablishment of an Indian reservation. In 2006, the Omaha Indian Tribe amended its Beverage Control Ordinance and attempted to tax and regulate non-Indian alcohol sales in the Village of Pender, Nebraska. Pender is located within the original borders of the tribe's reservation, which was established by an 1854 treaty and encompasses three hundred thousand acres. Pender and its alcohol retailers filed suit to prevent the tribal ordinance from being applied to them. Nebraska intervened in the case on behalf of Pender, and the United States intervened on behalf of the Omaha Tribe. The state joined the suit because the tribe also demanded that Nebraska share with it the taxes it received from fuel sales in Pender. The state, Pender, and the alcohol retailers claimed that the tribe had no jurisdiction in Pender because a western section of the original Omaha Reservation, where Pender was located, had been diminished by an 1882 act of Congress. The plaintiffs further contended that the tribe had not undertaken any attempts to enforce its sovereignty and jurisdiction in that part of the reservation or even been present in that area for over 120 years.[38]

The Supreme Court held in a 9 to 0 decision that Congress in fact had not diminished the Omaha Reservation. Seven of the nine justices on the *Parker* Court were also on the Court that decided *McGirt*. The unanimous decision in *Parker* was surprising because several justices who rarely vote for tribal positions agreed with it, and Justice Thomas, who very rarely votes for tribes, wrote the unanimous opinion.[39]

As with all diminishment cases, the Supreme Court began its analysis by looking at the relevant act to determine if Congress had intended to diminish the reservation. The Court held that the 1882 act in question, which provided for reservation lands to be allotted to Omaha Indians, only opened the Omaha Reservation for non-Indians to buy surplus lands and to settle on the reservation. The Court began "with the text of the 1882 Act, the most 'probative evidence' of diminishment." The *Parker* Court cited many of the cases we address above and recognized that Congress knew full well how to express its intent if it wanted to diminish or disestablish a reservation. Such evidence would include "[e]xplicit reference to cession [sale] or other language evidencing the present and total surrender of all tribal interests" and "the total surrender of tribal claims in exchange for a fixed payment" and a "commitment from Congress to compensate the Indian tribe for its opened land." However, the *Parker* Court said, "The 1882 Act bore none of these hallmarks of diminishment." Instead, the 1882 act only authorized the secretary of the interior, on behalf of the Omaha Indians, to sell lands within the reservation to non-Indians. This was a common specification in allotment acts at the time and did not diminish or disestablish reservations but "merely opened reservation land to settlement" by non-Indians. Consequently, the Supreme Court held that the Omaha Reservation was not diminished by the 1882 act.[40]

The Court then proceeded to *Solem* step two, examining evidence that might demonstrate whether Congress and others had an understanding, at the time the 1882 act was enacted, that Congress intended to diminish the reservation. Both parties produced historical evidence to support their arguments, but the Court concluded that this evidence was "mixed" and "in no way *unequivocally* reveal[s] a widely held, contemporaneous understanding that the affected reservation would shrink as a result of the proposed legislation" (emphasis added).[41]

The Court then turned to *Solem* step three and looked for any subsequent history and circumstances that might shed light on what Congress intended to do in the 1882 act. The Court looked specifically for evidence on the United States' "treatment of the affected areas, particularly in the years immediately following the opening." It also noted the demographic history of the opened part of the reservation because these factors serve as "one additional clue as to what Congress expected would happen once land on a particular reservation was opened to non-Indian settlers." But the Court found this evidence also to be mixed and inconclusive, and consequently, the demographic history had no effect on how the Court read the congressional intent expressed in the 1882 act.[42]

Several aspects of *Parker* are especially relevant to the *McGirt* decision. First, Nebraska, Pender, and the alcohol retailers pointed out that the Omaha Tribe had been almost totally absent from the Pender part of the reservation for more than 120 years. Apparently, until 2006 and its amended beverage ordinance, the tribe had not enforced any of its laws or regulations in Pender or the immediately surrounding area. After our review of some of the cases above, one might think that the Court would have placed great emphasis on this fact. Second, a significant point that the Supreme Court has often mentioned in diminishment cases concerns the demographic statistics. At the time, Pender had a population of 1,300 residents, most of whom were not citizens of the Omaha Tribe, and less than 2 percent of tribal citizens had lived in the area around Pender since the early twentieth century. But the *Parker* Court was not swayed by these demographic facts. This was so, the Court stated, because Congress did not expressly intend to diminish the reservation in 1882. "After all, evidence of the *changing demographics* of disputed land is 'the *least compelling' evidence* in our diminishment analysis, for '[e]very surplus land Act necessarily resulted in a surge of non-Indian settlement and degraded the 'Indian character' of the reservation" (emphasis added).[43]

The *Parker* Court held unanimously that Pender and the surrounding area were still part of the Omaha Reservation. As with any question of statutory interpretation, the Court began with the actual language of the 1882 act, and this act had none of the specific hallmarks of diminishment. And, significantly for *McGirt*, using steps two and three, the *Parker* Court held that the historical evidence could not overcome the clear statutory text in the 1882 act that Congress did not intend to diminish the reservation. In fact, even if some of this *Solem* step three evidence might have hinted at diminishment, Justice Thomas wrote that courts cannot "rel[y] solely on this third consideration to find diminishment."[44]

SHARP V. MURPHY (10TH CIRCUIT 2017)

The *McGirt* decision of 2020 was not the first federal case to hold that the MCN Reservation still exists in the twenty-first century. In 2017, in a case that was then called *Murphy v. Carpenter* but was subsequently renamed *Sharp v. Murphy*, the United States Court of Appeals for the Tenth Circuit analyzed past Supreme Court cases and congressional actions toward the MCN, and held that the MCN Reservation still exists. The *Murphy* case, even at the time, was considered difficult if not impossible to decide. In fact, Columbia University law professor Ronald Mann declared that it was "the single hardest case of the [U.S. Supreme Court 2018–2019] term—the one case that the justices could not decide."[45]

Patrick Murphy is a citizen of the MCN. In August 1999, he began making threats against another Creek man named George Jacobs. On August 28, 1999, Murphy and two companions forced a car containing Jacobs to stop on a rural road. Murphy and his friends castrated Jacobs and cut his throat. Jacobs subsequently bled to death. Murphy was charged with murder and tried in Oklahoma state court, where in 2000 a jury found him guilty and he was sentenced to death.[46]

Over the next seventeen years, Murphy and his lawyers launched a series of appeals. They filed multiple writs of habeas corpus in state and federal courts in which they requested that Murphy be released from the Oklahoma State Penitentiary. They raised multiple issues in these appeals, including that because Murphy was mentally disabled, he could not legally be executed. They also raised the issue that because he is a Creek Indian and because he committed his crime in Indian Country, on the MCN Reservation, the state had no criminal jurisdiction and no authority to prosecute or execute him.[47]

In 2004, the Oklahoma Court of Criminal Appeals ordered a state trial judge to conduct an evidentiary hearing on Murphy's jurisdictional claim. The state did not dispute that Murphy and the victim were both

Muscogee Indians, but the state argued that the crime was not committed on the MCN Reservation, and thus state jurisdiction, rather than federal jurisdiction under the Major Crimes Act, was proper. The Major Crimes Act is a federal law from 1885 that provides for federal jurisdiction over Indian-on-Indian crime in Indian Country. The trial judge agreed that the crime occurred on state land and not in Indian Country because the location of the crime was not an Indian or tribally owned allotment under federal law, 18 United States Code section 1151(c). But that judge inexplicably failed to also examine subsection 1151(a) of that statute to determine whether the MCN Reservation still exists.[48]

Murphy appealed that decision to the Oklahoma Court of Criminal Appeals (OCCA), and on December 7, 2005, that appellate court denied his jurisdictional claim. The state trial judge and the OCCA held that the piece of land where he committed his crime was not Indian Country because it was owned by non-Indians. At the heart of the appeal, though, was the 1866 Treaty with the Creek Nation. That treaty, as discussed in chapter 3, designated over 3.25 million acres as the Creek Reservation and defined its exact boundaries. According to the 1866 treaty, lands within these boundaries were Creek lands, governed by the sovereign Creek Nation. The jurisdictional question raised by Murphy depended on whether privately owned lands located within the 1866 boundaries were now part of the state of Oklahoma or part of the MCN Reservation. The OCCA "refuse[d] to step in" and decide that question.[49]

On December 28, 2005, Murphy brought his jurisdictional claim to the federal district court for the Eastern District of Oklahoma. In the federal judicial system, the U.S. district courts located within each state are the federal trial courts, while the regional circuit courts of appeals hear appeals from the district courts within their circuits. The Supreme Court then hears appeals from the circuit courts of appeals, and in certain situations it can also take appeals from state courts, as it did in *McGirt*.

Murphy's lawyers reiterated their argument to the federal district court that, no matter who individually owned the actual lot of land, the location of his crime was within the MCN Reservation, and accordingly the state of Oklahoma did not possess jurisdiction over his criminal conduct. But on August 1, 2007, the district court relied on the OCCA state court decision and held that the location of Murphy's conduct was not in Indian Country. The federal district judge ruled that the OCCA did not act contrary to established federal law in reaching its decision to deny Murphy's claim. Consequently, the federal district judge also denied Murphy's jurisdictional claim disputing Oklahoma's prosecution. After further proceedings in the Oklahoma state courts, Murphy's team once again brought a writ of habeas corpus to the federal district court of the Eastern District of Oklahoma on April 12, 2012. This court continued to deny his claims. Murphy then appealed that decision to the United States Court of Appeals for the Tenth Circuit.[50]

The United States Court of Appeals for the Tenth Circuit hears appeals from the U.S. district courts in the states of Oklahoma, Colorado, Kansas, New Mexico, Utah, and Wyoming. The Tenth Circuit consolidated all of Murphy's claims into one appeal. The court also allowed the MCN, the Seminole Nation of Oklahoma, and the United Keetoowah Band of Cherokee Indians to file briefs and thus to participate in a limited way in Murphy's appeal.[51]

More than five years later, on November 9, 2017, the Tenth Circuit issued a 138-page opinion and reversed the Eastern District of Oklahoma decision that Oklahoma had criminal jurisdiction over Murphy. In contrast, the Tenth Circuit held that the MCN Reservation, as designated in its 1866 treaty, still exists, and that Murphy's crime occurred on the MCN Reservation notwithstanding who owned the specific piece of land where the crime was actually committed. In other words, all lands, regardless of who owns them, that are within the territorial bounds of the MCN Reservation as specified in the 1866 Treaty with the Creeks still constitute the MCN Reservation. Consequently, Oklahoma's prosecution of Murphy was illegal and void *ab initio* (from the start) because he is a Creek Indian and his criminal conduct occurred within the boundaries of the MCN Reservation. Therefore, under the Major Crimes Act, only the federal government and the MCN had jurisdiction to prosecute Murphy in this situation.

In its lengthy opinion, the Tenth Circuit thoroughly examined Murphy's and the state's arguments, and carefully pored over the history of the MCN in the Indian Territory and in Oklahoma, the MCN treaties, and the acts of Congress concerning the MCN and the Creek Reservation. The Tenth Circuit analyzed in detail and applied the controlling U.S. Supreme Court case law on the question of how to determine whether an Indian reservation was diminished (reduced in size) or disestablished (completely erased) by Congress. As we have discussed in this chapter, the Supreme Court has determined that only Congress can abrogate Indian treaties and that only Congress has the power to diminish or disestablish reservations. In a series of eight cases from 1962 to 2016, the Court set out a test for federal courts to apply in answering whether a specific reservation has been diminished or disestablished by Congress. The Tenth Circuit carefully applied this test and considered numerous other Supreme Court and Tenth Circuit cases to analyze Murphy's and the MCN's argument that the MCN Reservation still exists. Oklahoma, on the other hand, argued that various acts of Congress, actions of the executive branch, and federal court cases proved that Congress had disestablished the reservation by the early 1900s.

The Tenth Circuit spent thirty pages of its opinion methodically analyzing eight federal laws from 1893 to 1906 that Oklahoma claimed had disestablished the MCN Reservation. The court closely analyzed these statutes and the historical facts that were relevant to the question of whether the MCN Reservation still exists. Ultimately, the Tenth Circuit applied the Supreme Court precedent and the Court's test in holding that the reservation still exists.[52]

The Tenth Circuit highlighted one particular point that is worth mentioning here, because the *McGirt* case does not address this point. Because of Oklahoma's mistaken belief that most of Indian Country and the Indian reservations in that state had disappeared, it ignored the opportunity in 1953 to legally acquire the very jurisdiction it illegally claimed and exercised for over a century, including in the *Murphy* and *McGirt* cases. As discussed in chapter 4, in 1953 Congress enacted a law known as Public Law 280, in which Congress granted certain states criminal jurisdiction, and a limited form of civil jurisdiction, over Indian individuals in Indian Country. Until 1968, this law allowed any state to voluntarily take on that jurisdiction on its own prerogative. Ironically, the Department of the Interior even wrote the governor of Oklahoma in 1953 suggesting that the state consider taking on this

Public Law 280 jurisdiction. But the governor and the state assumed they did not need Public Law 280 because they believed there were no reservations in Oklahoma and that the state already possessed criminal and civil jurisdiction over all Indians in the state.[53]

In 1953, Governor Johnston Murray, a Chickasaw Indian, responded to the letter from the assistant secretary of the interior:

> When Oklahoma became a state, all tribal governments within its bound-
> aries became merged in the State and the tribal codes under which the
> tribes were governed prior to Statehood were abandoned and all Indian
> tribes, with respect to criminal offenses and civil causes, came under State
> jurisdiction. Therefore, Public Law No. 280 will not in any way affect the
> Indian citizens of this state.[54]

Likewise, in 1979, the Oklahoma attorney general issued a legal opinion that claimed the Indian nations in the former Indian Territory had been dissolved, and that there was no "Indian Country" in eastern Oklahoma over which tribal and federal criminal jurisdiction could be exercised. But as *Murphy* and *McGirt* demonstrate, Oklahoma, Governor Murray, and the 1979 attorney general were badly mistaken. Only an act of Congress can diminish or disestablish an Indian reservation, and no such act has been passed in regard to the MCN Reservation since its founding in 1866.[55]

The *Murphy* opinion was necessarily long and detailed because of the significance of the issue to Oklahoma, to the MCN, and to the governance, people, and society of that state and the Indian nations. The decision was clearly a shock to the common understanding of most people. As mentioned below, the seriousness of the issue and the opinion the three Tenth Circuit judges issued in *Murphy* almost seemed to surprise the judges, too. Given the complexity and gravity of the case, one can easily understand why the decision took more than five years from the day Murphy appealed his case to the Tenth Circuit until the opinion was issued.

In fact, Chief Judge Timothy Tymkovich of the Tenth Circuit Court of Appeals, one of the judges on the three-judge panel that decided *Murphy*, felt compelled to alert the Supreme Court to the seriousness of the case. The U.S. Supreme Court has discretion over which appeals it will hear in the vast majority of cases, so Tymkovich urged the Court to take a close look at *Murphy*. He added a short concurrence to the *Murphy* opinion: "I write only to suggest this case might benefit from further attention by the Supreme Court." To ensure the Court did not miss his point, he even repeated it: "In sum, this challenging and interesting case makes a good candidate for Supreme Court review." Tymkovich could foresee the serious and substantial consequences that would follow from *Murphy* for Oklahoma, the MCN, the United States, and all the peoples involved with the MCN Reservation. In fact, many Natives and non-Natives in Oklahoma and beyond were acutely aware of the potential consequences of the *Murphy* case and the promise of significant issues to follow.[56]

To the surprise of no one, Oklahoma appealed *Murphy*, and the U.S. Supreme Court agreed to hear the case. Both parties filed briefs and documents with the Court. In an attempt to sway the Court, numerous other tribes, states, organizations, and business entities filed amicus briefs, which is a common practice in Supreme Court cases. And, as with almost all its cases, the Court heard oral arguments, in which the justices ask questions of the parties' attorneys.

Oklahoma's opening brief to the Court was clearly intended to alarm the justices and alert them to the ramifications of upholding the Tenth Court's ruling. Consequently, Oklahoma's legal team opened with a map of Oklahoma. However, the map they chose did not focus on the 1866 Creek Reservation boundaries, but instead highlighted approximately nineteen million acres of land in eastern Oklahoma that potentially could be recognized as Indian Country if the *Murphy* appeal was upheld and the boundaries of all the tribes' reservations were subsequently re-recognized in the future. Oklahoma then stated its reason for using the map:

> [O]ver three million acres in eastern Oklahoma are currently an Indian reservation of the Muskogee (Creek) Nation. Because the Creek Nation's history parallels that of the Choctaw, Chickasaw, Seminole, and Cherokee Nations, the decision below likely renders more than 19 million acres in eastern Oklahoma "Indian country."[57]

The state plainly feared that *Murphy*, if affirmed by the Supreme Court, would lead to the re-recognition of many more Indian reservations in eastern Oklahoma.

The state of Oklahoma then presented a photo of the Tulsa skyline. The implication was clear: four hundred thousand non-Indians who live in that city had found out after the *Murphy* decision that they now live within Indian Country. At the oral argument on November 27, 2018, Justice Breyer even noted this intended effect of the photo. He caused an outburst of laughter in the courtroom when he commented to the state's attorney, "I don't know how much trouble [*Murphy*] causes. And the reason there is a picture of Tulsa in the brief, I thought, was to stimulate me to ask such a question" ("Laughter" noted in the transcript of the argument). In its brief, the state, in strident language, admitted that the photo was included to increase the Court's shock and incredulity at the sheer audacity of the Tenth Circuit *Murphy* decision:

> If affirmed, the decision below would reincarnate Indian Territory in the form of "Indian country" under 18 U.S.C. § 1151(a), *cleaving the State in half.* The decision below would create the largest Indian reservation in America today, which would include Tulsa—Oklahoma's second-largest city[.] That *revolutionary result* would shock the 1.8 million residents of eastern Oklahoma who have universally understood that they reside on land regulated by state government, not by tribes. Affirmance would *plunge* eastern Oklahoma into civil, criminal, and regulatory *turmoil* and overturn 111 years of Oklahoma history. (Emphasis added)

The state's brief continued in this fevered vein and also warned the Supreme Court that "affirmance [of *Murphy*] would invite a *tsunami* of jurisdictional *consequences*" and "would immediately trigger a *seismic shift* in criminal and civil jurisdiction" (emphasis added).[58]

Oklahoma continued with its doomsday scenario and relied on a parade of horrible outcomes by claiming that *Murphy* would lead to rampant crime and chaos and would unsettle justified expectations. At the argument, the state's attorney, Lisa Blatt, pointed out "two *earth-shattering* consequences that Congress can't fix" and claimed that "*this will stimulate you* [the justices]" (emphasis added). In addition to drastic criminal jurisdictional changes, she argued that *Murphy* "would *plunge the region into criminal, tax, and regulatory chaos*" (emphasis added). She also highlighted "the *earth-shattering consequence on the civil side* . . . Affirmance [of *Murphy*] *raises a specter of tearing families [apart] all across eastern Oklahoma,* and probably beyond, *for years and years and years and years* after the fact" (emphasis added).[59]

Several of the justices took Oklahoma's chaos theme seriously. Court observers and legal commentators often dissect questions and answers between the justices and attorneys in an effort to predict how the Court might rule and to assess the thoughts of the justices. In this case, Oklahoma had succeeded in drawing attention to the broader implications of the *Murphy* case, beyond those of the MCN Reservation. Justices Alito, Ginsburg, Breyer, and Kavanaugh and Chief Justice Roberts expressed concerns about the "practical effects" on all of Oklahoma and on a wide array of jurisdictional issues raised by *Murphy*. Some justices emphasized the "*consequences* for criminal justice, taxation and regulatory authority of extending a reservation over the *eastern half of the state*" (emphasis added). Justice Breyer asked about "criminal law . . . municipal regulations, property law, dog-related law, thousands of details." He also asked: "What if the tribe decides not to allow the type of business in which you're engaged, such as alcoholic beverages?" Obviously, the justices were focused on the numerous and broad potential consequences of *Murphy*.[60]

Moreover, Oklahoma's dramatic arguments in regard to the changes that *Murphy* could potentially cause did persuade many legal commentators. After analyzing the oral argument and Oklahoma's dire predictions, some commentators were convinced that the Court was very concerned about the possibility of hundreds or even thousands of convicted felons like Murphy and McGirt being released from prison and about changes to the criminal and civil governance structures of eastern Oklahoma. One reporter wrote that "several justices appeared extremely uncomfortable with" ruling for the MCN because of the "possible practical implications for non-Indian Oklahomans." Another veteran Court watcher and legal commentator opined that the Court would surely reverse *Murphy* and the Tenth Circuit: "I have the strong impression that the court, one way or the other, is not going to disrupt the long-settled allocation of authority . . . The justices might struggle to coalesce around a rationale, and it might take them several months to produce a decision, but the argument did not leave much doubt about the ultimate outcome."[61]

At the time, we shared this viewpoint that the Supreme Court—which currently leans conservative, as almost everyone would agree—was probably not going to affirm *Murphy*. The impacts and the future consequences appeared to be so dramatic and significant that it was easy to envision even some "liberal" members of the Court, like Justices Ginsburg and Breyer, based on their questions at oral argument, voting to reverse *Murphy*. In addition, most considered Justice Ginsburg sympathetic to the Oklahoma argument. In 2005, she authored the Court's ruling in the *City of Sherrill* case, in which the Supreme Court protected the settled expectations of non-Indian cities, counties, and citizens over a new claim by an Indian nation to have restored land to "Indian Country" status by buying it on the open market, and that these lands were now free from state and county taxation and regulation.[62]

In fact, the Supreme Court did struggle with deciding *Murphy*. On December 4, 2018, in a rare occurrence, it directed the parties to file supplemental briefs and to answer two more questions. Finally, on June 27, 2019, and without announcing its reason, the Court set *Murphy* over for reconsideration and reargument in the 2019–2020 U.S. Supreme Court term, which would start in October 2019. Such a reconsideration and reargument is highly unusual, and the Court has done this only in extraordinarily significant cases such as *Brown v. Board of Education* (ending legalized school segregation), *Roe v. Wade* (legalizing abortion), and *Citizens United* (political campaign contributions). The Court gave no reason for holding *Murphy* over until its next term. Commentators believe, however, that the Court was split 4 to 4 on whether to affirm the Tenth Circuit Court decision. A tie vote in the Supreme Court automatically affirms the lower court decision, and thus the Court would have affirmed the Tenth Circuit decision that the MCN Reservation still exists if it was deadlocked at 4 to 4. A tie vote was certainly a possibility, because only eight justices sat on the *Murphy* case. Justice Gorsuch had recused himself from the case because he had been involved in some of Murphy's earlier legal proceedings in the Tenth Circuit Court of Appeals when he was a judge on that court. Commentators also assumed that the Supreme Court considered the case far too important, far too significant, to let the Tenth Circuit decision be affirmed by a tied Supreme Court vote.[63]

But instead of hearing a second oral argument in *Murphy*, in which Gorsuch would still have been recused, the Court decided to hear a case from the Oklahoma state court system that raised the identical issue about the continuing existence of the MCN Reservation: *McGirt v. Oklahoma*. Because it was a state court case, Justice Gorsuch would not have to recuse himself. We will see, indeed, that Gorsuch thereafter played an absolutely crucial role in deciding *McGirt*. On July 9, 2020, the U.S. Supreme Court held in *McGirt* that the MCN Reservation still exists, and on that same day it also affirmed the Tenth Circuit's decision in *Murphy* in a one-sentence order that simply cited the *McGirt* opinion.[64]

6

McGIRT v. OKLAHOMA

I don't think there's ever been a bigger issue that's hit a state before.

—Oklahoma governor Kevin Stitt, Fox 25 interview, May 17, 2021

The United States Supreme Court hears on average two to three Indian law cases every year. These appeals are crucial for the parties involved, and sometimes they change federal Indian law for all Indian nations and Indian peoples across the country. Rarely, though, does an Indian law case drop with the impact of *McGirt v. Oklahoma.* On July 9, 2020, the Supreme Court held by a 5 to 4 vote that the Muscogee (Creek) Nation's reservation, as defined in its 1866 treaty with the United States, still exists. Overnight, the MCN Reservation was re-recognized as covering 3.25 million acres and including about one million Oklahomans, including four hundred thousand people in Tulsa. With these lands now being within a reservation, this entire area is "Indian Country" as defined by federal law.

Consequently, these one million Oklahomans now live on an Indian reservation, and the city of Tulsa, dozens of other counties and towns, and the state itself will have to deal with MCN jurisdiction over an amount of land and a population perhaps twenty-five times larger than was previously assumed. The ruling involves, and will involve for years to come, the MCN, the United States, Oklahoma, and other tribes in that state, and perhaps across the country, in negotiations, lawsuits, and federal, tribal, and state legislative efforts to address the multiple issues that arise from the case.

Oklahoma state courts have already relied on *McGirt* to rule that the reservations of the Cherokee Nation, Chickasaw Nation, Choctaw Nation, Seminole Nation, and the Ottawa, Eastern Shawnee, and Miami tribes also continue to exist, and litigation regarding the existence of other reservations is ongoing. *McGirt* is certainly one of the most significant and impactful Supreme Court Indian law cases in more than one hundred years. But if the state, the Indian nations, and the United States can adjust to this new reality, it is possible that under well-understood case law, and with the example of other states that also have numerous Indian nations and large reservations within their borders, this situation can ultimately work out well for all the governments and peoples concerned.[1]

In the previous chapter we considered eight pivotal U.S. Supreme Court cases and the U.S. Tenth Circuit Court of Appeals case *Murphy v. Carpenter* that led to the *McGirt* decision. In four of those eight Supreme Court cases, the Court ruled that an Indian reservation had been diminished or disestablished, and in the other four cases, the Court ruled that an Indian reservation had not been diminished or disestablished. This chapter explores how the justices decided the *McGirt* case, what it is that makes it so different from the other Supreme Court diminishment and disestablishment cases, and why it is hailed as a landmark case.

In 1997, Jimcy McGirt, a citizen of the Seminole Nation of Oklahoma, was prosecuted and convicted in an Oklahoma state court of sexual abuse of a child and was sentenced to one thousand years plus life. Thereafter, he filed court proceedings in which he alleged that the state of Oklahoma did not have jurisdiction over him because he is an Indian and his alleged crime was committed in Indian Country, on the MCN Reservation. The Oklahoma courts held that the state possessed criminal jurisdiction over McGirt because his crime was committed on state, not MCN, lands.[2]

The U.S. Supreme Court agreed to hear his appeal to answer "whether the land these [Creek] treaties promised remains an Indian reservation for purposes of federal criminal law." Oklahoma argued that all Indian reservations within the state had been disestablished (erased) by the time of statehood in 1907. The state claimed that everyone, including the Indian nations and Indian peoples in Oklahoma, assumed that the Indian reservations in that state had disappeared.[3]

As in the *Murphy* appeal discussed in chapter 6, the state vigorously pressed the argument that if the Supreme Court were to rule for McGirt and hold that the MCN Reservation still existed, it would cause "chaos" and "staggering ramifications" and a "sea change," and that state and local tax revenues would be reduced, which would "decimate state and local budgets." Oklahoma continued its sky-is-falling line of attack at oral argument before the Court, which was held May 11, 2020, over Zoom due to the COVID pandemic. The parties argued at length about the possible ramifications of *McGirt*, and the justices asked multiple questions about its potential consequences.[4]

The attorneys for the parties and the justices discussed "Oklahoma's rhetoric about disruption" and "hundreds of prosecutions, for murder, for terrible sexual offenses" that could be impacted, and the "tsunami" of court proceedings that had been predicted would follow the *Murphy* Tenth Circuit case. Justice Gorsuch asked about the "terrible practical consequences" and the "parade of horribles generally," and Justice Alito discussed a section of McGirt's brief that was "labeled The Sky Is Not Falling" and asked Oklahoma's attorney whether "you and the federal government are exaggerating the effect of this decision." The state responded by claiming "over 3,000 inmates we may have to turn over [to federal and tribal governments]." Justice Gorsuch asked the state, though, why the courts had not "seen a tsunami—of cases" after the *Murphy* case. The attorney for the United States, who supported Oklahoma in the *McGirt* appeal, claimed that a decision for Jimcy McGirt "would impose great burdens on the federal government . . . a 1300 percent increase in criminal prosecutions."[5]

In the end, the Supreme Court surprised many people and legal commentators and held for McGirt: "Because Congress has not said otherwise, we hold the government to its word." In fact, the Court opened its opinion with this poetic line: "On the far end of the Trail of Tears was a promise." The promise the Supreme Court referenced was the treaties the Creek Nation signed with the U.S. between 1832 and 1866 that promised the MCN a permanent reservation in what is now the eastern part of Oklahoma. Since Congress had never disestablished the 3.25-million-acre MCN Reservation, the Court held that it continues to exist today.[6]

As we set out in part 1, the MCN signed several treaties with the U.S. in the nineteenth century, and Congress enacted several laws in the nineteenth and early twentieth centuries that defined the MCN's rights and the boundaries of its reservation in the area that came to be called the Indian Territory and then later became part of the state of Oklahoma. Under these treaties, legislative acts, and federal Indian law, only the MCN and the United States were authorized to exercise sovereignty and jurisdiction within that reservation. In fact, the Supreme Court held in 1832 that states had no jurisdiction at all within Indian Country, which includes reservations, and that was the strict rule for 140 years. Even today, states have limited jurisdiction in those areas even though reservation lands are within state borders. But, as we have seen, for more than one hundred years after Oklahoma became a state in 1907, the state illegally exceeded its authority and applied its jurisdiction and laws inside the MCN Reservation and in other areas of Indian Country within the state. These actions were in express violation of the requirements Congress placed on the Oklahoma Territory and Indian Territory to enter the Union as the state of Oklahoma in its federal Enabling Act of 1906. These actions also violated the Oklahoma Constitution of 1907, in which the new state expressly disclaimed any jurisdiction over Indians and the lands and property of Indian nations. Regrettably, the federal government and officials purposely and negligently allowed those illegal activities.[7]

McGirt challenged Oklahoma's exercise of criminal jurisdiction over him and argued that the U.S. Major Crimes Act only allows the federal government to prosecute an Indian for criminal conduct in Indian Country. (See chapter 3 for a discussion of the MCA.) His attorneys asserted that based on the MCA, "State courts generally have no jurisdiction to try Indians for conduct committed in 'Indian country.'" The Supreme Court understood the "key question" in the case to be "Did [McGirt] commit his crimes in Indian country?" Oklahoma argued that a Creek reservation had never been created in the first place, and thus the location where McGirt committed his acts could not be within

Indian Country. However, the U.S. solicitor general, who supported Oklahoma in this appeal, refused to join the state's argument that the Creek Nation had never had a reservation, and that its lands had never been Indian Country. Oklahoma also argued that if a Creek reservation had once existed, then "the land once given to the Creeks is no longer a reservation." The U.S. solicitor general joined Oklahoma in this second argument.[8]

The Supreme Court began its analysis by asking whether the U.S. and the MCN had created a reservation. The Court relied on the Creek treaties with the United States, and focused on the removal-era treaties in which the U.S. guaranteed a permanent homeland for the Creek Nation to entice the nation to remove west of the Mississippi River. The Court quoted the treaties and readily concluded that in these treaties "Congress established a reservation for the Creeks" and "guarantied" them their homelands west of the Mississippi, and "establish[ed] boundary lines [to] secure a country and permanent home to the whole Creek Nation of Indians." It is also important to remember that the U.S. did not "give" these lands to the Creek Nation out of the goodness of its heart. Rather, the western lands were in payment for the Creek Nation's agreement to sell its lands in present-day Alabama and Georgia and to remove west. Thereafter, the 1833 Treaty with the Creeks defined the seven-million-acre Creek lands, in what came to be called the Indian Territory, as the "permanent home" of the MCN.[9]

Admittedly, the early Creek treaties do not use the word "reservation," probably because, as the Court noted, the term only came into common usage in Indian policy after 1849. The 1866 U.S. Treaty with the Creeks, however, in article IX, did expressly use the word "reservation" in relation to the Creek homelands, removing any doubt that the U.S. considered the Creek Nation's lands to be an Indian reservation. Thereafter, numerous federal laws and treaties expressly referenced the Creek Reservation. In light of these facts, the Supreme Court held that there was "no question that Congress established a reservation for the Creek Nation."[10]

The crucial issue that now faced the Supreme Court was whether the MCN Reservation still exists. The Court stated there was only one place to look, "the Acts of Congress." This is correct because, as the

Court has long stated, "only Congress can divest a reservation of its land and diminish its boundaries." One problem with answering this issue, however, is that the Court has never required Congress to use specific language to indicate its intention to diminish or disestablish an Indian reservation. In reviewing the range of possible congressional language that could diminish or disestablish a reservation, the Court only set forth the requirement "that Congress clearly express its intent to do so." We recounted in the previous chapter that the Supreme Court has deemed a variety of statutory language sufficient to determine congressional intent.[11]

The *McGirt* Court then analyzed numerous federal laws for evidence of specific congressional intent to disestablish the Creek Reservation. Oklahoma pointed to the same eight federal laws that it had cited to the U.S. Court of Appeals for the Tenth Circuit in *Murphy*, and which that court had rejected. The Tenth Circuit held that none of those laws showed that Congress ever intended to disestablish the Creek Reservation. Once again, Oklahoma made the same arguments to the *McGirt* Court and relied heavily on its claim that the 1901 Creek Allotment Act proved that Congress intended to disestablish the MCN Reservation.

As detailed in part 1 and briefly summarized here, in 1887 Congress began a new era of federal Indian policy and adopted a new strategy to acquire Indian lands by enacting the General Allotment Act. This act and the subsequent tribally specific allotment acts were designed to destroy tribal communal ownership of lands, thus undermining the territorial base of the tribal nations. They did so by dividing tribal communal lands into privately owned lots, owned by tribal citizens. But, as we also have seen, much of this land fell into non-Native private ownership. The GAA itself, however, only set out the new policy and did not allot any particular Indian reservation. Thereafter, Congress had to enact specific laws to allot specific reservations, such as the 1901 Creek Allotment Act. According to the allotment acts, any reservation lands left over after the allotting of land to tribal citizens were defined as "surplus lands" and were sold to non-Indians who then moved onto the reservation. Almost always, these acts required that the federal government hold the legal title to the allotments "in trust" for the individual Indians, usually for twenty-five years. Ultimately, however, these allotments were to be held by individual Indians in fee simple absolute private ownership, the usual form of landownership in the U.S.[12]

The GAA and the tribe-specific allotment acts, specifically the 1901 Creek Allotment Act, did not, in fact, diminish or disestablish Indian reservations, as Oklahoma argued. Indeed, one can say that the state was incorrect in claiming both that the Creek Allotment Act disestablished the Creek Reservation and that the 1901 act was even relevant to the question in *McGirt*. This is true because the Supreme Court has often stated that allotting a reservation did not diminish or disestablish it and had no effect on its borders. In the 1973 *Mattz* case discussed previously, for example, the Court stated that "allotment . . . is completely consistent with continued reservation status." In addition to this general principle, the specific factual and historical process that occurred when Congress allotted the Creek Reservation in 1901 clearly proves the exact opposite of what Oklahoma argued. The negotiations and enactment of the 1901 Creek Allotment Act show that Congress did not intend to disestablish the reservation, and that Congress knew it had not disestablished or diminished the reservation's borders in the Creek Allotment Act.[13]

The *McGirt* Court, therefore, closely analyzed how the 1901 act came to be enacted to try to discern Congress's intentions for the Creek Reservation in 1901. In 1893, as we discussed previously, Congress charged the Dawes Commission with the task of attempting to convince the Creek Nation to sell land to the United States. The Creeks, however, consistently refused to sell even a single acre. This outcome was not a surprise to Congress. In 1893, Congress was well aware that this might happen because there was much Native resistance to allotment. Therefore, when Congress assigned the commission to negotiate with the Creek Nation, it "charged the Dawes Commission with negotiating changes to the Creek Reservation [and] identified two goals: Either persuade the Creek to cede [sell] territory to the United States, as it had before, or agree to allot its lands to Tribe members." As Congress expected, the Dawes Commission could not convince the Creek Nation to sell any land at all, and the commission reported back to Congress that the nation "'would not, under any circumstances, agree to cede [sell] any portion of their lands.'"[14]

Accepting that the Creek Nation would not sell any of its land, Congress gave up trying to buy Creek land and instead "turned [its] attention to allotment rather than cession." The Dawes Commission then concluded an allotment agreement with the Creek Nation that Congress enacted into law in the 1901 Creek Allotment Act. The *McGirt* Court held, as its precedent required, that this allotment act had no impact at all on the boundaries of the MCN Reservation. The *McGirt* opinion states: "Missing in all this, however, is a statute evincing anything like the 'present and total surrender of all tribal interests' in the affected lands . . . [and] because there exists no equivalent law terminating what remained, the Creek Reservation survived allotment." The *McGirt* majority charged that "the dissent fails to mention the Commission's various reports acknowledging that those efforts were unsuccessful precisely because the Creek refused to cede their lands." The dissenting justices even conceded these points: "No one here contends that any individual congressional action or piece of evidence, standing alone, disestablished the Creek reservation."[15]

Just as in the *Murphy* case, instead of pointing to one federal statute, Oklahoma and the dissent in *McGirt* relied on the alleged cumulative effect of numerous federal laws to argue that Congress had ultimately revealed an intention to disestablish the Creek Reservation by the time of statehood in 1907. There is no question, as addressed in chapters 3 and 4, that Congress repeatedly attacked tribal sovereignty, governance, and landownership in the Indian Territory. Many of these laws were directed specifically at the Five Tribes to try to force allotment and other changes on these nations. But the *McGirt* Court was not convinced by the alleged overall effect of these laws. In contrast, the majority relied on and quoted a 1906 act of Congress that predated Oklahoma statehood: "Despite these additional incursions on tribal authority, however, Congress expressly recognized the Creek's 'tribal existence and present tribal governmen[t]' and 'continued [them] in full force and effect for all purposes authorized by law.'" The Court also noted that starting in the 1920s, Congress began supporting Indian nations and tribal sovereignty in Oklahoma, and that it authorized the MCN and other tribes in 1936 to draft constitutions and to engage in governance and economic development. After reviewing this history and all these acts of Congress, the *McGirt* Court concluded: "in all this history there simply arrived no moment when any Act of Congress dissolved the Creek Tribe or disestablished its reservation."[16]

In light of the evidence that Congress never intended to disestablish the MCN Reservation, and never enacted a law to disestablish the reservation, the Court held, not surprisingly, that the reservation has never been disestablished and that it is still intact. The Court's analysis was straightforward. The United States and the Creek Nation created a reservation in their treaty of 1833, and it was reaffirmed and re-recognized in later U.S. and Creek treaties. The Supreme Court then examined the evidence put forward by the state but did not find any express or ambiguous statements that even hinted at a congressional intent to disestablish the Creek Reservation. Consequently, under Supreme Court case law, the MCN Reservation continues to exist.[17]

The majority opinion began and ended its analysis with the relevant congressional language, what most legal commentators would call step one of the *Solem* test for reservation diminishment and disestablishment questions. The dissent, however, pointed to the evidence covered in steps two and three of the *Solem* test to claim that the intent of Congress was to disestablish the Creek Reservation. Contrary to the dissenting opinion and what many people believe, however, the Supreme Court did discuss and ultimately rejected the necessity and the value of considering this evidence. The majority opinion noted that Supreme Court case law shows that the "value" of step two and three evidence "can only be *interpretative*—evidence that, at best, might be used to the extent it sheds light on what the terms found in a statute meant at the time of the law's adoption, *not as an alternative means of proving disestablishment or diminishment*" (emphasis added). The majority correctly stated that step two and three evidence cannot be used to contradict clear and explicit congressional statutory language and turn it into ambiguous language that then requires a court to use interpretive tools such as *Solem* step two and three evidence. "The only role such materials can properly play is to help 'clear up . . . not create' ambiguity about a statute's original meaning." The Supreme Court unanimously applied this principle in *Parker* in 2016, and in other diminishment cases in 1998, 1977, and 1975, because it has "acknowledge[d] that extratextual sources may help resolve ambiguity about Congress's directions." As the *McGirt* majority noted, "Oklahoma does not point to any ambiguous language in any of the relevant statutes." Consequently, the majority opinion did not need to use any *Solem* step two or three evidence.[18]

The majority did not ignore these steps and did not ignore the evidence on which Oklahoma and the dissent relied. In fact, it is worthwhile to quote at length what the *McGirt* majority stated after it finished analyzing the relevant federal laws and found no statutory proof that Congress ever intended to disestablish the MCN Reservation:

> Oklahoma even classifies and categorizes how we should approach the question of disestablishment into three "steps." It reads *Solem* as requiring us to examine the laws passed by Congress at the first step, contemporary events at the second, and even later events and demographics at the third. On the State's account, we have so far finished only the first step; two more await.
>
> This is mistaken. When interpreting Congress's work in this arena, no less than any other, our charge is usually to ascertain and follow the original meaning of the law before us. New Prime Inc. v. Oliveira, 586 U. S.——,——, 139 S.Ct. 532, 538–539, 202 L.Ed.2d 536 (2019). That is the only "step" proper for a court of law. To be sure, if during the course of our work an ambiguous statutory term or phrase emerges, we will sometimes consult contemporaneous usages, customs, and practices to the extent they shed light on the meaning of the language in question at the time of enactment.[19]

This statement is not at all surprising considering that it was written by Justice Gorsuch. He is an avowed advocate of the judicial interpretive approach called originalism and textualism. In a nutshell, this theory holds that a court should only read the text of the Constitution, or of a statute enacted by a legislature, and apply the meaning of the words used by those authors. Originalists and textualists argue that if the drafters of the Constitution or an act of Congress have written a law using language that is clear, and their intent is clear, then courts should never rely on outside evidence to try to refute or render that original intent ambiguous. Courts are not legislatures, and they do not write laws. Obviously, then, an originalist and textualist like Justice Gorsuch would disagree that *Solem* requires a court to consider and apply steps two and three–type evidence in every case to interpret the written words. In contrast, under the theory of originalism and textualism, if Congress's intent and language are clear, outside or extrinsic evidence should not even be considered to try to contradict the clear language of a statute. That would be sacrilege because the judge might now be making law. In fact, giving proper credence to what Congress actually meant to do is exactly what the *McGirt* majority did. As already pointed out, the 1901 Creek Allotment Act and the other federal laws cited by Oklahoma did not disestablish the MCN Reservation.

Consequently, a textualist like Gorsuch would say, as he did, that a court need not, and in fact must not, consider outside evidence to try to contradict clear congressional language and intent. Justice Gorsuch thus disparaged any assumed requirement that a court must always use *Solem* step two and three evidence. What is actually quite surprising in *McGirt* is that the four dissenters, Chief Justice Roberts and Justices Thomas, Alito, and Kavanaugh, who are all self-avowed originalists and textualists, did not join the majority opinion. Instead, Oklahoma and the dissenters relied on outside evidence to attempt to contradict the clear intent demonstrated in the actual language used by Congress not to disestablish the Creek Reservation.[20]

Justice Gorsuch emphasized that exact point, and he even "restate[d] the point" that "[t]here is no need to consult extratextual sources when the meaning of a statute's terms is clear. Nor may extratextual sources overcome those terms." He added about *Solem* step two and three evidence that "[t]he only role such materials can properly play is to *help 'clear up . . . not create' ambiguity* about a statute's original meaning" (emphasis added).[21]

The *McGirt* majority, then, did consider the three steps of *Solem*. But it concluded that the step one evidence, the statutory language Congress actually used, was clear and demonstrated that Congress never intended to disestablish the Creek Reservation. Consequently, there was no reason to use step two and three evidence to try to contradict Congress's clear intent.

The majority opinion also addressed the dissent's and Oklahoma's "chaos" theory and its "sky-is-falling" argument if the MCN Reservation was re-recognized. "In the end, Oklahoma abandons any pretense of law and speaks openly about the potentially 'transform[ative]' effects of a loss today." The opinion noted Oklahoma's argument that "[i]f we dared to recognize that the Creek Reservation was never disestablished, Oklahoma and dissent warn, our holding might be used by other tribes." More-over, Oklahoma and the dissent argued that if the Court ruled in favor of McGirt, the ruling "could unsettle an untold number of convictions and frustrate the State's ability to prosecute crimes in the future." The majority countered that this argument was "admittedly speculative . . . [and] even Oklahoma admits that the vast majority of its prosecutions will be unaffected whatever we decide today." Thus, the Court easily discounted these potential issues.[22]

Additionally, Oklahoma and the dissenting opinion went beyond the criminal jurisdiction issue *McGirt* brought before the Court and argued civil law and civil jurisdictional matters. The majority quickly refuted those points, because "dire warnings are just that, and not a license for us to disregard the law." In addition, the Court made an excellent point in response to Oklahoma's and the dissent's arguments that since Oklahoma had exercised jurisdiction over Indian Country in Oklahoma for more than a century, it had therefore established its jurisdiction. The Court pointed out that Oklahoma never had legal jurisdiction in Indian Country and that any practice of such was, in fact, illegal. The majority opinion simply stated that "the *magnitude* of a *legal wrong* is no reason to perpetuate it" (emphasis added). The Supreme Court, in other words, would not allow Oklahoma to benefit from its illegal actions in exercising jurisdiction in Indian Country for over one hundred years and prosecuting and regulating people over whom it had no legal jurisdiction.[23]

The majority further rejected the state's and dissent's argument about potential chaotic changes that might follow the re-recognition of the MCN Reservation by stating that even the possibility of major conse-quences would not be an excuse to ignore the inequities and the viola-tions of law that occurred in the past. Should the Supreme Court, for example, have refused to end more than one hundred years of illegal racial segregation in schools in *Brown v. Board of Education* in 1954 due to the absolute certainty that that case would be followed by many decades of turmoil, disputes, lawsuits, violence, and even murders? Should the Court not have decided *Roe v. Wade* in 1973, or should it consider reversing that decision now, because of the decades of protests, demonstrations, and even murders that have occurred over the issue of abortion, and that would perhaps also occur if the Court were to reverse *Roe*? Just posing those questions mandates the answer: the Supreme Court must state what the law is, what the law requires, and it must uphold the law, no matter the consequences that might follow.

The Court also refuted Oklahoma's and the dissent's arguments that it should consider the possible "costs" of its decision. "By suggesting that our interpretation of Acts of Congress adopted a century ago should be inflected based on the costs of enforcing them today, the dissent tips its hand." The Court also used this point to refute Oklahoma's and the dissent's arguments about the step three–type evidence of *Solem*: "Yet again, the point of looking at subsequent developments seems not to be determining the meaning of the laws Congress wrote in 1901 or 1906, but emphasizing the costs of taking them at their word." Consequently, the Court said it does not matter if there are "costs" to enforcing the law; such costs must be paid. And the majority opinion also noted that if "chaos" truly were to ensue, if the "costs" of enforcing *McGirt* were to become too burdensome to society, "Congress remains free to supplement its statutory directions about the lands in question at any time."[24]

In fact, the majority was actually more hopeful about the future consequences that might follow *McGirt* than the dissent and Oklahoma. The Court recognized that Oklahoma and Indian nations have for decades negotiated and enforced hundreds of compacts on multiple topics such as "taxation, law enforcement, vehicle registration, hunting and fishing, and countless other fine regulatory questions," and that these successful agreements were a positive indication that Oklahoma and the tribes could also handle the criminal and civil issues that might arise from *McGirt*.[25]

In concluding its discussion on the chaos argument, the majority emphasized that "[i]n reaching our conclusion about what the law demands of us today, we do not pretend to foretell the future and we proceed well aware of the potential for cost and conflict around jurisdictional boundaries, especially ones that have gone unappreciated for so long." But the Court noted that it had an overriding obligation to answer the issue before it and to uphold the law:

> [M]any of the arguments before us today follow a sadly familiar pattern. Yes, promises were made, but the price of keeping them has become too great, so now we should just cast a blind eye. We reject that thinking . . . *Unlawful acts*, performed long enough and with sufficient vigor, are *never enough to amend the law*. To hold otherwise would be to elevate the most brazen and longstanding injustices over the law, both *rewarding wrong and failing those in the right*. (Emphasis added)[26]

The *McGirt* Court searched for and applied the intent of Congress in regard to the MCN Reservation and as expressed in the relevant laws. It did not find express or even ambiguous statements that demonstrated that Congress ever intended to disestablish the reservation. The Court addressed but ultimately ignored the *Solem* step two and three evidence highlighted by Oklahoma and the dissent. To use that unclear and uncertain evidence to try to disprove the clear language and statutory intent of Congress, the Court said, would allow Oklahoma to benefit from its illegal actions, and in fact "would be the rule of the strong, not the rule of law."[27]

Since the *Solem* test figures so prominently in the *McGirt* ruling, we consider here *McGirt*'s impact on *Solem*. The *Solem* test has been presumed by courts and legal commentators to allow, or even to require, courts to go beyond what Congress expressly said or did not say in a particular statute about diminishing or disestablishing a specific Indian reservation. Step two of *Solem* allowed a court to examine the contemporaneous history and events surrounding a newly enacted statute that arguably diminished or disestablished a reservation. A court would look at contemporaneous evidence to determine whether there had been a common understanding by Congress, federal officials, the tribal government and its citizens, states, and even the average American citizen that "the . . . reservation would shrink." Then, under step three of *Solem*, a court could examine subsequent history and events, even those that occurred many decades after the opening of a reservation to non–Indian settlement, to try to determine if the Congress that enacted the original law at issue had intended, at that time, that the reservation's borders were to be diminished or disestablished.[28]

One can argue that the *McGirt* opinion did modify the long-accepted *Solem* three-step test. The dissent claimed that the majority "announce[d] a new approach" and "[did] not even discuss the governing approach reiterated throughout [Supreme Court] precedents." In fact, though, the majority opinion plainly discussed the *Solem* three steps and briefly analyzed the step two and step three evidence that Oklahoma and the dissent relied upon. But the majority disapproved of the idea that *Solem* had created three mandatory steps of analysis and that those "steps" have to be applied in every diminishment or disestablishment case. So it is possible that *McGirt* can be read as limiting the *Solem* analysis to some extent.[29]

The dissenting justices, as discussed below, clearly believed that the majority ignored and altered the *Solem* test. The dissent charged that *McGirt*'s "new approach sharply restrict[ed] consideration of contemporaneous and subsequent evidence of congressional intent." The dissent also claimed that the majority had ignored precedent and "'our traditional approach . . . [which] *requires* us' to determine Congress's intent by 'examin[ing] *all* the circumstances surrounding the opening of a reservation.' Yet the Court refuses to confront the cumulative import of all of Congress's actions here" (emphasis in the original).[30]

The dissent surely overstated its argument. One can argue that the majority did alter the *Solem* approach somewhat, but it is just as valid to state that it applied *Solem* and even applied in reverse another judicial interpretive principle stated in that case. This is in fact a strong point in favor of the *McGirt* majority. In *Solem*, the Supreme Court stated that if a law clearly diminished or disestablished a reservation, then that creates an "almost insurmountable presumption" that the reservation was diminished or disestablished. That principle means that it would then be nearly impossible for step two and step three evidence to overcome the presumption that the reservation was diminished. But that principle also applies in *McGirt*, in reverse. Since the laws regarding the Creek Nation and the MCN Reservation clearly did not disestablish the reservation, that situation created an "almost insurmountable presumption" that the reservation was not disestablished and that *Solem* step two and step three evidence cannot be used to overcome that presumption. Remember, the MCN expressly refused to sell any land to the United States or to change its reservation borders. Thus, *Solem* step two and step three evidence should not, and could not, be considered in an effort to overcome the "almost insurmountable presumption" that Congress did not intend to disestablish the Creek Reservation in the laws it actually enacted.[31]

It does appear, however, that *McGirt* will impact the future application of the *Solem* test. The majority did not reverse *Solem*, but it did expressly disapprove of there being a mandatory three-step approach that courts must apply in every disestablishment case, and it expressly disapproved of using step two and three–type evidence to try to contradict clear congressional language and intent.

In contrast, the dissenting opinion by Chief Justice Roberts claimed that the majority opinion altered the application of *Solem*, ignored steps two and three of its analytical format, and ignored decades of Supreme Court case law on how to apply *Solem*. In a lengthy dissent, four justices (Chief Justice Roberts and Justices Thomas, Alito, and Kavanaugh) discussed what they contended were the required three steps of *Solem*. The dissent (and the state of Oklahoma) admitted that there was no single stand-alone federal law that they could cite to argue that Congress had disestablished the Creek Reservation. Instead, the dissent relied on a "relentless series of statutes" that Congress enacted regarding the Creek Nation and other tribes in the Indian Territory. It argued that this series of laws, taken as a whole, demonstrated sufficient proof of congressional intent to disestablish the Creek Reservation.[32]

The dissent continued its argument, under *Solem* step two, that it was the contemporary understanding of everyone—Congress, the state, Oklahomans, the Creek Nation, and the other tribes in the Indian Territory—that by Oklahoma statehood in 1907, Indian reservations were disestablished. The dissent argued that "[t]he available evidence overwhelmingly confirms that Congress eliminated any Creek reservation."[33] We are compelled, however, to point out that this statement is incorrect. In fact, in the 1906 Oklahoma Enabling Act, in which Congress authorized the Oklahoma Territory and the Indian Territory to form a state, Congress expressly recognized that there were currently many Indian reservations in existence in those territories. In the 1906 act, Congress used the word "reservation" at least nine times to refer to the "Osage Indian Reservation," which was located within those territories. Congress also recognized that the "Kansas Indian Reservation," the "Tonkawa Indian Reservation," the "Pawnee Indian Reservation," and nine unnamed "Indian reservations lying northeast of the Cherokee Nation" were still in existence and located within the Indian and Oklahoma Territories. The lands of the Creek, Cherokee, Choctaw, Chickasaw, and Seminole nations were also recognized by Congress in that act as currently being in existence in the Indian Territory. The Enabling Act then required the new state to recognize and respect all the Indian reservations and all the tribal nations and their landownership and sovereign rights. And as Congress required, in 1907 Oklahoma included a provision in its constitution disavowing any state jurisdiction over Indians and tribal nations and their lands and assets. Logic tells us that if there were no Indian nations and no Indian reservations within that new state, then why would the state have had to disclaim jurisdiction over Indian nations and their lands? This point is so crucial that we quote the Oklahoma Enabling Act of June 16, 1906, and the 1907 Oklahoma Constitution here. As Congress stated in the Enabling Act,

> nothing contained in the [Oklahoma] constitution shall be construed to limit or impair the *rights of person or property pertaining to the Indians of said Territories* (so long as such rights shall remain unextinguished) or to limit or affect the authority of the Government of the United States to make any law or regulation *respecting such Indians, their lands, property, or other rights by treaties.* (Emphasis added)

Congress further required that

> the people inhabiting said proposed State do agree and declare that they forever disclaim all right and title in . . . all *lands . . . owned or held by any Indian, tribe, or nation;* and that . . . the same shall be and remain subject to the jurisdiction, disposal, and control of the United States. (Emphasis added)

Congress also prohibited the new state from introducing

> intoxicating liquors within those parts of said State now known as the
> Indian Territory and the Osage Indian Reservation and within any other
> parts of said State which existed as Indian reservations on the first day of
> January, nineteen hundred and six, . . . for a period of twenty-one years.

In addition, as a new state, Oklahoma was awarded five seats in the
House of Representatives, and Congress instructed that the third district
of the state must "comprise all the *territory now constituting the Cherokee,
Creek, and Seminole nations,* and the *Indian reservations lying northeast of the
Cherokee Nation,* within said State" (emphasis added).[34]

Pursuant to these requirements for entering the Union, when Oklahoma adopted its 1907 Constitution, it expressly disavowed any jurisdiction over or ownership of the lands of the Indian nations. The Oklahoma
Constitution states:

> The people inhabiting the State do agree and declare that they forever
> disclaim all right and title . . . to all lands lying within said limits owned
> or held by any Indian, tribe, or nation; and that until the title to any such
> public land shall have been extinguished by the United States, the same
> shall be and remain subject to the jurisdiction, disposal, and control of the
> United States.[35]

The dissent not only ignored these crucial points, it also ignored a 1906
act in which "Congress expressly recognized the Creek's 'tribal existence and present tribal governmen[t]' and 'continued [them] in full
force and effect for all purposes authorized by law.'"[36]

Instead of focusing on the *Solem* step one evidence—what Congress
actually stated about Indian nations and reservations in Oklahoma—
the dissent leaned on *Solem* step two evidence (contemporaneous
understandings) and then relied heavily on step three evidence. In step
three, the dissent examined the subsequent history of various laws that
were enacted after the 1901 allotment of the Creek Reservation and
Oklahoma's 1907 statehood. It cited numerous statements by tribal,
federal, and state officials, congressional language in later statutes, and

Congress's treatment of the allegedly disestablished Creek Reservation. From this evidence, the dissent inferred that Congress intended to disestablish the Creek Reservation by 1907. The dissent also relied on modern-day demographic data showing that Indians constitute about 10 percent of the population within the MCN Reservation area, and "a century of settled understanding" that the reservation had been disestablished by the early 1900s.[37]

The dissent also relied heavily on future predictions that were part of the "chaos theory" advocated by Oklahoma. The dissent declared that an MCN Reservation encompassing over three million acres, one million Oklahomans, and part of the city of Tulsa would harm "the State's ability to prosecute serious crimes," and that "decades of past convictions *could* well be thrown out" (emphasis added). It then stated that with the *McGirt* majority ruling, "the Court has profoundly destabilized the governance of eastern Oklahoma." The reference to "eastern Oklahoma" went beyond the bounds of the appeal because the *McGirt* case concerned only the three-million-plus acres of the MCN Reservation.[38]

In continuing with its chaos argument, the dissent also went beyond the criminal issue facing the Supreme Court to address potential issues in the civil law arena. The dissent worried that "[b]eyond the criminal law, the decision may destabilize the governance of vast swathes of Oklahoma." The dissent also fretted about the "significant uncertainty" the decision could cause regarding "the State's continuing authority over any area that touches Indian affairs, ranging from zoning and taxation to family and environmental law." Similarly, it lamented that possible questions about tribal civil jurisdiction, judicial jurisdiction, and regulatory authority would require complicated legal analysis to answer whether Oklahoma, the MCN, or the United States would be in control. Obviously, the dissent and Oklahoma foretold looming disasters on the horizon. The majority, however, discounted these "dire warnings" and emphasized that even if the warnings were to come true, Congress has the power to legislate on these topics.[39]

The dissent also emphasized a disturbing subtext that we must address. The dissenters surprisingly relied on the intent and effects of some disconcerting historical events, and they even seemed to praise illegal aspects of Oklahoma history. These events highlight the history of ethnocentric settler-colonial confiscation of Indian nations' lands and assets. Yet the dissent used this history to support its argument that the Creek Reservation was, for all intents and purposes, disestablished by Congress by the early 1900s. The *Solem* three-step test is a mechanism for discerning congressional intent at the time Congress enacted the statute at issue. It is difficult to understand, however, how this unsettling history that the dissent addressed is even relevant to what Congress might have intended in 1901 or 1906 in regard to the MCN Reservation.

The dissent further relied on a manifest destiny trope and praised Americans' "'determination to thrust the nation westward'" into the Indian Territory, and to "rapidly transfor[m] vast stretches of territorial *wilderness* into farmland and ranches . . . [and] '[f]lourishing towns'" (emphasis added). (We are compelled to mention that the Indian Territory was not a "wilderness" and that the Five Tribes and their citizens were utilizing their lands to support themselves through farming and ranching and other economic endeavors.) The dissent also made a bizarre suggestion that because some individual Creek Indians were more successful than others, and came to control large portions of the reservation, this was somehow additional evidence that the reservation had been disestablished. This statement seems both illogical and ludicrous in the face of the robber barons of late nineteenth- and early twentieth-century America, and it seems even more ironic and ridiculous today, considering that there are three Americans who alone are richer than the bottom 50 percent of all Americans combined.[40]

Most of this American expansion into the Indian Territory that the dissent praised and its attendant so-called progress was, as we have documented, illegal trespass, invasion, and theft of treaty-protected and tribally and Indian-owned lands and assets. The dissent, though, inexplicably bemoaned that the trespassers, who had invested "millions" in towns and farms, "had no durable claims to their improvements" and did not have "meaningful access to private property ownership, as the unique *communal titles of the Five Tribes precluded ownership by Indians and non-Indians alike*" (emphasis added). The dissent omitted the obvious answer to this statement: Indian nations held the titles and owned these lands, and it was their rightful and legal ownership that "thwarted" many non-Indians from acquiring ownership.[41]

In contrast to this odd statement by the dissent, research by historians and lawyers and reports to Congress in the early 1900s demonstrate that the American takeover of Indian lands and assets in the Indian Territory, and afterward in Oklahoma, included fraud, coercion, and even murders. Tribal governments, stripped of most of their legal and even political authority by various federal laws, were hard-pressed to control the corruption and violence. Tribal governing bodies during these years were "decimated and nearly inactive for many decades." In fact, historian Angie Debo wrote in 1950 that "the whole legal system of Eastern Oklahoma was warped to strip [Indians] of their property." But instead of condemning this history, the dissent inexplicably cited it as further "proof" that Congress had disestablished the Creek Reservation.[42]

The majority opinion in *McGirt* commented briefly on this disturbing history and the dissent's argument. The Court noted that the historical evidence shows

> that the loss of Creek land ownership was accelerated by the discovery of oil . . . A number of the federal officials charged with implementing the laws of Congress were apparently openly conflicted, holding shares or board positions in the very oil companies . . . And for a time Oklahoma's courts appear to have entertained sham competency and guardianship proceedings that divested Tribe members of oil rich allotments. Whatever else might be said about the history and demographics placed before us, they hardly tell a story of unalloyed respect for tribal interests.[43]

In hindsight, one can see that the dissent's decision to highlight these specific events as part of its argument for disestablishment backfired. The *McGirt* majority criticized and dismissed this type of evidence because "[n]one of these moves would be permitted in any other area of statutory interpretation, and there is no reason why they should be permitted here. That would be the rule of the strong, not the rule of law." The majority added, "To hold otherwise would be to elevate the most brazen and longstanding injustices over the law, both rewarding wrong and failing those in the right."[44]

In contrast to the dissent's "historical" arguments and its inaccurate statement that the Indian Territory was a "wilderness," the actual evidence shows that after removal from the American Southeast in the 1830s, the Five Tribes and their citizens "showed tremendous resilience in reestablishing an orderly and productive existence" in the Indian Territory. They operated their governments and engaged in beneficial governance and economic efforts. But their valuable lands, minerals, and oil assets were just too attractive for Americans to ignore.[45]

In conclusion, the dissenting justices vigorously attacked the majority opinion. This impassioned dissent, the close 5 to 4 vote in *McGirt*, and the change in the composition of the Court after the death of Justice Ginsburg lead one to wonder how the Court might use *Solem* and *McGirt* to decide similar cases in the future. And, in fact, the change in the Court makes one wonder about the continuing existence of the *McGirt* decision itself. Since Justice Gorsuch wrote the majority opinion, there is little doubt that he was instrumental in coalescing four other justices around the ruling.

Gorsuch was appointed to the Supreme Court in April 2017. He was born and raised near Denver, Colorado, and educated at Columbia University and Harvard Law School. He then received a doctorate in law from the University of Oxford in 2004. After graduating law school in 1991, he clerked for a federal judge on the U.S. Court of Appeals for the District of Columbia Circuit in 1991–92 and then clerked for Supreme Court justices Byron White and Anthony Kennedy in 1993–94. Afterward, he worked in private practice in Washington, D.C., for a decade and then became the principal deputy to the associate attorney general and the acting associate attorney general in the U.S. Department of Justice in 2005–6. In 2006, President George W. Bush nominated Gorsuch to the U.S. Court of Appeals for the Tenth Circuit. President Donald Trump nominated him to be an associate justice on the U.S. Supreme Court in February 2017, and he was confirmed by the Senate in April 2017.[46]

Gorsuch's appointment to the Court was controversial for two reasons. The seat he filled had become vacant with the death of Justice Antonin Scalia in February 2016, but for over nine months, Republican senators refused to consider President Barack Obama's nomination for the Court. After President Trump was elected, he nominated Gorsuch. In addition, many Democrats objected to some of Judge Gorsuch's opinions while he was on the Tenth Circuit, and to some of his political positions. Democratic senators filibustered his nomination until the Republican senators in the majority amended the Senate's rules to prevent filibusters on Supreme Court nominations. Gorsuch was subsequently confirmed by a vote of 54 to 45.[47]

Under the United States Constitution, the president nominates candidates for federal judgeships and the Senate confirms or denies them. This is an inherently political process and can become quite partisan. As one might expect, presidents nominate people who no doubt share their political ideals. The law, and the interpretation of law in the United States, is influenced by the composition of the federal courts, and especially of the Supreme Court. All of these judges are dedicated to the law, and swear to uphold the law, of course, but the meaning of "law" and the interpretation of the U.S. Constitution and federal statutes is always subject to divergent interpretations. And judges, like everyone else, have their own inherent beliefs and biases. It matters, then, in the long run what president, of what political party, nominates a person to the Supreme Court because it foretells to some extent the political and legal leanings of a particular federal judge. Justices appointed by "conservative" presidents can correctly be presumed to lean at least somewhat in that direction, and justices appointed by "liberal" presidents can be presumed to lean in that direction. Some justices, however, have turned out quite differently than this general rule predicts. For example, William Brennan Jr., appointed to the Supreme Court by Republican president Eisenhower, and Harry Blackmun, appointed by Republican president Nixon, were ultimately among the most "liberal" justices to ever sit on the Court.

While many liberals were upset over Gorsuch's nomination to the Supreme Court in 2017, many Indian nations and organizations were hopeful because Gorsuch was from the West, and he had written numerous Indian law opinions during his eleven years on the Tenth Circuit Court of Appeals. The analysis of his opinions left many tribes and commentators optimistic because of his knowledge of Indian law. For example, the general counsel for the leading tribal organization in the United States, the National Congress of American Indians (NCAI), noted that Judge Gorsuch had extensive experience in Indian law, since the Tenth Circuit's jurisdiction covers six western states, including Oklahoma, and "the territory of 76 federally recognized Indian tribes." In addition, this commentator noted that "Gorsuch wrote 18 legal opinions and participated in an additional 42 cases relating to federal Indian law or Indian interests" and that "Gorsuch's experience with Indian law and federal lands issues may be useful in examining other sources of federal authority in Indian Country." "With his Western experience and inclination toward textual interpretation," the NCAI attorney argued, "we can hope that Justice Gorsuch will champion this more fundamental understanding of federal authority in Indian Country." He then concluded, "It is encouraging, however, that Justice Gorsuch has signficant [*sic*] experience with federal Indian law and appears to be both attentive to the details and respectful to the fundamental principles of tribal sovriegnty [*sic*] and the federal trust responsibility."[48]

As predicted, Justice Gorsuch has lived up to the hopes of Indian law advocates and tribal nations. Even before writing *McGirt*, he had made a dramatic difference in the outcomes of Supreme Court Indian law cases. For many decades previously, Indian nations, Indian individuals, and tribal positions before the Supreme Court had a dismal losing record. In the thirty-one years from 1986 to 2017, tribes lost perhaps 75 percent of their cases in the William Rehnquist and John Roberts Courts. In contrast, in the first four years that Gorsuch has been on the Court, he has voted for tribal positions, individual Indian litigants, and Indian nations in five out of six cases, and tribes actually won all six of the cases. In addition, Gorsuch was the crucial fifth pro-Indian vote in three of these cases and was quite often on the opposite side from the Court's conservative justices. He also, of course, was the author and in the 5 to 4 majority in *McGirt v. Oklahoma*.[49]

A concurring opinion that Gorsuch wrote in one case gives some insight into his views on Indian law and the history of U.S. and Indian relations and no doubt impacted his views in *McGirt*. In 2019, he disparaged the State of Washington's arguments when it was trying to justify taxing Yakama Nation citizens in violation of their treaty rights:

Really, this case just tells an old and familiar story. The State of Washington includes millions of acres that the Yakamas ceded to the United States under significant pressure. In return, the government supplied a handful of modest promises. The State is now dissatisfied with the consequences of one of those promises. It is a new day, and now it wants more. But today and to its credit, the Court holds the parties to the terms of their deal. It is the least we can do.[50]

One can hear echoes of this statement in Gorsuch's *McGirt* opinion.

Finally, the primary reason that President Trump nominated Gorsuch to the Supreme Court is that Gorsuch is a leading advocate of the judicial interpretive theory called originalism and textualism. He applied that principle in *McGirt* and relied almost exclusively on congressional language regarding the MCN Reservation. Therefore, it seems absurd to criticize him for using that analytical process in *McGirt* and to be surprised that he did not assign much value to the evidence that the dissent and Oklahoma wanted to use to ignore the actual language Congress used in the laws it enacted regarding the MCN and its reservation.

The outcome in *McGirt* surprised many people. One reason, as already mentioned, is that the Supreme Court in general was very unfavorable to tribal and Indian litigants from 1986 to 2017. A second reason to doubt that Jimcy McGirt would succeed at the Supreme Court was the size of the MCN Reservation and the magnitude of the consequences that will follow, as we will discuss in chapter 8. Third, the *McGirt* case clearly raised the potential that most of eastern Oklahoma could also be re-recognized as Indian Country, as it has been. Thus, the MCN and Indian advocates had valid reasons to be uncertain about the outcome.

A fourth reason why some doubted whether McGirt would prevail was uncertainty over the position of Justice Ginsburg. Although she is largely perceived as having been a liberal justice, a recent study demonstrates that she voted in favor of tribal positions only 49 percent of the time in her twenty-seven years on the Court. Another liberal justice, Stephen Breyer, has voted for Indian nations and Indian litigants only 39 percent of the time during his twenty-seven years on the Court. As is borne out with Justices Ginsburg, Breyer, and Gorsuch, Indian law at the Supreme Court has never been strictly a conservative/liberal issue, and it is hard to predict how a particular justice will vote in any individual case. (Other than Gorsuch, however, the other four conservative justices currently on the Court have the worst voting records for tribal litigants in the past seventy years.) Consequently, the votes of Ginsburg and Breyer in the *McGirt* case were by no means a foregone conclusion.[51]

Fifth, and foremost with respect to Justice Ginsburg, McGirt and his lawyers had to consider the impact of a Ginsburg opinion from 2005, in *City of Sherrill v. Oneida Indian Nation*, which was decided by the Supreme Court on an 8 to 1 vote. In *Sherrill*, the Oneida Indian Nation (OIN), located in New York State, was attempting to restore its sovereignty over lands that were within the boundaries of its 1788 reservation. The OIN began buying land within that area and then refusing to pay state, county, and city taxes, rejecting those governments' regulatory authority over the parcels it now owned. But Justice Ginsburg and seven other members of the Court took a different view of that strategy. The *Sherrill* Court used an ominous line that could have reverberated equally in *McGirt*: "We . . . hold that 'standards of federal Indian law and federal equity practice' preclude the Tribe from *rekindling embers of sovereignty that long ago grew cold*" (emphasis added). In *McGirt*, it sure looks like the MCN and McGirt himself were trying to rekindle tribal sovereignty over the reservation.[52]

In addition, the *Sherrill* Court considered the "settled expectations" and the "justifiable expectations" of New York State, the county and city governments, and the predominantly non-Indian population within the Oneida Indian Nation's original 1788 reservation. The Court emphasized that New York and the counties and cities had governed, organized, and increased the value of the lands in this area in the absence of any tribal presence for nearly two hundred years. Due to the OIN's long absence from this area, the centuries that had passed in which the Oneidas had made no attempt to regain or govern their reservation lands, the Court prevented them from reasserting their sovereignty merely by repurchasing various parcels of land. Eight justices held that the OIN was precluded from making its "ancient" claims because of the defendants' defenses of laches (that the nation had waited too long to raise its claim), acquiescence (that for centuries the Oneidas had, in essence, allowed or agreed with the changed circumstances), and impossibility (that returning the lands to reservation status and tribal sovereignty was impossible). Thus, due to the settled and justified expectations of non-Indian governments and people, the Court prevented the Oneida Indian Nation "from rekindling embers of a sovereignty that long ago grew cold." Previous diminishment cases had also mentioned that the "justifiable expectations" of non-Indians can be an issue.[53]

Obviously, the *Sherrill* decision raised concerns for how Justice Ginsburg would vote, since Oklahoma and its citizens had operated and governed eastern Oklahoma for over a hundred years as if there were no MCN Reservation. Settled expectations in Oklahoma, similar to those in New York in *Sherrill*, might have arisen during this time even if they were in violation of federal and state laws, the Creek and U.S. treaties, and the borders of the MCN Reservation. In fact, at oral argument in the *Murphy* case on November 27, 2018, Justice Ginsburg asked the attorney for the United States what "the ramifications . . . [would be] in areas other than criminal jurisdiction," and one commentator noted that she and Justice Alito placed a heavy emphasis at that argument on "the consequences for criminal justice, taxation and regulatory authority of extending a reservation over the eastern half of the state."[54]

As expected, the majority opinion in *McGirt* did address the *Sherrill* case. Justice Gorsuch wrote that "reliance interests" had arisen in the *McGirt* situation and that these interests might have to be litigated in the future. These "reliance interests" look identical to the "settled expectations" that were protected in *Sherrill*. It is possible that this paragraph in the majority opinion about these interests and the statement that they might have to be litigated in the future were insisted upon by Justice Ginsburg, or at least were included to attract her vote to Gorsuch's opinion. The dissent also raised this topic, no doubt in an attempt to attract Ginsburg's support. In the end, however, Justice Ginsburg voted with the majority.[55]

Because of Ginsburg's record, the conservative makeup of the Supreme Court, and the Supreme Court's history regarding Indian law, and despite the appointment of Gorsuch, when the *McGirt* case came before the Court, legal experts found it difficult to predict the outcome. Instead, the decision dropped like a bombshell in federal Indian law. The ramifications and consequences from the case will play out over many decades to come. As the opinion pointed out, the United States, Indian nations, and Oklahoma can address these issues through negotiations and cooperative agreements, or they can choose to litigate them for decades. And as the Court stated in its ruling, Congress can always step in to resolve any problems that linger. We leave it for the next chapter to analyze the conflicts and issues that have already arisen since *McGirt* was decided in 2020 and to predict other issues that will no doubt arise.

7

THE CONSEQUENCES
OF *McGIRT*

In this chapter, we examine the consequences of the *McGirt* case, both those that have already occurred and those that may occur in the future. The *McGirt* decision has helped define and apply the law in Oklahoma and has changed many people's perceptions about the state's society and life.

All United States Supreme Court cases affect the law and society to some extent: consider the abortion rights case *Roe v. Wade* or the abolishment of segregated schools in *Brown v. Board of Education*. The re-recognition of the 3.25-million-acre MCN Reservation and the subsequent re-recognition of seven other reservations has provoked changes and fears and will create major consequences in the coming decades. The state of Oklahoma argued to the Supreme Court that *McGirt* would cause enormous turmoil, chaos, and a "sea change" in the state. The state contended that the ruling would lead to all of eastern Oklahoma being re-recognized as Indian Country, and that has, in fact, occurred. State courts have applied the same analysis to re-recognize the reservations of the Cherokee Nation, Choctaw Nation, Seminole Nation, Chickasaw Nation, and Ottawa, Eastern Shawnee, and Miami tribes. The four large reservations of the Muscogee (Creek), Cherokee, Choctaw, and Chickasaw nations are now the second-, third-, fourth-, and sixth-largest Indian reservations in the United States.

Oklahoma governor Kevin Stitt, who is an enrolled Cherokee Nation citizen, has repeatedly spread alarm about *McGirt*. He has called it a "huge issue" and a "nightmare" and stated that eastern Oklahoma is less safe now than it was before the case. In May 2021, he called it the most significant challenge Oklahoma has ever faced. Oklahoma's then attorney general, Mike Hunter, said in 2018 that re-recognizing the Creek Reservation, which covers eleven counties and a million people, would "result in the largest abrogation of state sovereignty by a federal court in American history." Furthermore, in September 2020, the Oklahoma Tax Commission estimated that *McGirt* and similar decisions for other Indian nations would cost the state well over $300 million in sales and income tax revenues in the first year and approximately $200 million every year thereafter. A well-known international credit rating service commented that the case could affect the state's and counties' credit ratings in the future. Governor Stitt has taken several steps to combat *McGirt*. He organized a commission that he said was about "cooperative sovereignty," but he did not appoint a single tribal leader or Indian person to serve on it. Not surprisingly, this commission offered five suggestions that took a hardline approach against *McGirt*, including that all Oklahomans should pay their share of taxes "without regard to race, gender or affiliation" and that state laws and regulations should apply to all "regardless of race, gender or affiliation." These suggestions ignore the fact that Indian nations are independent governments and enact laws that apply within their borders for their own citizens and for other persons and entities that fall under tribal jurisdiction. Tribal laws are enacted and applied without state input, permission, or interference. The U.S. Constitution, Supreme Court decisions, tribal nations, and acts of Congress have defined and enforced those legal principles since 1789.[1]

The Oklahoma state legislature is also fighting *McGirt*. On May 21, 2021, at the governor's request, the legislature set aside $10 million to pay attorneys' fees to continue litigating the issue, and the state has signed contracts retaining outside counsel for this purpose. In July 2021, Oklahoma sued the United States over the regulation of surface mines on reservations in eastern Oklahoma because the U.S. was reclaiming this authority after *McGirt*. And, as of April 2022, the state had filed over forty petitions with the Supreme Court asking it to reverse *McGirt*. So far, the Court has denied the state's attempt to reverse the case.[2]

As we have stated, *McGirt* presents serious issues and challenges for Indian nations, too. In fact, two of the Five Tribes, the Cherokee Nation and the Chickasaw Nation, are apparently in favor of a congressional legislative fix for *McGirt* that might preserve the status quo from before the case. But at the same time, these two tribal governments and the others that have had their reservations re-recognized are actively taking steps to implement *McGirt*. They are hiring new prosecutors and court personnel and filing more criminal prosecutions than ever before. The principal chief of the Cherokee Nation, Chuck Hoskin Jr., stated on May 15, 2021, that his nation had "carefully been planning and adding resources so we were ready for this new chapter in history. We have continued to upgrade criminal codes, appoint more district court judges, and hire more deputy marshals, prosecutors and victim advocates." And as of February 2022, the Chickasaw Nation Office of Tribal Justice Administration had added "five new criminal prosecutors, five new legal support staff, one criminal investigator and one supervisory probation officer" and, with grant money from the U.S. Department of Justice, "was able to hire a Special Assistant U.S. Attorney to prosecute federal cases in the U.S. District Court as well as tribal cases in the Chickasaw Nation District Court." There is no question that *McGirt* poses significant operational and monetary challenges for tribal governments.[3]

Clearly, there is much uncertainty and trepidation about the consequences of *McGirt*. For the benefit of Oklahoma society and the welfare of all Oklahomans, one hopes that instead of conflicts, roadblocks, and lawsuits, the governments of all three entities—Oklahoma, the Indian nations, and the United States—might intelligently address these issues. Instead of unleashing decades of litigation, hopefully these governments will negotiate agreements that address the challenges and solve problems for the greater benefit of all.

In our opinion, the largest and most immediate impact and challenge from *McGirt* and the subsequent state cases is in the criminal law arena. This impact will primarily affect Indians who commit crimes or are the victims of crime and non-Indians who commit crimes against Indians within the re-recognized reservations. In the area of civil and regulatory law, tribal citizens will also feel the greatest impacts from *McGirt*. Non-Indians who live and work on non-Indian-owned fee simple lands on these reservations should not see much, if any, change in their day-to-day lives. State laws and regulations will continue to apply to them. The uncertain question, however, is just how much impact tribal laws and jurisdiction will have on them, both now and in the decades to come.

Criminal jurisdiction is the power and authority that governments exercise to keep the peace and control serious antisocial behavior within their territories. Historically, Indian nations exercised similar sovereign and governmental powers over their populations and territories. The diverse array of indigenous governments, communities, and cultures exerted varying levels of political power and jurisdiction over many centuries, and undertook steps, as all governments must, to control and punish criminal conduct. Most Indian tribes had some form of dispute and conflict resolution system, with sanctions ranging from social pressure to corporal punishment to capital punishment.[4]

As we have seen, however, from the late nineteenth through the twenty-first centuries, the U.S. Congress and the U.S. Supreme Court have set the interface between tribal governments and the federal government by defining the parameters of federal criminal jurisdiction in Indian Country and in limiting tribal criminal jurisdiction. Congress has enacted numerous laws creating federal jurisdiction over criminal conduct in Indian Country by Indians and non-Indians. We will briefly set out that law and the law governing tribal and state criminal jurisdiction in Indian Country. We will then concentrate on the specific ramifications of the *McGirt* decision on Indians and non-Indians in eastern Oklahoma in the field of criminal law.

Federal, tribal, and state criminal jurisdiction in Indian Country has been characterized as a maze: it is difficult to understand, and it is often difficult for the three governments to enforce these laws in a cooperative and coordinated manner. It is not our intention to write an encyclopedia on the topic here. Instead, we lay out the basic principles and the three primary federal laws that will guide the impact of *McGirt* on criminal law for both Indians and non-Indians in the re-recognized reservations. We will also explain tribal criminal jurisdiction that almost exclusively impacts Indian individuals.

After the founding of America and for the first one hundred years of interactions between Indian nations, the U.S., and the states, tribal governments exercised almost exclusive jurisdiction over criminal activity by Indians in Indian Country. As early as 1790, Congress expanded federal jurisdiction over non-Indians who committed crimes against Indians inside Indian Country and vice versa, which was codified in the 1817 General Crimes Act (also called the Indian Country Crimes Act and the Inter-Racial Crimes Act).[5] In the 1883 case *Ex parte Crow Dog*, the U.S. Supreme Court held that tribal governments possessed exclusive jurisdiction to prosecute an Indian-on-Indian murder on a reservation and that the U.S. government had no jurisdiction over the matter. Two years after *Ex parte Crow Dog*, Congress enacted a law that is at the heart of the *McGirt* case. The 1885 Major Crimes Act created a specifically defined and limited federal jurisdiction in Indian Country over Indian defendants who committed any of seven specific crimes. The statute has since been expanded, and today it includes thirty different crimes.

Since these laws were enacted, various legislative acts have revised and amended them. In 1947, for example, Congress amended an 1825 act known as the Assimilative Crimes Act (ACA), which attempted to clarify federal and state jurisdictions within a state but carried implications for criminal jurisdictions in Indian Country. In 1968, Congress limited the lengths of sentences and the amounts of fines that tribal governments and courts can impose on Indian criminal defendants. And in 1978, the Supreme Court hampered criminal law enforcement in Indian Country when it held that tribal governments cannot criminally prosecute non-Indians. In 2013, however, Congress took a tentative step to ameliorate the impact of that 1978 decision and granted tribal governments the option of taking criminal jurisdiction over non-Indians in domestic violence situations.[6]

Furthermore, federal criminal jurisdiction could be expanded exponentially in the newly re-recognized areas of Indian Country under the ACA. In 1825, when this law first was enacted, Congress was surely not thinking about Indian Country, but in 1946 the Supreme Court simply assumed that it applied there. The ACA could have an enormous impact on Indians and non-Indians in eastern Oklahoma. It allows the federal government to prosecute anyone who commits a crime within the jurisdiction of the U.S. if the conduct "would be punishable if committed or omitted within the jurisdiction of the State . . . in which such place is situated." In other words, under the ACA, the U.S. can borrow the state laws of Oklahoma to prosecute in federal court non-Indians or Indians who allegedly violate an Oklahoma criminal law within Indian Country. We must note, however, that while the Major Crimes Act, the General Crimes Act (Indian Country Crimes Act), and the Assimilative Crimes Act are the three major federal laws that expanded federal criminal jurisdiction into eastern Oklahoma, there are other federal laws that criminalize conduct in Indian Country, such as hunting or fishing without authority and theft of tribal assets.[7]

In contrast to tribal and federal governments, state governments generally have limited jurisdiction and authority in Indian Country, and almost none over Indian nations and the Indian peoples located there. The Supreme Court has clearly stated that "tribal sovereignty is dependent on, and subordinate to, only the Federal Government, not the States." But the Court did hold in 1881 that state governments can prosecute non-Indians who commit crimes against non-Indians in Indian Country. The Court was plainly concerned about a vacuum of law enforcement and jurisdiction over such crimes if no government was able to prosecute these non-Indians, since tribal and federal governments could not prosecute them. Consequently, Oklahoma still possesses jurisdiction over non-Indian-on-non-Indian crime in the newly re-recognized areas of Indian Country. But the state is bemoaning its loss of jurisdiction over Indian defendants in Indian Country, and also over non-Indians who commit crimes against Indians. These results from *McGirt* and federal Indian law are the primary reasons that Oklahoma claims there will be criminal law chaos in eastern Oklahoma. In April 2022, the Supreme Court heard oral arguments in *Oklahoma v. Castro-Huerta*, in which Oklahoma asked the Court to allow state criminal jurisdiction over non-Indians who commit a crime against an Indian in Indian Country. The Court ruled in favor of Oklahoma.[8]

So, what are the current and potential criminal law issues that tribal, state, and federal governments will now face? Such issues are not new, and the Indian nations and Oklahoma already have more than a thousand agreements with city, county, and state authorities that will help these governments work together to handle any emerging issues. The *McGirt*

Court, in fact, relied on this long history of state and tribal negotiations and agreements on a multitude of issues as an omen that they can also successfully work to address the issues arising from that case.

Contrary to the fearmongering in which some state politicians have engaged, as of summer 2021 relatively few criminals have been released from state prisons. The state and federal governments coordinated in regard to Jimcy McGirt and Patrick Murphy, and both were taken into federal custody directly from state incarceration. Both men were then tried, convicted, and sentenced to long terms in federal prison. The federal, tribal, and state governments and courts have also mostly worked in this same fashion with other state convicts and pretrial detainees. In July 2021, the Oklahoma Department of Corrections reported that fifty-seven convicts had been released "to the street," and another seventy-two had had their state convictions vacated or dismissed but were turned over directly to federal or tribal officials for prosecution. A more detailed analysis from April 2022 demonstrates that only thirty-three inmates have "gotten off free and clear" due to *McGirt*. These numbers are a far cry from the "thousands" predicted by Governor Stitt.[9]

Even so, it is possible that the number of persons who might be released from state, county, or city incarceration could become overwhelming for tribal and federal governments. One news report, for example, highlighted that Ottawa County, Oklahoma, planned to lower bail amounts for incarcerated criminal defendants, or even to release them without bail, because, as a judge in that county stated, the federal and tribal governments are not "used to dealing with the humongous numbers of cases . . . and many cases will simply just go unprosecuted."[10] This possibility makes it crystal clear that these governments must coordinate in good faith to ensure that persons who have been convicted by state courts or who are in pretrial detention do not fall through the cracks and get released by the state before a tribal government or the federal government can take them into custody. If state, county, or city agencies release such persons without providing adequate notice to federal and tribal authorities, this will create an unnecessary and inexcusable risk to society. Obviously, these governments need to work cooperatively and not develop competitive and antagonistic positions.

Despite the dire predictions, the release of prisoners has not, to date, been an unmanageable problem. A more pressing concern is the jurisdictional shift in criminal caseloads. Thousands of state court cases are now being reassigned to federal courts. In the summer of 2021, the federal law enforcement departments were overwhelmed by their new caseloads. For example, in 2018, during the *Murphy* case, the U.S. informed the Supreme Court that the Federal Bureau of Investigation (FBI) had seven agents for eastern Oklahoma, handling about fifty cases per year. Now, after the *McGirt* ruling, the FBI office in Oklahoma City is being inundated with thousands of cases involving Indians. In addition, the U.S. Attorney's Office for the Eastern District of Oklahoma, which was formerly the smallest in the fifty states, filed a record number of criminal indictments in April 2021, and its lead attorney stated that while it "normally prosecutes about 100 to 110 felony cases each year," the federal grand jury had "returned 90 indictments" in the month of April alone. Because of the overload, the office also narrowed its focus primarily to people in state custody "whose charges are being dismissed or convictions set aside as a result of McGirt." Not surprisingly, that office went on a hiring spree and added forty new lawyers and staff. Moreover, the chief judge of the U.S. District Court for the Eastern District of Oklahoma declared a judicial emergency due to the "unprecedented increase in criminal filings" after *McGirt*. That court even had to lease an extra courtroom from a county court because the federal courthouse was filled to capacity. Assistant U.S. attorneys from across the country have volunteered to assist the Eastern District of Oklahoma with prosecutions, and federal public defenders have also offered to work on these cases. Likewise, the U.S. Attorney's Office for the Northern District of Oklahoma has had to hire significantly more prosecutors and staff and to borrow prosecutors from other U.S. attorneys' offices. By July 2021, the Northern District had expanded its staff by over 58 percent, and its caseload had doubled.[11]

While the lack of courtrooms is certainly a serious issue, the limited number of federal district court judges, who are appointed under article III of the U.S. Constitution, is even more crucial. Appointing new federal judges is a time-consuming and costly proposition, but not doing so could be a serious roadblock for the federal court system in Oklahoma, which is absorbing this significant increase in criminal trials, because only article III judges can preside over federal criminal trials. In recognition of this fact, the U.S. Judicial Conference requested in September 2021 that five more district judges be appointed for Oklahoma. In addition to a judge shortage, the Eastern District faces a lack of parole and probation services, courtroom security, secure transport for inmates, and federal public defenders.[12]

Federal agencies and courts are not the only ones affected. Indian nations' law enforcement agencies and courts have also been hit with an enormous increase in new cases and responsibilities. Principal Chief Hoskin of the Cherokee Nation said in May 2021 that his nation had filed over eight hundred criminal cases in only the first ten months after *McGirt* was decided: "That represents more Cherokee Nation District Court cases in the past year than were filed in the *previous 10 years combined*" (emphasis added). Two months later, a deputy attorney general for the Cherokee Nation updated those statistics. She stated that the nation typically files about sixty-two criminal cases a year, but it had filed twelve hundred criminal cases in just four months, from March to July 2021. Before this, the nation had one prosecutor, but six more full-time prosecutors have since been hired. Similarly, the MCN court system and law enforcement agencies have also faced a dramatic increase in cases and responsibilities. The territory where that nation's jurisdiction and law enforcement duties apply increased perhaps twenty-five times after *McGirt* re-recognized the Creek Reservation. One MCN judge says the nation has had a 5,000 percent increase in criminal cases since *McGirt*. Previously, about seventeen felony cases were filed a year, but since *McGirt* the MCN has filed a thousand felony cases. Consequently, the nation has invested over $2.5 million to hire four more prosecutors, a new district court judge, and forty other officers, investigators, and dispatchers.[13]

In contrast, Oklahoma state courts, jails, prosecutors, and police departments should see significant decreases in their caseloads and responsibilities. The *McGirt* Court foretold that result and noted that there would be a period of readjustment for these governments to realign their obligations and capacities. One example of this kind of readjustment and intergovernmental cooperation that will benefit tribal, state, and federal governments is that the Bureau of Indian Affairs, to help enforce federal and tribal laws, swore in a dozen Chickasha city police officers in June 2021 and Johnston County officers in July 2021 to serve on the Special Law Enforcement Commission. In the opinion of the Johnston County sheriff, "Johnston County isn't weaker because of *McGirt*." In fact, he believes that "the justice system is now stronger."[14]

The increased obligations and duties are driving up costs for the federal and tribal governments. Attorney General William Barr announced in August 2020 that the Trump administration would fund four new federal prosecutors in Oklahoma. In June 2021, the Biden administration offered $82 million in additional federal funding to hire more assistant U.S. attorneys, FBI agents, marshals, and court staff to handle the "spike in caseloads" resulting from *McGirt*.[15]

Tribal governments are in the same position. As part of the Cherokee Nation's preparations for implementing *McGirt*, Principal Chief Hoskin reported, "we've increased spending on our criminal justice system by record setting amounts, all using our own tribal revenue. We will spend a minimum, annually, of $35 million on our criminal justice system above the millions that we already spend." After the MCN police department's $2 million budget increase and forty new hires in 2021, the MCN court system requested a $12 million annual budget from the nation instead of its usual $2.5 million. The other Indian nations impacted by *McGirt* face similar financial issues.[16]

Incarceration and emergency facilities are also impacted. None of the Five Tribes had jails as of 2021, and it was probably true that few if any of the tribal governments in Oklahoma had jails. Most of these governments contract with state, county, and city jails to hold criminal defendants before trial and to incarcerate them if they are convicted in tribal courts. The Cherokee Nation, for example, as of July 2021 had agreements with thirteen counties to rent jail space. Similar agreements will have to be utilized by all the Indian nations as tribal criminal jurisdiction has expanded. These arrangements are also beneficial to state and county governments because their facilities remain occupied and they can recoup some of the tax revenues they will lose due to *McGirt*. After *McGirt*, there also were reports of delays in the handling of 911 calls. Callers were shuttled between police agencies and sometimes left on hold for long periods. Obviously, delays in handling emergency calls and a lack of prompt police, fire, and medical response create dangerous situations.[17]

The change in recognized jurisdictional boundaries after *McGirt* and the enormously expanded landmass where federal and tribal officials exercise their criminal responsibilities and authority are also an issue. If tribal police officers are cross-deputized by state and county authorities, they now have criminal jurisdiction over all peoples, not just Natives, within the expanded borders of Indian Country. Moreover, even if tribal officers are not cross-deputized, they possess criminal authority on reservations to stop, search, and detain non-Indians based on a June 2021 decision of the U.S. Supreme Court, *United States v. Cooley*. In that case, the Court held unanimously that tribal police officers have the authority to stop and search non-Indians in Indian Country, and to turn them over to state or federal agencies for suspected violations of state or federal laws.[18]

In tandem, federal criminal authority has expanded exponentially, from the hundreds of thousands of acres of Indian Country that were presumed to exist in eastern Oklahoma to now encompass the nearly nineteen million acres that have been re-recognized. Consequently, state officers and law enforcement agencies have less jurisdiction in eastern Oklahoma now because they have no authority to prosecute Indian defendants. However, in a weakening of *McGirt*, the June 2022 decision in *Oklahoma v. Castro-Huerta* gave jurisdiction to the state over non-Indian defendants who have allegedly criminally injured Indians in Indian Country.

Related is the issue of "hot pursuit"—when criminal suspects cross jurisdictional borders while being pursued by law enforcement officers. Whether a suspect does this purposely or accidentally, it raises questions about the authority of the pursuing officers and the jurisdictional powers of their governments. Many courts across the country have had to decide questions of state and tribal authority when fleeing suspects cross into or out of Indian Country. This situation could arise more frequently after *McGirt*. State and tribal governments need to cooperate to avoid conflicts and confusion in these situations. Once again, cross-deputization agreements that allow law enforcement officers to enforce both state and tribal laws seem to be a reasonable solution that should be considered.[19]

Moreover, the laws are written in such a way that federal, tribal, and state criminal jurisdiction depend on whether a suspect is Indian. But police officers at every level will frequently not know whether a criminal suspect is an Indian or a non-Indian and whether they have jurisdiction over that person in Indian Country. In this situation, offenders sometimes lie about their status as Native or non-Native. In July 2021, an Ottawa County district attorney noted that "gangs" were already taking advantage of the gaps in criminal jurisdiction that appeared after *McGirt* by lying about their status as "Indians." Compounding this problem, there are several possible legal tests for determining whether someone is an "Indian." Enrollment as a citizen in a federally recognized tribe is the norm and the most easily verified method to prove Indian status. However, many Indian nations still require some set amount of blood quantum for a person to be enrolled as a tribal citizen. Because of the confusion that can result from this nineteenth-century nonscientific criterion, the Bureau of Indian Affairs has long issued certificates of degree of Indian blood.[20]

Several federal courts across the United States, however, have also adopted two-part tests to define who is an "Indian" for federal criminal jurisdiction. These tests complicate the issue for law enforcement, and even for the courts. In the test used by the U.S. Court of Appeals for the Tenth Circuit, which encompasses Oklahoma, a person must (1) have some Indian blood and (2) be recognized as an Indian by a tribe or the federal government. The Tenth Circuit makes the determination even more difficult by using a multifactor test for the second prong. In determining whether a person is recognized by a Native community as an Indian, this court looks at whether the person is enrolled in a tribe; whether the person is recognized by the government on the basis of receiving some form of tribal assistance reserved for Indians; whether the person enjoys the benefits of tribal affiliation; or whether the person is socially recognized as an Indian by living on a reservation or participating in Indian social life. Oklahoma state courts apply this same test. It is unclear whether the Indian nations in Oklahoma will use a similar test in applying tribal criminal jurisdiction. What is clear is that these different definitions of "Indian" are imprecise, and police officers in the field are often unable to determine whether or not a suspect is an Indian. When they arrive at an accident or crime scene and see a tribal license plate on a car, an emergency dispatcher reported, they first have to figure out who is Native and who is not. This kind of confusion in the jurisdiction of tribal, state, and federal governments is not an ideal situation.[21]

Confusion, complexity, and change—the *McGirt* case entails all three, and there is much public and private uncertainty about its on-the-ground impacts. The lack of clarity about legal authority and jurisdiction and territorial boundaries leads to uncertainty and perhaps the under-enforcement of criminal law and increased risk for everyone. In fact, the Supreme Court stated in a disestablishment case that police officers should not be required to look at maps to determine whether they have the authority to respond to criminal activity or to arrest someone. It goes without saying that when courts, governments, and police departments have to change their long-established strategies and tactics, mistakes are more frequent. That eventuality is of concern to all Oklahomans.[22]

Civil jurisdiction also is affected. Indigenous governments exercise extensive jurisdiction and control over civil matters within Indian Country. Many Indian tribes operate court systems and governmental bureaucracies and exercise administrative, regulatory, and judicial authority over their reservations. Tribes have the sovereign authority to regulate the conduct of their own citizens, and they also have extensive authority within their territories over the conduct of Indians enrolled in other tribes. Indian nations also have some civil jurisdiction over non-Indians and their activities on reservations. For example, they can tax and regulate anyone involved in on-reservation activities on lands owned by the tribe or its citizens, and disputes that arise on reservations involving Indians or non-Indians will often be decided in tribal courts. In fact, the Supreme Court stated in the 1980s that tribal courts are the primary forum for adjudicating civil disputes in Indian Country because that is where jurisdiction "presumptively lies" even if non-Indians are involved. Civil jurisdiction encompasses a wide array of sovereign powers that governments exercise over people's daily life and activities. We will only briefly survey this topic to highlight the powers that tribal, federal, and state governments exercise in Indian Country, the expanded jurisdiction that Indian nations now exercise in eastern Oklahoma, the expanded role of the federal government, the jurisdictional limitations that Indian Country status imposes on Oklahoma, and some of the civil issues and conflicts that will arise for Indian nations, Oklahoma, and the U.S.[23]

In part 1, we document that the United States and the U.S. Constitution have long recognized Indian nations as sovereign entities that govern their territories, and that the U.S. Supreme Court has acknowledged that Indian governments possess inherent sovereign powers that exist separately from the U.S. and from the Constitution. In the 1832 *Worcester v. Georgia* case, the Court famously stated that the entire course of the United States' history with Indian nations shows that it "manifestly consider[s] the several Indian nations as distinct political communities, having territorial boundaries, within which their authority is exclusive, and having a right to all the lands within those boundaries." In 1959, in *Williams v. Lee*, the Court reiterated this position and precluded state court civil jurisdiction from reaching into Indian Country when it stated in the ruling that Indian nations and their citizens have the power and the right "to make their own laws and be ruled by them" and "to enforce that law in their own [courts]." In 1975, the Court again repeated that tribes possess "attributes of sovereignty over both their members and their territory." In short, state civil law has had no, or very little, application in Indian Country.[24]

The civil jurisdiction of tribal governments in Indian Country, on the other hand, is extensive. The federal courts have reaffirmed this point many times. Tribal nations possess the power to enact laws regarding taxation, gambling, land use, zoning, administrative and regulatory matters, economic issues, and other subjects. These laws control member Indians (citizens of that tribe), often control non-member Indians (Indians enrolled in a different tribe), and sometimes even control non-Indians who live and work in Indian Country. In contrast, the federal government, despite a few high-profile cases, rarely interferes with internal tribal issues.[25]

State civil laws and regulations did not apply in Indian Country at all from 1832 to 1973, but in 1973 the Supreme Court altered its test for the application of state laws there, while maintaining that state civil laws and jurisdiction would still play a minor role. "State laws generally are not applicable to tribal Indians on an Indian reservation," the Court stated, and "[s]tate jurisdiction is pre-empted . . . if it interferes or is incompatible with federal and tribal interests." The Court has also "consistently guarded the authority of Indian governments over their reservations." These principles limit Oklahoma's civil jurisdiction and sovereignty to varying degrees over Native lands and Native peoples, and sometimes even over non-Indians within the re-recognized reservations. They also expand tribal authority.[26]

The day the *McGirt* opinion was issued, some non-Indian Oklahomans who now live and work on the re-recognized reservations were fearful that their homes and rights were at risk because they were now under tribal civil authority as well as state authority.[27] To be clear, for non-Indian Oklahomans who own fee simple lands within the re-recognized reservations, there will be little, if any, change in the government exercising civil jurisdiction over them and the laws and rules governing their properties and actions. State laws and state taxes will still apply to them. In fact, in recent decades, the Supreme Court has limited tribal civil jurisdiction over non-Indians in these situations. These limitations will apply to the non-Indians who now find themselves living inside a reservation after *McGirt* and the state court cases.

The Supreme Court explicitly limited tribal civil jurisdiction in 1981, in the famous case of *Montana v. United States.* In *Montana*, the Crow Nation attempted to regulate fishing and hunting within its reservation borders by non-Indians on lands owned in fee simple by non-Indians. Previously, the state of Montana had regulated these activities. The Supreme Court held that the Crow Nation could not assert regulatory jurisdiction over hunting and fishing when the persons to be regulated were non-Indians and their conduct occurred on their fee simple owned lands. It advanced a general rule that Indian nations do not have civil authority to regulate or control non-Indian activities on such lands in Indian Country unless Congress has stated otherwise.[28]

However, the Court allowed two exceptions that are worth noting because they will apply in Oklahoma. The first *Montana* exception allows a tribal government to civilly regulate non-Indian activities through taxation, licensing, or other methods if the non-Indian has entered into a consensual relationship with the Indian nation or its citizens through contracts, leases, or other commercial and noncommercial arrangements. This exception has been applied by federal and tribal courts many times to hold that a tribal government had civil jurisdiction over a non-Indian for conduct that occurred on non-Indian-owned fee lands.[29]

The second exception allows a tribal government to exercise civil jurisdiction over non-Indians and their conduct on non-Indian-owned fee lands if that conduct "threatens or has some direct effect on the political integrity, the economic security, or the health or welfare of the tribe." This exception has rarely been applied to approve tribal jurisdiction over non-Indians. Under *Montana*, therefore, it is unlikely that the MCN and the other tribes will have jurisdiction over the actions of non-Indians on fee owned lands within reservations. Oklahoma will instead be the government that exercises civil jurisdiction over those non-Indians and their conduct within the reservations.[30]

But under the two *Montana* exceptions, Indian nations will sometimes have civil jurisdiction over non-Indian conduct on non-Indian-owned fee lands. Other courts have occasionally used the second exception to approve tribal jurisdiction over non-Indians, but the Supreme Court used it for the first time in June 2021, when it approved a tribal police officer stopping and detaining a non-Indian criminal suspect within a reservation on land that is analogous to non-Indian-owned fee lands. The application of the *Montana* test is not easy to predict. Consequently, confusion and questions will arise as to the extent of Oklahoma's and Indian nations' civil jurisdiction on the re-recognized reservations.

These changes in civil and criminal jurisdiction also have multiple financial implications. Although the state of Oklahoma will save significant amounts of money on criminal law enforcement and incarceration of prisoners, *McGirt* undoubtedly will lead to a significant drop in tax revenues for the state and local governments. At the same time, tribal governments will need to ramp up their tax collection efforts to fund the new and expanded duties that have now been placed on them. Obviously, this situation presents challenges, opportunities, and conflicts for both state and tribal governments.

Many tribes, for example, charge sales taxes at their hotels and impose those taxes on all consumers, but few, if any, tribal nations impose income taxes or other taxes on their citizens even though they possess the authority to do so. Most tribal operating funds come from tribally owned enterprises such as casinos, tourism, timber, and mining. One of the challenges *McGirt* has created for tribal governments is creating and implementing mechanisms to impose an income and sales tax regime on their own citizens if they so choose.[31]

A wrinkle in this process is that Indian nations are limited in their power to impose taxes on Indians from other tribes and on non-Indians living within their reservations. Numerous Supreme Court cases have set out these restrictions. Thus, Oklahomans who are not citizens of a tribe can live and work on non-Indian-owned fee simple lands within a reservation without having their incomes taxed by that tribal government unless one of the *Montana* exceptions applies. Tribal governments will therefore not be able to impose a general sales tax or business taxes on non-Indians for their economic activities with other non-Indians on non-Indian-owned fee lands on reservations. Indian nations can, however, impose these taxes on all persons who voluntarily engage in business with an Indian nation or a tribal citizen in Indian Country or who engage in such conduct on tribally or individually owned trust lands.[32]

On the other hand, the *McGirt* ruling does not affect the federal government's power to tax Indians and non-Indians if they live and/or work within Indian Country. Indians pay the same federal taxes as all Americans, except in the limited situation where an Indian derives income directly from land that is owned in trust with the United States. Indians and non-Indians living on the re-recognized reservations will continue to pay federal taxes. One of the most important and immediate issues raised by *McGirt*, obviously, concerns Oklahoma's collection of income and sales taxes from individual Indians and Indian-owned businesses inside the newly re-recognized reservations. In September 2020, the Oklahoma Tax Commission estimated that the state not only could lose almost $73 million in income taxes each year if all of the Five Tribes' reservations were re-recognized, but also could possibly face refund requests for another $200 million and would lose an additional $132 million in sales taxes each year. As expected, by summer 2021, many tribal citizens had filed challenges to state income taxation, and one can anticipate that multiple other tax issues will arise between

Oklahoma and Indians who live in Indian Country, and between the state, local, and tribal governments.[33]

In point of fact, the state of Oklahoma is prevented from taxing the incomes of Indians who live and work on their own tribes' reservations and from imposing sales and use taxes on Indians for goods purchased anywhere on their reservations. That prohibition will apply whether or not the goods are purchased at a non-Indian-owned business located on fee owned lands. A variety of Supreme Court cases have defined the limits that now apply to Oklahoma's taxation authority on the newly re-recognized reservations.

Many of these limitations are set out in three Supreme Court cases that Oklahoma lost by unanimous decisions in 1991, 1993, and 1995—cases in which the state attempted to tax Indians within Indian Country. In 1991, in *Oklahoma Tax Commission v. Citizen Band Potawatomi Indian Tribe*, the Court held that Oklahoma could not tax cigarette sales to tribal members in a tribally owned store located on tribal trust lands. Citizen Band Potawatomi, however, did have to collect, document, and remit to the state the cigarette taxes on any sales to non-Indians and Indians enrolled in other tribes. Likewise, in 1993, in *Oklahoma Tax Commission v. Sac & Fox Nation*, the Court reaffirmed the legal principle that a state generally lacks the authority to tax Indians in Indian Country. Specifically, that decision held that Oklahoma could not impose income taxes, use taxes, sales taxes, motor vehicle taxes, or registration fees on tribal citizens who live within their own tribe's Indian Country. Moreover, in 1995, in *Oklahoma Tax Commission v. Chickasaw Nation*, the Supreme Court held invalid a state tax on motor fuels sold by a tribe at its retail stores located on trust lands, but found that the state could impose income taxes on tribal citizens if they lived outside of Indian Country.[34]

Despite these restrictions, Oklahoma will still exercise ample taxation authority on the re-recognized reservations. States can impose income and sales taxes on non-Indians who live and work in Indian Country and can usually tax Indians who live and work on a reservation if that reservation does not belong to their own tribe, that is, if they are non-member Indians. In addition, Oklahoma has the legal right to expect tribal governments to collect and remit permissible sales taxes to the state for sales made at tribal businesses to people who are not exempt from state taxation. Moreover, Oklahoma can tax all Indians who live, work, and shop off reservations. The state and local governments can even collect annual property taxes on lands owned by tribal governments and individual Indians on reservations if the lands are held in unrestricted fee simple ownership. Further lessening the state's pain at losing tax revenue is that its governmental duties and obligations have been lessened to a considerable extent within the re-recognized reservations because of the newly expanded jurisdictions of the federal and tribal governments.[35]

One particularly pressing issue revolves around the 1978 Indian Child Welfare Act (ICWA). Oklahoma and Indian nations have often worked together on social issues regarding child welfare, and the MCN and other tribes have negotiated and entered various compacts with the state covering ICWA issues. *McGirt* alters this preexisting relationship by increasing tribal jurisdiction over these issues and concomitantly decreasing state jurisdiction.[36]

Under the ICWA, when questions about foster care placements, adoptions, or termination of parental rights arise regarding an "Indian child" who is domiciled or resides on a reservation, jurisdiction over those decisions and that child is exclusively in the tribal court. The ICWA is explicit on this count: "An Indian tribe shall have jurisdiction exclusive as to any State over any child custody proceeding involving an Indian child who resides or is domiciled within the reservation of such tribe." In addition, the ICWA requires states to honor and enforce tribal court child custody decisions. Consequently, the sovereign, jurisdictional, and human dimensions of *McGirt* are well demonstrated. Now that the Creek Reservation and other reservations are re-recognized, *all Indian children of any tribal nation* who are undergoing the above-named proceedings and who reside or are domiciled within a reservation or are already wards of a tribal court are subject to the exclusive jurisdiction of that tribal court. Thus, ICWA now applies to all Indian children who reside on the nineteen million acres of re-recognized Indian Country in Oklahoma. This is an enormous increase in jurisdiction for Indian nations and grants them far more control over child welfare issues.[37]

Tribal advocates will undoubtedly see this expanded jurisdiction as a victory, but it also presents these Indian nations with the challenge of effectively exercising their greater jurisdiction over a large increase in the number of cases and of funding the array of social and judicial services necessary to handle it. In apparent recognition of these facts post-*McGirt*, the Five Tribes signed agreements with Oklahoma for the state to continue caring for some Native children in ICWA situations and for the state and the tribes to cooperate and collaborate on these issues.[38]

One of the most potentially explosive effects of *McGirt* concerns water rights. Water rights have long been a source of agitation and contestation between tribal nations, the federal government, and state governments, and the mere mention of them foretells acrimonious disputes. There is an old adage that applies here: "In the west, whiskey is for drinking and water is for fighting." Drew Kershen, a retired Oklahoma attorney and professor emeritus at the University of Oklahoma College of Law, wrote that *McGirt* will have "far-reaching effects" on water rights on the reservations for Indian nations, Indian individuals, and non-Indians, and that "the impact of this decision will be very broad and affect every aspect of legal and political life in eastern Oklahoma." Rhett Larson, an expert on water issues who also taught at the University of Oklahoma College of Law, agrees and thinks "it's possible that the tribe's water rights will increase in quantity." These possible changes and any increase or decrease in water rights for tribes, Indians, and people who live on reservations will absolutely also affect other water users outside Indian Country.[39]

The Supreme Court case law on Indian and tribal water rights is clear. In 1908, the Court held that when Indian nations and the U.S. reserved land for reservations, those governments also reserved the amount of water necessary to support the tribal nations and citizens on those lands into the future. This was true even if the specific treaty was silent on the issue of water. The Court reasoned that neither the U.S. nor Indian nations could have intended for Native peoples to survive and thrive on reservations without water for farming, ranching, and survival. It took until 1963, however, for the Supreme Court to address the issue again. At this time, the Court was faced with the issue of how much water was reserved for reservations and tribal nations. In the ensuing case, *Arizona v. California*, the Court established a legal test for how to quantify the amount of water each tribal nation owned and could use on its reservation. The ruling adopted the "practicably irrigable acreage" (PIA) test—that is, an Indian nation owns the amount of water needed to irrigate the number of acres within its reservation that can be practicably (reasonably) irrigated. Obviously, assessing a test of this kind requires many branches of scientific inquiry, and many Indian tribes have not yet had their water rights quantified according to the PIA. The uncertainty about Indian water rights, then, is a hot-button issue in many states.[40]

In Oklahoma, the majority of tribal nations still need to have their water rights quantified. In 2012, the Oklahoma Water Resources Board recommended that the state "address uncertainties relating to the water rights claims by the Tribal Nations of Oklahoma." In 2016, Oklahoma, the United States, and the Chickasaw and Choctaw nations followed that suggestion and entered into an agreement in which both the Chickasaws and the Choctaws secured rights to use water and confirmed the rights of their individual citizens on trust lands to access water resources. In addition, the parties committed to greater involvement and collaboration on future water-planning efforts. To reach that agreement, however, the U.S. and the two Indian nations waived claims to other waters and some water management. Notwithstanding this 2016 agreement, Indian water rights are a nearly unanswered question for the state and its citizens as well as for the other tribal nations and their citizens, and the impacts of *McGirt* on water rights will have to be addressed and accommodated.[41]

The first step, of course, will be to subject the expanded reservations to the PIA test and to quantify the amount of water each of these reservations owns and uses. This issue is absolutely crucial for Indian and non-Indian Oklahomans who live inside and outside of Indian Country. It is unknown at this time whether the amount of water owned by Indian nations, and by Indians and non-Indians who own lands on those reservations, will increase or decrease. This quantification, however, is not a simple mathematical equation; rather, implementation of the PIA bumps up against court decisions about land and resource rights in Indian Country. Federal courts, for example, have held that individual Indian landowners, as well as non-Indians who bought land on reservations from the U.S., from tribal nations, or from individual Indians, own a percentage of the water reserved for that reservation equal to the percentage of the reservation land that they own. For example, an individual Indian or non-Indian who owns 1 percent of the landmass of a reservation also owns 1 percent of the PIA water amount that was reserved for that reservation. Consequently, some landowners on the re-recognized reservations might now own more or less water than they currently assume they own. Plainly, this situation could lead to serious disputes.[42]

In addition, other issues concerning water rights might arise. First is the question of the "priority" date of a water right. Several western states, including Oklahoma, follow the "prior appropriation" water rights system. Under prior appropriation law, in the event of a drought, people who own what are called "senior" water rights—a right that has an older priority date—are allowed to use all the water they have normally used since their rights were created. "Junior" water rights users—those with more recent priority dates—cannot access any water at all until those with senior priority dates have used their full amounts. Federal courts have long held that the priority date for Indian water rights is the date of the establishment of a reservation, or even earlier in some circumstances. The treaty establishing the MCN Reservation, for example, is dated 1833. That is a senior and a solid priority date in Oklahoma and predates almost all non-Indian settlers in the state. The other tribes with re-recognized reservations also have senior priority dates for water use. A second issue is whether the tribes, Indians, and non-Indian purchasers of reservation lands have rights to groundwater. This question is currently unsettled because some courts across the country have held that tribes possess rights to groundwater, whereas others have said they do not.[43]

Finally, some of the Five Tribes have already litigated the question of who owns the bed of the Arkansas River. Because of their unique treaty provisions, the Cherokee, Chickasaw, and Choctaw nations won a 1970 Supreme Court case that declared them the owners of the riverbed. Ownership of the bed also constitutes ownership of the gravel and minerals located there, the right to sell those assets, the right to lease oil and gas wells on those lands, and the right to regulate activities on the waters that run through the channel. However issues such as these get resolved, *McGirt* opens the door for tribal governments to have greater jurisdiction over, input into, and rights to the waters in Oklahoma.[44]

On the other hand, because of the general rule set out in the 1981 *Montana* decision that a tribal government cannot regulate non-Indian activities on non-Indian-owned fee lands within a reservation, the *McGirt* decision may not impact hunting and fishing rights in any significant way. About 95 percent of the land within the Creek Reservation is estimated to be owned by non-Indians, and thus the MCN will not have the authority to regulate hunting and fishing on those lands unless the specific conduct of a non-Indian meets one of the two exceptions delineated in *Montana*.

But one factor complicates this relatively straightforward answer. In 2016, Oklahoma signed compacts with the Choctaw Nation and the Cherokee Nation recognizing tribal authority in the arena of hunting and fishing rights. The state expressly recognized the Cherokee Nation's authority over "the lands, waters, fish, wildlife and persons subject to the jurisdiction of the Nation." In addition, the compact with the Choctaw Nation said that the tribe's authority extends over lands "defined as 'Indian country' per 18 United States Code section 1151." With Oklahoma state courts having re-recognized the reservations of these two tribes, their reservations now encompass perhaps ten million acres combined. Hence, obvious questions arise as to whether these 2016 jurisdictional definitions apply to the newly re-recognized Indian Country and whether these two Indian nations now exercise far more authority over hunting and fishing issues on their reservations than the *Montana* case would seem to allow. Nevertheless, these compacts and their jurisdictional provisions may ultimately not raise any serious issues, because even before the *McGirt* case, the Cherokee and Choctaw nations were negotiating a procedure for their tribal citizens to acquire state licenses and to allow the two nations to work with Oklahoma in managing these resources. There does appear to be a legitimate argument that the Cherokee and Choctaw nations have the authority to regulate hunting and fishing issues everywhere within their newly re-recognized reservations under these compacts.[45]

Oil and gas rights, too, will need serious deliberation in the wake of *McGirt*. The oil and gas industry is near and dear to Oklahoma, and industry representatives and pipeline operators are quite concerned that *McGirt* could potentially increase federal and tribal jurisdiction over their activities. The oil and gas industry supported Oklahoma and filed briefs with the Supreme Court in both the *McGirt* and *Murphy* cases. It was also represented on a commission that Governor Stitt created to study *McGirt*. Then, in December 2020, after the Seminole Nation Reservation was re-recognized, the Seminole Nation sent tax notices to oil companies, which put the industry on notice. Governor Stitt and the state attorney general downplayed the possibility of the nation taxing the industry, and industry spokespersons vigorously pushed back on the tax notices. Although the Seminole Nation's efforts have not come to fruition, some law firms warned their energy clients that *McGirt* could lead to tribal jurisdiction, taxation, regulation, water disputes, and the application of federal instead of state environmental regulations.[46]

One piece of legislation that may shield the oil and gas industry from *McGirt* is the 1947 Stigler Act. It granted Oklahoma regulatory authority over oil and gas operations on the Five Tribes' lands, and since then, the state and the Oklahoma Corporation Commission have exercised authority over the majority of oil and gas activities across eastern Oklahoma on the lands of the Five Tribes and their citizens.[47]

However, three Indian nations in addition to the Five Tribes have had their reservations re-recognized—the Ottawa, Eastern Shawnee, and Miami tribes. The Stigler Act applies only to the Five Tribes, so the Ottawa, Eastern Shawnee, and Miami tribes should be able to control oil and gas issues on their reservations in coordination with the U.S. In addition, the state's authority under the Stigler Act over the lands of the Five Tribes does not displace concurrent tribal powers in this arena and remains subject to federal oversight and approval, as well as federal leasing and regulatory authority over the lands of the Five Tribes. So it is possible that our preliminary prediction that this subject will remain mostly in the background could prove to be incorrect.[48]

McGirt calls into question much about state and tribal jurisdiction over resource rights, criminal law, and civil law in Indian Country. In addition, the majority of federal Indian law applies in Indian Country. Thus, by re-recognizing enormous areas of eastern Oklahoma as reservations, *McGirt* increases the application of federal law in those areas, increases the involvement of the federal government in traditional state affairs, and increases the sovereign authority of Indian nations. The application of these federal laws could lessen or even totally preempt the application of some Oklahoma laws within the nineteen million acres. Nine months after the *McGirt* ruling, for example, on April 2, 2021, the U.S. Office of Surface Mining Reclamation and Enforcement, an agency in the Department of the Interior, referenced the 1977 Surface Mining Control and Reclamation Act when it announced that, due to *McGirt*, Oklahoma "may no longer exercise regulatory jurisdiction under the [act] on Indian Lands within the State."[49]

The agency specifically relied on *McGirt* in making this decision and announced that it would "work with . . . Oklahoma and consult with the Muscogee (Creek) Nation towards a responsible and orderly transition of [the act's] responsibilities on the Muscogee (Creek) Reservation to [the federal office]." This decision was not a surprise because the 1977 Surface Mining Act applies on "Indian lands," which the act defines as "[a]ll lands, including mineral interests, *within the exterior boundaries of any Federal Indian reservation*, notwithstanding the issuance of any patent [title], and including rights-of-way [highways and pipelines, for example], and all land including mineral interests held in trust for or supervised by an Indian tribe" (emphasis added). That definition is broad and expressly includes all minerals located in Indian Country. Oklahoma responded immediately. Governor Stitt met with the secretary of the interior and thereafter called this decision "a huge issue for our state" and "a degradation of the state sovereignty." One reporter noted that it was a "significant loss of power by Oklahoma." On July 16, 2021, the state sued the United States to overturn the decision. This example portends future complications regarding surface mining between federal, state, and tribal controls and regulations.[50]

In addition, several federal laws that protect cultural resources will now apply to the re-recognized Indian Country. Prior to *McGirt*, federal cultural resource laws were inapplicable to most of these lands because the lands were (incorrectly) presumed to be under exclusive state jurisdiction. In particular, the 1990 Native American Graves Protection and Repatriation Act (NAGPRA) provides heightened protections for Native American human remains, funerary objects, and sacred objects when they are located on federal and tribal lands. NAGPRA defines the term "tribal lands" broadly as "all lands within the exterior boundaries of any Indian reservation." Hence, the protections provided by NAG-PRA now apply to all lands and all peoples in the re-recognized Indian Country in eastern Oklahoma. NAGPRA also applies to the conduct of all persons who live within a reservation even if they are non-Indians or own their lands in fee simple.[51]

In addition, the Archaeological Resources Protection Act of 1979 grants all tribal nations the right to be consulted and to consent to permits for archaeological excavations and similar activities conducted on "Indian lands." However, it more narrowly defines the term "Indian lands" than does NAGPRA. Under this act, Indian lands are limited to lands that an Indian nation or its citizens own in trust with the United States. This more limited territorial definition will probably prevent this act from impacting how Oklahoma and Indian nations handle these issues and might not alter pre-*McGirt* federal, state, and tribal jurisdiction on this topic.[52]

In 1992, the 1966 National Historic Preservation Act (NHPA) was amended to include the protection of tribal historic and cultural properties. The NHPA requires the federal government to work in concert with tribal leaders to develop programs to protect such objects and sets out a federal policy to assist Indian nations in developing their own historic preservation goals and programs. It also allows tribes to assume some of the functions and duties of the state historic preservation officers that were created by the act in 1966. If a tribe qualifies to assume the NHPA's functions within its lands, this increases tribal jurisdiction and influence over the functions and objectives of the act and lessens state control and authority in Indian Country. The NHPA defines "Indian lands" as "all land within the exterior boundaries of any Indian reservation." Consequently, the Indian nations of Oklahoma can apply to exercise the powers and responsibilities under the NHPA over all lands and all peoples within reservations and Indian Country.[53]

In addition to cultural resource management, Congress has enacted laws and created programs that encourage and sometimes even require other departments and agencies of the U.S. to cooperate, consult, and plan with Indian nations regarding the management of federal lands, facilities, and programs. The Department of Defense has had official policies in place since at least 1998 that require consultations with Indian nations. Pursuant to those general policies, the U.S. Air Force enacted tribal consultation policies in 2014 that require base commanders to meet regularly with tribal leaders and to jointly plan programs and operations as far as is practicable. In addition, numerous executive orders and directives, beginning with President Clinton in 1993 and extending through the Biden administration, require executive branch departments to consult with tribal governments about their plans before proposing new federal regulations. These executive orders also provide for Indian nations and peoples to have access to sacred sites located on federal lands. Other provisions grant tribes the right to consult with federal agencies about agency plans and programs and even about the operation of facilities.[54] There are several federal facilities and federally owned lands within the Muscogee (Creek) Reservation, including Department of Defense sites, Army Corps of Engineers reservoirs, and a Fish and Wildlife Service refuge. No doubt there are many others within the other re-recognized reservations. Federal duties to the MCN at these facilities are increased because they are now located within the MCN Reservation. Indian nations have taken advantage of these laws, programs, and executive orders, and they have expanded their roles and input in planning and decision-making regarding federal facilities and resources within and outside their boundaries. In July 2021, for example, the Reno-Sparks Indian Colony in Nevada intervened in a lawsuit challenging the federal approval of a lithium mine, claiming that its rights under federal consultation duties and the NHPA had been violated. Tribal consultations and input often impact state and non-Indian interests, too.[55]

Some federal laws grant stronger rights to Indian nations by allowing them to control and operate certain federal programs and some federal facilities. One particularly controversial case involved the 1975 Indian Self-Determination and Education Assistance Act and the 1994 Tribal Self-Governance Act. Under these acts, Indian nations can contract and compact with the federal government to operate federal programs that were created to assist Indian peoples and tribes. They can even control and operate federal lands, facilities, and Department of Interior programs that have some "special geographic, historical, or cultural significance" to an Indian nation. Pursuant to these laws and policies, in 2005 the Confederated Salish and Kootenai Tribes in Montana assumed the control and operation of the National Bison Range, which is located within its reservation. In 2020, Congress transferred the ownership of the range from the U.S. Fish and Wildlife Service to the Bureau of Indian Affairs, and then transferred the range to the ownership of the tribes to be held in trust with the U.S. The precedent and the principles behind these federal laws and policies raise questions in Oklahoma about whether the MCN and other Indian nations will take over the operations of federal programs and physical facilities in eastern Oklahoma. In particular, questions have already arisen about various dams and reservoirs operated by the Army Corps of Engineers that are now within the boundaries of reservations.[56]

We pause here to make a distinction between administrative law and regulatory law. Administrative law is "the body of law that regulates the operation and procedures of government agencies," while regulatory law is "promulgated by an executive branch agency under a delegation from a legislature." Both administrative and regulatory laws affect the rights and duties of people who are under the jurisdiction of a specific government or bureaucracy. State and federal governments exercise both administrative law and regulatory laws, and tribal governments do so as well. The scope of tribal administrative and regulatory authority on reservations has been addressed by courts a few times, but many questions remain. Federal courts have held on numerous occasions that tribal governments can enact administrative and regulatory laws, rules, and regulations that will apply on a reservation even if they ignore or contradict state regulatory jurisdiction and rulings. For example, the Supreme Court invalidated state attempts to tax and regulate individual Indians on reservations and to override tribal gambling laws. Moreover, lower federal courts have held that a city's mobile home rent-control ordinances did not apply to non-Indian lessees on a reservation, and that Indian-owned trust lands on a reservation were exempt from non-Indian building and zoning ordinances. In one unique factual situation, a tribal court and the federal court that reviewed that court's decision held that tribal laws could regulate logging on non-Indian-owned fee land within a reservation to protect a tribal sacred site.[57]

We will briefly examine two specific areas of administrative and regulatory law as they might apply to the re-recognized reservations in Oklahoma. The first involves zoning. "Zoning is the process whereby a community defines its essential character. Whether driven by a concern for health and safety, esthetics, or other public values, zoning provides the mechanism by which the polity ensures that neighboring uses of land are not mutually—or more often unilaterally—destructive." Indian nations enact zoning laws to improve their citizens' quality of life and to create standardized, logical, and beneficial community planning and development on their reservations just as all governments do. State, county, and city governments have long exercised zoning authority in most of eastern Oklahoma. The re-recognition of Indian reservations, however, and the revitalization of tribal jurisdiction in these areas, creates the potential for conflicting zoning policies, laws, and regulations.[58]

The presence of nearly 1.8 million Oklahomans living on these reservations, roughly 90 percent of whom are non-Indians, complicates zoning. The ownership of lands in fee simple by both non-member Indians and non-Indians on many reservations has resulted in a "checkerboard" pattern of settlement in eastern Oklahoma, which causes complex jurisdictional problems regarding who—the state or the tribe—has authority over which lands. The complexity, confusion, and conflict inherent in these situations, and the issues that might arise on the re-recognized reservations, are well represented by the 1989 decision of the Supreme Court in *Brendale v. Confederated Tribes & Bands of Yakima Indian Nation*. In this case, the Court had to answer whether Yakima County or the Yakama Nation (as it is now spelled) had jurisdiction to zone and control the development of two parcels of land owned in fee by a non-member Indian and by a non-Indian within the reservation. In this case, Philip Brendale was an Indian but not a member, or citizen, of the Yakama Nation. He owned his land in fee simple in what was called the "closed area" of the reservation, where access was restricted to only tribal citizens and permittees. Stanley Wilkinson, in contrast, was a non-Indian who owned his land in fee simple in the "open area" of the reservation, where three towns were located and where almost 50 percent of the land was owned in fee simple. In dueling opinions and dissents, four Supreme Court justices argued that the county had jurisdiction to zone both Brendale and Wilkinson, and three justices argued instead that the Yakama Nation had jurisdiction to zone them both. Justices Stevens and O'Connor cast the deciding votes and controlled the judgments issued in the two cases. The Court ruled that the county could zone Wilkinson, the non-Indian, who owned his land in the "open area" of the reservation, and the Yakama Nation could zone Brendale, the non-member Indian, who owned his land in the "closed area."[59]

Because the Court could not produce a majority opinion, *Brendale* raises more questions about tribal zoning authority than it answers for Oklahoma and the re-recognized reservations, and we can only guess how a future court might apply *Brendale* to the re-recognized reservations. Since about 90 percent of the population of these reservations is non-Indian and the vast majority of the lands are probably owned in fee simple by non-Indians, a court might consider these reservations to be "open areas." Thus, the judgment in *Brendale* might allow state, county, and city governments to apply their zoning laws and rules to the exclusion of tribal laws. Would any court consider parts of these reservations to be "closed areas" analogous to the Yakama Nation Reservation, where the tribal government was allowed to zone? Perhaps not. But according to the two exceptions in the 1981 *Montana* ruling regarding civil jurisdictions, tribes can zone their own lands and the lands owned by their citizens in trust with the U.S. within their reservations to the exclusion of the state and counties.

Tribal governments are also interested in exercising regulatory jurisdiction over utility companies that operate in Indian Country, even though the companies might be physically located outside a reservation. This topic has been litigated in some state and federal courts across the country and could arise in eastern Oklahoma. In February 2021, for example, the federal district court in Montana held that tribal law applied to the operations of an off-reservation utility company, and thus the company was prohibited from cutting off electric power in the winter to a tribal citizen living on tribal trust land within the reservation. This same utility company had won a case in 2000 against Crow Nation officials who were trying to regulate the company by imposing taxes on the utility's transmission lines within the Crow Reservation.

The U.S. Court of Appeals for the Ninth Circuit relied on the 1981 *Montana* case in holding that the Crow Nation did not possess this regulatory jurisdiction.[60]

Indian nations in North Dakota have also litigated the issue of utilities services on their reservations and have received apparently contradictory state court opinions. In 1990, the North Dakota Supreme Court held that the Devils Lake Sioux Tribe did not possess regulatory jurisdiction to override the North Dakota Public Service Commission's decision regarding electric service in areas that included the reservation. Yet in 2013, that same court appeared to change its position when it held that the same Public Service Commission lacked the authority to regulate the Turtle Mountain Band of Chippewa Indians' decision regarding which utility would provide electric service to its tribally owned facility on tribally owned trust land within the reservation. Similarly, in 1995, a federal district court in North Dakota held that the Devils Lake Sioux Tribe had the authority to contract with whatever utility it wanted for services to a tribally owned business within its reservation.[61]

The *McGirt* ruling also has implications for federal environmental laws. The U.S. Congress has included Indian nations in most of the major federal environmental laws since the mid-1980s. When it comes to controlling environmental issues within a specifically defined area, like a reservation, Congress has recognized the value of having a single government make those decisions. Accordingly, Congress and the Environmental Protection Agency (EPA) depend on tribal governments to assist the EPA in exercising environmental control and jurisdiction over reservations. Tribes across the United States have taken advantage of these laws to qualify for "treatment as a state" status, in which they propose air and water quality standards for their reservations. If the EPA adopts those standards, it enforces them against every person and business living and working on that reservation, whether or not they own their lands in fee simple. One federal court of appeals even held that the water standards recommended by a tribe and adopted by the EPA applied to non-Indians outside of Indian Country. States and non-Indians have litigated the exercise of this tribal and EPA power; so far, though, they have lost all their cases. The environmental reach of this indirect form of tribal jurisdiction and the potential impact of

McGirt are demonstrated by Congress's broad definitions of tribally controllable areas in the Clean Water Act and the Clean Air Act. In *City of Albuquerque v. Browner*, for example, Isleta Pueblo proposed new, stricter water quality standards, and the EPA adopted them. The EPA then enforced the new standards against the off-reservation upriver city of Albuquerque, and the U.S. Court of Appeals for the Tenth Circuit approved this decision.[62]

But this scenario will probably not occur in Oklahoma. These federal laws and the significant tribal role in setting federal environmental standards should be a major topic in connection with the MCN's and other Indian nations' jurisdiction and authority on their reservations. The laws will apply differently in Oklahoma, however, because in 2005, current Oklahoma U.S. senator James Inhofe attached what is called a "midnight rider" to a massive transportation bill that Congress enacted. The Inhofe rider gave the state of Oklahoma the right to request federal approval to control any Indian nation that attempted to use the federal environmental laws described above.[63]

The very month *McGirt* was decided, Governor Stitt used the Inhofe rider and requested that the Trump administration approve this state control over tribal attempts to work with the EPA to regulate the environment in Oklahoma. In October 2020, Oklahoma was granted this authority over all Indian nations within the state. In December 2021, however, the EPA proposed that it would withdraw and reconsider that Trump administration decision. Consequently, Indian nations in Oklahoma will not be able to exercise the rights and powers provided under these federal laws, and assume their role in controlling the environment of their reservations, unless the Biden administration withdraws that October 2020 approval, or Oklahoma approves of tribal control, or Congress revokes that "midnight rider" provision.[64]

Another body of law that *McGirt* affects is adjudicatory jurisdiction—the power and authority of a court system to hear specific disputes and issues that arise between persons within specific geographical boundaries. Even before *McGirt*, the federal government, Indian nations, and Oklahoma faced overlapping judicial jurisdiction and possible conflicts. *McGirt* and the subsequent court cases have greatly magnified the possibility that such disputes will become more common.

The U.S. judicial system is a court of limited jurisdiction, and it can only decide cases that the Constitution and Congress authorize. Yet the presence of a vastly increased area of Indian Country in eastern Oklahoma expands dramatically the possibility that federal courts will be called on to handle many more disputes that arise within that geographical area.

In contrast to the principle of the limited jurisdiction of the federal court system, every state has a court of general jurisdiction, and civil procedure professors in American law schools will say that these courts are allowed to hear any dispute that arises between anyone within the state's borders. However, this principle does not apply to Indian Country within a state. A state court system does not have general jurisdiction in Indian Country even though those geographical areas are located within that state's borders.

As we have discussed, the Supreme Court has made that principle clear. In 1959, in *Williams v. Lee*, the Court held that a state court's jurisdiction is limited over Indian peoples and their conduct inside Indian Country even though they are also citizens of that state and the reservation is located within its borders. The plaintiff in *Williams* was a non-Indian who operated a business on the Navajo Nation Reservation. He sued two Navajo defendants in Arizona state court, no doubt because he thought state court would be more favorable to him. But the Supreme Court restated the longstanding and well-recognized legal principle that tribal nations and peoples make their own laws and are governed by them. The Court held that allowing the state court to hear this case "would infringe on the right of the Indians to govern themselves." Therefore, it dismissed Lee's state court case because the Arizona state court did not have jurisdiction to hear the case even though the Williamses were citizens of Arizona and lived within that part of the Navajo Reservation that is also within Arizona. The ruling held that such cases must be heard only in tribal or federal courts.[65]

In addition, in the 1980s, the Court developed a rule that litigants must exhaust their tribal court remedies before they can even file their cases in federal court. This rule has also been extended to state courts. Thus, even where a federal or state court might have concurrent jurisdiction with a tribal court, out of the respect shown between separate judicial systems, federal and state courts must allow tribal courts to hear cases first and review their own jurisdiction over the matter and the litigants before the cases can be heard in state or federal courts. Consequently, under these authorities, Oklahoma state court adjudicatory jurisdiction will be significantly affected on the Muscogee (Creek) Reservation and the other re-recognized reservations because what Oklahoma previously assumed to be its general adjudicatory jurisdiction over the re-recognized Indian Country will be significantly limited.[66]

Even so, Oklahoma courts will still play a role in adjudicating disputes on the reservations. Non-Indians who live or work on reservations or who travel through them will often have any lawsuits that arise on these reservations heard in state courts. This is so because of the *Montana* rule, under which tribal governments generally do not have jurisdiction over non-Indians and their conduct on non-Indian-owned fee lands. For example, in 1997, in *Strate v. A-1 Contractors*, the Supreme Court analyzed *Montana*, its rule against tribal jurisdiction over non-Indians, and its two exceptions, and held that a tribal court lacked jurisdiction to hear a lawsuit between two non-Indians regarding an auto accident that had occurred within the reservation on tribally owned land. The accident occurred on a state highway built on a right-of-way, an easement granted to the state by the tribe and the federal government. The Court held that the location was analogous to non-Indian-owned fee lands on a reservation and thus applied its *Montana* test.

In this case, the Court relied on its general rule from *Montana* that Indian nations do not have jurisdiction over non-Indians for their conduct on non-Indian-owned fee lands even though they are located within a reservation. The *Strate* Court also analyzed the two exceptions to the *Montana* general rule but held that neither of them applied. Consequently, the tribal court lacked adjudicatory jurisdiction in this situation, and the state court had jurisdiction to hear the case.[67]

In 2001, the Supreme Court expanded on the *Strate* case and continued to hold that tribal courts' adjudicatory jurisdiction over non-Indians on reservations was limited. In *Nevada v. Hicks*, the Court stated, "Tribal courts, it should be clear, cannot be courts of general jurisdiction." Here the Court held that the tribal court did not have jurisdiction over a lawsuit against state game officers even though the suit was about conduct they had engaged in on land on the reservation owned by the tribe in trust with the United States. Similarly, in 2008, the Court held that the Cheyenne River Sioux tribal court did not have jurisdiction over a discrimination tort lawsuit concerning an off-reservation bank's sale of fee simple land within the reservation.[68]

Despite the limits set by the *Montana* rulings, with *McGirt* the federal and tribal courts will see their adjudicatory jurisdiction increase while the state's will decrease. The costs of the federal and tribal court systems will increase significantly, and Oklahoma's judicial expenses will decrease to some unknown extent. This new uncertainty and these changes will create challenges both for Oklahoma and for Indian nations. However, there are signs that the state and the Indian nations can and will address these issues. Pre-*McGirt*, Oklahoma had already agreed to honor and enforce tribal court judgments if a tribal government reciprocates. In turn, the MCN enacted a tribal law that it would honor court judgments of all Indian nations, states, and territories that also recognize the judgments of MCN courts. These are encouraging signs.[69]

Adjusting sovereign and jurisdictional boundaries and the impacts on governments and individuals are inherently fraught with tension. In fact, just about every issue mentioned above could lead to decades of acrimonious disputes and litigation. The Supreme Court was well aware that *McGirt* could lead to changes for Oklahoma and Indian nations and to litigation. But the Court also cited the path that Indian nations and Oklahoma have been following for many decades. Instead of litigation, these governments have primarily settled their differences by negotiating intergovernmental issues and settling them through contract-like agreements called compacts. The *McGirt* Court cited the hundreds of cooperative compacts these governments had already entered into on every topic imaginable, including taxation, courts, and criminal and civil law issues. The ruling noted that this kind of intergovernmental respect, negotiation, and cooperation could ameliorate and perhaps even prevent the most draconian effects of *McGirt*. Many states, many state attorneys general, and scholarship on Indian law written by state attorneys general concur that intergovernmental agreements with Indian nations "resolve the core uncertainties" about jurisdiction and tax issues, for example, and result in more effective services for all.[70]

Of the potential issues we have discussed in this chapter, criminal jurisdiction appears to be the most important and of the most immediate concern. Tribal, federal, city, county, and state police officers must be able to act with certainty and with authority in ongoing criminal situations. In recognition of exactly these kinds of concerns, many Indian nations and state, county, and city police departments across the country had already entered cross-deputization agreements, which authorize police officers of all these governments to act under the laws of all the governments and to at least arrest suspected criminals and transport them to the proper authorities for processing. As of late 2018, the MCN had entered into forty cross-deputization agreements with the forty-four county and municipal jurisdictions within the MCN Reservation, as well as with the United States and Oklahoma. The Cherokee Nation has cross-deputization agreements with all relevant local and county governments. Most of the Indian nations in Oklahoma have similar agreements. Such arrangements are a win-win situation for Indian nations and Oklahoma because enforcing law and order and protecting all citizens is in everyone's best interest. One point is worthy of special attention: in the year after the July 2020 *McGirt* decision, the Five Tribes and state, county, and city agencies in Oklahoma entered into more than 210 new cross-deputization agreements and jurisdiction-sharing agreements. This, too, is an encouraging development.[71]

Still, controversy surrounds the *McGirt* ruling. The Five Tribes and Oklahoma officials were engaged in discussions about the case before it was even decided. In fact, within days of the decision being issued, the Oklahoma attorney general announced that he had reached an agreement-in-principle with the Five Tribes. It called on the U.S. Congress to enact a law to alter *McGirt* and maintain the status quo from before the case was decided. This announcement surprised almost everyone, and it shocked many tribal citizens. Some of them immediately pushed back and put pressure on the Five Tribes to repudiate this agreement, claiming that it totally threw away the great victory that *McGirt* represented. Three of the Five Tribes quickly disavowed the agreement, and it went no further.[72]

But the Cherokee Nation and the Chickasaw Nation are apparently still interested in the agreement-in-principle and have continued negotiating with the state over *McGirt*. On May 11, 2021, Oklahoma congressman Tom Cole (Chickasaw) introduced a bill in the U.S. House of Representatives to address *McGirt* and to "support clarity and consistency with regard to the exercise of criminal jurisdiction and authority in Indian country, and for other purposes." It appears, however, to only allow the Cherokee and Chickasaw nations the option to negotiate and perhaps enter into compacts with Oklahoma and to address criminal law issues. What leaves us uncertain about this bill is that these tribes already possess that sovereign power, and they have already negotiated and entered into hundreds of such agreements with Oklahoma. Consequently, it is unclear why Congressman Cole, Oklahoma, and the two tribes even proposed this legislation. Moreover, in October 2020, Governor Stitt created a "sovereignty commission" that one might hope would have been a serious attempt to negotiate issues surrounding *McGirt*. However, the governor did not appoint any tribal leaders to the commission. Instead, it represents the state's economic and oil and gas interests. It seems difficult to call this commission a sincere attempt to address *McGirt*.[73]

Notwithstanding these apparent missteps, the clear path forward for Indian nations, Oklahoma, and the United States seems to be sincere, honest, and open negotiations. The alternative is decades of acrimony and expensive litigation with uncertain outcomes. Of great concern is that litigation has already begun, with Oklahoma suing the United States on July 16, 2021, over surface mining regulation, the state filing more than forty petitions with the Supreme Court to reverse *McGirt*, the legislature's allocation of $10 million to litigate to reverse *McGirt*, and Governor Stitt's and the state's new attorney general's statements in July 2021 that they will fight to reverse the decision.[74]

In contrast, the governor and state appear to be open to negotiations. On January 22, 2021, Governor Stitt appointed a state negotiator and invited the Five Tribes to the negotiating table. One hopes that this was a sincere and good-faith attempt to deal with Indian nations on the important issues presented by *McGirt* and the subsequent state cases. Hopefully such negotiations will lead the federal, state, and tribal governments to enter into agreements that protect the populations, sovereignty, and powers of all three governments.[75]

The range of issues discussed in this chapter highlight the significance and impact of the *McGirt* decision. Oklahoma, Indian nations, and the United States are now faced with implementing the ruling and dealing with the consequences and challenges that have already ensued and others that will arise. The land within Oklahoma's borders is now 43 percent Indian Country, and this is a fact that all persons and all governments have to face. Over the next several decades, we will see how these governments deal with the challenges and consequences, and whether they are dealt with by decades of anger and litigation or by negotiations and consensual agreements.

CONCLUSION

The *McGirt v. Oklahoma* decision was a long time in the making and derived from a complex and inconsistent five-hundred-year historical relationship between Natives and newcomers in the New World. We endeavor here to chronicle the events, policy decisions, avarice, and destructions, as well as the opportunities, trust, and obligations, that have characterized the long history of the Muscogee (Creek) Nation, and especially its bonds with the United States. We then offer an analysis of the *McGirt* case through a microscopic lens in order to follow the twists and turns of American Indian policy and statutes as well as the interventions of the state of Oklahoma to turn those policies and statutes to its advantage over the Creeks. We hope through these analyses to convince millions of non-Native Oklahomans and others that the Court's decision is simply an upholding of the treaty obligations between the United States of America and the MCN. These obligations were first enunciated soon after the American Revolution and have been repeated in legally binding documents many times since. Despite subsequent large and small efforts to undermine and erase them, the United States has sometimes remained true to its promises in the intervening 250 years. The *McGirt* ruling reminds us of that.

Many have called this case a "bombshell" since the day it was decided. While the specific issue before the Court was a narrow one, the holding that the 1866 MCN Reservation still exists portends enormous and significant changes for Oklahoma and the MCN for decades to come. Oklahoma state courts have since held that other tribal reservations still exist as well, with their boundaries as stated in the treaties of the early to mid-nineteenth century. Thus, *McGirt* has become even more of a bombshell than first predicted, and about 43 percent of eastern Oklahoma is now Indian Country under 18 U.S.C. section 1151(a).

In one of the first legal reviews of the case, Miller and Dolan point out that "any 'shock' arising from *McGirt* was not caused by the U.S. Supreme Court decision but by Oklahoma's illegal actions and incorrect assumptions over the past century and the United States' acquiescence and failure to support Indian nations." In other words, the Court's ruling points to the decades-long efforts by the state of Oklahoma in the first half of the twentieth century to erase Creek legal jurisdictions and self-governance, oftentimes illegally and with the support of the federal government. The Court, as should be expected, exposed the well-known unlawfulness of these efforts and corrected course.[1]

For Native peoples, the *McGirt* decision not only corrected illegal jurisdictional trespassing on the part of the state of Oklahoma, it also reaffirmed U.S. obligations to and territorial rights of the Creeks (and, by extension, of other Native nations) as constitutionally guaranteed by treaty, and it confirmed Native sovereignties and reiterated and underscored the particular and lawful relationship between Native nations and the U.S. Congress. For the non-Native, the *McGirt* decision looks problematic—what to do with those millions of non-Natives and population centers that are suddenly in Creek country? It is a good question, and one that cannot be addressed through reaction, alarm, and fear. The question needs serious, thorough, and deliberate pondering, discussion, negotiation, and goodwill between all who are affected by the ruling. The history of the MCN and the analysis of the *McGirt* case show us that previous decisions concerning Native lands, resources, and economic rights that were made in haste and without goodwill and tribal participation had disastrous short- and long-term consequences for Native peoples, the states, and the federal government.

We point out, though, that after 1975, with the passage of the Self-Determination Act, the state of Oklahoma entered into a more lawful relationship with the Indian nations within its borders. The

Self-Determination Act gave Indian nations a powerful, congressionally approved tool with which to promote tribal interests, and the state of Oklahoma subsequently reconfigured its frame of reference regarding Indian policy. Instead of approaching Indian and state negotiations from a place of inequality and flagrant violations of federal treaties and statutes, both now proceed from a place of equality and legality. The result has been multiple mutually beneficial compacts over the past several decades addressing a wide variety of legal and jurisdictional concerns. Complexity and dense details are certainly inherent in the compacts, but as Miller and Dolan observe, "This same process should be relatively easy to continue." They also are "very encouraged by the fact that on January 22, 2021 Governor Stitt appointed a state negotiator and invited the Five Tribes to start negotiating about *McGirt*."[2]

The way forward will not be easy, and undoubtedly many in the coming years will offer opinions and models for how to proceed. There will be failures and there will be successes, but a path into and through this new political and policy terrain can and will be forged. Our modest recommendation is that the MCN, Oklahoma, and the United States begin a cooperative and mutually beneficial discussion about anticipated and emergent issues, and then once issues have been identified, begin a flexible negotiation process through which to address them. Flexibility is an essential ingredient because the full scope and consequences of the *McGirt* ruling are still unfolding, and those involved must be able to change tack if and when needed.

We also, however, recognize lurking dangers. For one, as of early 2022, Oklahoma had filed at least forty-five petitions repeatedly asking the Supreme Court to reverse *McGirt*. This is a possibility, although a remote one given that the Court does not usually care to revisit a ruling. In fact, in over 230 years of history under our current Constitution, the Court has partially or outright reversed only about 300 of its own cases, less than 1 percent. Thus, to ask the Court to reverse *McGirt* within the first year or two of its existence seems farfetched. But we have to note that the Court did reverse one case within just one year in 1872, and it has reversed others in just two and three years. Unquestionably, the passing of Justice Ginsburg puts the *McGirt* 5 to 4 decision on shaky ground, as discussed in chapter 7.[3]

The other danger to the *McGirt* decision comes from the ability and the legal right of Congress to diminish or disestablish the MCN Reservation. In fact, when Governor Stitt first received news of the ruling, he publicly announced that he would seek this option. The governor, the Oklahoma attorney general, and others have continued to suggest that Congress should disestablish the re-recognized reservations and are waging a public relations campaign against *McGirt* that they appear to be winning. In early 2022, the governor was reported as saying that the case is "a threat to the future of our state."[4]

Using Congress to disestablish the MCN Reservation and the other re-recognized reservations would not be as simple as it may seem. Congress would have a poisonous and protracted fight on its hands. The MCN and other Indian nations have strong allies in Congress; there is a vocal and growing activist arm of Native political operatives and their allies who could mobilize an organized opposition; and many corporate and business ventures with political lobbyists have lucrative partnerships with Indian nations. All would have a vested interest in opposing any such legislation. In our opinion, any effort toward disestablishment would be at best foolhardy, and at worst severely damaging, because it would create untold legal and social disturbances, not to mention enormous costs, that would linger for decades. We know this because, plainly speaking, any efforts to disestablish the MCN Reservation would be a repeat of some of the most shameful and dramatic episodes of American history—Indian removal, ethnic cleansing, and allotment. Those episodes left the United States with deep wounds, severe disadvantages, and enormous costs, all of which we are still working to rectify two hundred years later.

The saying goes that history is made and written by the victors, but that is not correct. How history gets written sometimes derives from the perspective of the victor, but the events and structures that are history are generated through the encounters and entanglements of myriad players through the flow of power and resources and the tumult of time. More importantly, history is made by people, and the people of the United States have an opportunity to keep a promise made almost two centuries ago. Will the Supreme Court and Congress continue to enforce the treaty and the constitutionally guaranteed promise that *McGirt v. Oklahoma* reaffirmed?

EPILOGUE

In re-recognizing numerous Indian reservations across Oklahoma, *McGirt* and the state court cases that followed have created a fluid and evolving process that will continue to develop over the next several decades. We analyze many of these political, jurisdictional, economic, and legal ramifications in chapter 7. Potential economic changes are, of course, an extremely important part of this evolutionary process.

In its arguments to the U.S. Supreme Court, Oklahoma protested vigorously that if the Court affirmed the existence of the MCN Reservation, it would disrupt jurisdiction and governance in that state and seriously injure the state's economy. In his dissenting opinion in *McGirt*, Chief Justice Roberts apparently accepted those anecdotal statements at face value and bemoaned the dramatic impacts that the existence of the Creek Reservation would surely create.[1] Since *McGirt* was decided in July 2020, Oklahoma governor Kevin Stitt and the state have continued to allege that the decision is harming and will continue to harm the state's economy. Some in the media have accepted those bare statements as fact, especially as demonstrated in multiple editorials by the *Wall Street Journal*.[2]

This epilogue provides an update on recent empirical and economic research conducted by well-respected economists that disproves the arguments and erroneous assumptions put forth by Oklahoma. Posted online in April and May 2022, the conclusions of these two in-depth studies prove that the state's fears and arguments are false. The facts show that there have been almost no economic changes in Oklahoma in the two years since the *McGirt* decision and in the nearly five years since the U.S. Circuit Court of Appeals for the Tenth Circuit decided the *Murphy* case, which first held that the MCN Reservation still exists.

In an article entitled *Restoring Indian Reservation Status: An Empirical Analysis*, authors Michael K. Velchik and Jeffery Y. Zhang compiled and reviewed the economic evidence available to date and concluded that there is "no statistically significant effect of the Tenth Circuit or Supreme Court opinions on economic output in the affected [Oklahoma] counties."[3] In reaching this conclusion, the authors examined economic data from counties in Oklahoma that were impacted by the *Murphy* and *McGirt* cases and compared it against Oklahoma counties unaffected by those decisions. They measured three economic variables: monthly county-level employment differences between the two groups of Oklahoma counties, annual county-level GDP based on information from the U.S. Department of Labor and from the Bureau of Economic Analysis, and daily financial data for public companies incorporated in the state.[4] From the data, they conclude that the *McGirt* decision has not had any negative economic impact on Oklahoma.

A second study, by University of Wisconsin economics professors Dominic Parker and Sarah Johnston, also concludes that there has been no negative economic impact on Oklahoma from *McGirt*.[5] This study was posted online on May 31, 2022. These authors studied Zillow home sales and price data, along with evidence regarding oil well starts, and compared them for the eastern Oklahoma counties implicated in *McGirt* against the counties that are not involved. The authors "find very little evidence of a systematic negative response of investment to *McGirt*. Neither home prices nor sale quantities in eastern Oklahoma appear to have systematically declined." They also found "no evidence that the number of new [oil] wells decreased in eastern Oklahoma. On the contrary, there is some evidence that developers in the east adjusted by drilling more oil wells and drilling them more quickly."[6]

These studies are important and worthy of special attention. Their authors relied on facts and verifiable data to show that so far, *McGirt* has had no adverse effect on Oklahoma's economy.

NOTES

INTRODUCTION

1. We note that the name "Muscogee" is also spelled "Muskogee." We have opted to use "Muscogee" because that is the spelling the Muscogee (Creek) Nation uses today.

2. *McGirt v. Oklahoma*, ___U.S.___, 140 S.Ct. 2452, 2459, 2482 (2020); Miller and Dolan, "Indian Law Bombshell," 2090n318.

3. The Osage Nation has also asserted its reservation boundaries under the *McGirt* case, and if that reservation is reestablished, part of Tulsa will be within the Osage Nation Reservation, as well.

4. Snyder, "Gov. Stitt."

5. *McGirt v. Oklahoma*, ___U.S.___, 140 S.Ct. 2452, 2481 (2020).

6. Oklahoma Tax Commission, "Report of Potential Impact"; Standard & Poor's Financial Services, "Bulletin."

7. *Johnson and Graham's Lessee v. McIntosh*, 21 U.S. 543, 572–73 (1823); George Washington to James Duane, September 7, 1783, in Prucha, *Documents of United States Indian Policy*, 1–2.

8. Washington to Duane, 1–2.

9. Miller, *Native America*, 78, 92–94, 115–61, 200n98. Calloway, in *The Indian World of George Washington*, details Washington's long relationship with American Indians.

10. *United States v. Winans*, 198 U.S. 371 (1905).

11. *Cohen's Handbook*, 183–90; 18 U.S.C. § 1151; *DeCoteau v. District County Court for Tenth Judicial District*, 420 U.S. 425, 428n2 (1975).

CHAPTER 1

1. Hudson and Ethridge, "Early Historic Transformation," 4.

2. Hahn, "Cussita Migration Legend," 60–64; Grantham, *Creation Myths*, 134–58; Swanton, *Social Organization*, 34–66.

3. Hahn, "Cussita Migration Legend," 60–64; Grantham, *Creation Myths*, 134–58; Swanton, *Social Organization*, 34–66.

4. Anderson and Sassaman, *Recent Developments*, 36–65; Ethridge, Thompson, and Meyers, "Indian Eras, Paleoindian Period."

5. Anderson and Sassaman, *Recent Developments*, 66–111; Ethridge, Thompson, and Meyers, "Indian Eras, Archaic Period."

6. Anderson and Sassaman, *Recent Developments*, 85–86; Ethridge, Thompson, and Meyers, "Indian Eras, Archaic Period," 136.

7. Anderson and Sassaman, *Recent Developments*, 101–7; Ethridge, Thompson, and Meyers, "Indian Eras, Late Archaic Domestication."

8. Anderson and Sassaman, *Recent Developments*, 112–51; Ethridge, Thompson, and Meyers, "Indian Eras, Late Archaic Domestication."

9. For the Woodland Period, see Pluckhahn, *Kolomoki*; Pluckhahn and Thompson, *New Histories*; Wright and Henry, *Early and Middle Woodland Landscapes*.

10. Anderson and Sassaman, *Recent Developments*, 155–63.

11. Ethridge, "Rise and Fall"; Ethridge and Meyers, "Indian Eras, Mississippian Period."

12. See the essays in Sharp, *Hero, Hawk, and Open Hand*.

13. Hally, "Platform Mound Construction"; Hally, "Territorial Size of Mississippian Chiefdoms"; Hally and Chamblee, "Temporal Distribution and Duration."

14. Smith, *Coosa*, 34–49, 85–87.

15. Biedma, "Relation of the Island," 1:232; Elvas, "Account by a Gentleman," 1:92–94; Rangel, "Account of the Northern Conquest," 1:284–88; Priestley, *Luna Papers*, 1:291–95; Ethridge, *From Chicaza to Chickasaw*, 62–66; Jenkins, "Tracing the Origins," 218–19; Smith, *Coosa*, 103–4, 107–9. See also Nelson, "Material Evidence."

16. Biedma, "Relation of the Island," 1:232–36; Elvas, "Account by a Gentleman," 1:95–105; Rangel, "Account of the Northern Conquest," 1:290–94; Priestley, *Luna Papers*, 1:291. Atahachi is most likely the Charlotte Thompson site. Hudson, *Knights of Spain*, 230–31; Jenkins, "Tracing the Origins," 214–16, 221, 223; Regnier, *Reconstructing Tascalusa's Chiefdom*, 81; Sheldon, "Present State of Archaeological Survey," 120; Waselkov, Derry, and Jenkins, "Archaeology of Mabila's Cultural Landscape," 230–31.

17. Jenkins, "Tracing the Origins," 228; Jenkins and Sheldon, "De Soto and Luna y Arellano Expeditions," 186–98, 200; Knight, "Formation of

the Creeks," 383; Knight, *Tukabatchee*; Waselkov and Smith, "Upper Creek Archaeology," 250–52; Wesson, "Prestige Goods," 118–20. DePratter, Hudson, and Smith, "De Soto Expedition," 120, place Talisi on the Coosa River, near Childersburg, Alabama, probably corresponding to the Kymulga phase people. However, a recent reevaluation of central Alabama archaeology during the late sixteenth and early seventeenth centuries places Talisi on the lower Tallapoosa. See Jenkins, "Tracing the Origins," 205–8, 233–34; and Jenkins and Sheldon, "De Soto and Luna y Arellano Expeditions," 170–71.

18. Jenkins, "Tracing the Origins," 214–15, 221, 233–34. Knight, in "Formation of the Creeks," 185, argues that the Abercrombie phase developed *in situ* as local Stewart phase people borrowed from numerous external influences. However, later work in the Chattahoochee shows that the Abercrombie phase most likely resulted from immigration into the valley. See Braley, *Yuchi Town*, 9–11; Worth, "Lower Creeks," 268–69.

19. Blitz and Lorenz, *Chattahoochee Chiefdoms*, 70–72; Jenkins, "Tracing the Origins," 228–29; Knight, "Formation of the Creeks," 383, 384; Worth, "Lower Creeks," 269, 271–72, 274.

20. Ethridge, *From Chicaza to Chickasaw*, 60–61.

21. Waselkov and Smith, "Upper Creek Archaeology," 250–52; Knight, "Formation of the Creeks," 383; Knight, *Tukabatchee*; Wesson, *Households and Hegemony*, 58–88, 127–34; Wesson, "Prestige Goods," 118–20.

22. Ethridge, *From Chicaza to Chickasaw*, 78.

23. Ethridge, 78–79. There has been much historical and archaeological study of La Florida; for a summary of that work, see Ethridge, 78–82.

24. Ethridge, 79.

25. Ethridge, 79–82.

26. Ethridge, 81.

27. Ethridge, 82.

28. Ethridge, 82–83.

29. Ethridge, 86–88; Ethridge, "Introduction," 10–13.

30. Ethridge, *From Chicaza to Chickasaw*, 92–93; Ethridge, "Introduction," 16–19, 20–25.

31. Ethridge, "Introduction," 26–42. See also Ethridge, *From Chicaza to Chickasaw*.

32. Ethridge, *From Chicaza to Chickasaw*, 60–115.

33. Ethridge, 112–13; Knight, "Formation of the Creeks," 384; Shuck-Hall, "Alabama and Coushatta Diaspora"; Waselkov, "Seventeenth-Century Trade."

34. Shuck-Hall, "Alabama and Coushatta Diaspora"; Hudson, *Knights of Spain*, 229; Worth, "Lower Creeks," 271–72; Boyd, "Expedition of Marcos Delgado," 14, 26; Ethridge, *From Chicaza to Chickasaw*, 162; Galloway, *Choctaw Genesis*, 177–79; Smith, *Coosa*, 80.

35. Ethridge, *From Chicaza to Chickasaw*, 99–100, 112, 164–67.

36. Ethridge, "Introduction," 34–36; Ethridge, *From Chicaza to Chickasaw*, 148–93.

37. Ethridge, *From Chicaza to Chickasaw*, 165–66.

38. Ethridge, 232–54.

39. Ethridge, *Creek Country*, 95–97.

40. Ethridge, 95–96, 102–4.

41. Ethridge, 74–76, 109–11.

42. Ethridge, 74–75.

43. Ethridge, 25.

44. Ethridge, 25.

45. Ethridge, 25–26.

46. Ethridge, 9–10.

47. Ethridge, 9–10. For a full-length and definitive treatment of the deerskin trade era among the Creeks, see Braund, *Deerskins and Duffels*; for an examination of this new exchange economy, see Usner, *Indians, Settlers, and Slaves*.

48. Perdue, *"Mixed Blood Indians."*

49. Hahn, *Invention of the Creek Nation*, 110–20; Green, *The Creeks*, 35.

50. Miller, "Legal Adoption of Discovery."

51. This agreement was later reiterated in a 1721 and 1732 treaty. Juricek, *Colonial Georgia and the Creeks*, 17.

52. Hahn, *Invention of the Creek Nation*, 103, 151–60; Juricek, *Colonial Georgia and the Creeks*, 12, 38–41. Oglethorpe negotiated two treaties with the Creeks, the one in 1733 and the Treaty of Savannah in 1739; both confirmed land grants that Tomochichi had bestowed on Oglethorpe as gifts. Juricek, *Colonial Georgia and the Creeks*, 36–40, 110–13. For a full-length biography of Mary Musgrove, see Hahn, *Life and Times of Mary Musgrove*.

53. Calloway, *Indian World*, 171–90; Edmunds, Hoxie, and Salisbury, *The People*, 143–45.

54. Calloway, *Indian World*, 171–90; Edmunds, Hoxie, and Salisbury, *The People*, 143–45; Perdue and Green, *North American Indians*, 38–39.

55. Hahn, *Invention of the Creek Nation*, 259, 262, 263 ("as a territorially" at 263); Perdue and Green, *North American Indians*, 39.

56. Green, *The Creeks*, 38–40; Hahn, *Invention of the Creek Nation*, 267–68; Juricek, *Endgame for Empire*, 180 ("Native framework").

CHAPTER 2

1. Braund, *Deerskins and Duffels*, 164–88; Ethridge, *Creek Country*, 10, 13.

2. Ethridge, *Creek Country*, 30.

3. Ethridge, 31.

4. Ethridge, 30–31.

5. Ethridge, 219.

6. Ethridge, 13; Royce, *Indian Land Cessions*, 670–71.

7. Ethridge, *Creek Country*, 15.

8. Braund, *Deerskins and Duffels*, 164–88; Ethridge, *Creek Country*, 10–11.

9. Nichols, *Engines of Diplomacy*, 8–9, 71–72, 127–29, 151–71. In 1849, Congress transferred the administration and oversight of Indian affairs to the U.S. Department of the Interior.

10. Ethridge, *Creek Country*, 11–12; Saunt, *New Order of Things*, 67–89.

11. Ethridge, *Creek Country*, 12.

12. Braund, *Deerskins and Duffels*, 164–88; Ethridge, *Creek Country*, 15; Saunt, *New Order of Things*, 139–229.

13. Cronon, *Changes in the Land*, 54–81.

14. Calloway, *Indian World*, 321–45; Ethridge, *Creek Country*, 15; Hawkins, *Letters, Journals, and Writings*, 1:402 ("that the U.S.").

15. Ethridge, *Creek Country*, 77–78, 161. For a thorough discussion of Indian countrymen among the Creeks, see Frank, *Creeks and Southerners*.

16. Ethridge, *Creek Country*, 118–19, 161, 181; Saunt, *New Order of Things*, 175–77; Perdue, "*Mixed-Blood Indians.*"

17. Braund, "Creek Indians, Blacks, and Slavery," 623–31; Ethridge, *Creek Country*, 115–17; Saunt, *New Order of Things*, 111–35, 273–90; Zellar, *African Creeks*, 3–40. For a comprehensive history of American Indians and slavery, see Snyder, *Slavery in Indian Country*.

18. Ethridge, *Creek Country*, 116–17. For a detailed analysis of Africans among the Creeks pre- and post-removal, see Saunt, *Black, White, and Indian*, and Zellar, *African Creeks*.

19. Littlefield, *Africans and Creeks*, 17–46; Ethridge, *Creek Country*, 116–17; Perdue, "*Mixed Blood Indians,*" 90–95; Saunt, *New Order of Things*, 111–35; Zellar, *African Creeks*, 15–16.

20. Ethridge, *Creek Country*, 175–94.

21. Ethridge, 158–74; Hawkins, *Letters, Journals, and Writings*, 1:288–316.

22. Ethridge, *Creek Country*, 169–74.

23. Ethridge, 215–18.

24. Ethridge, 175–94.

25. Ethridge, 196–200, 211–12; Saunt, *Unworthy Republic*, 217–21. For a comprehensive examination of land speculation in Georgia and Alabama leading up to removal, see Winn, *Triumph of the Ecunnau-Nuxulgee*.

26. Ethridge, *Creek Country*, 208–11.

27. Ethridge, 195–215.

28. Ethridge, 238–41.

29. Ethridge, 238–41.

30. Ethridge, 238–41.

31. Ethridge, 240–41. For modern analyses of the Red Stick War, see Braund, *Tohopeka*, and Waselkov, *Conquering Spirit*.

32. Ethridge, *Creek Country*, 241; Green, *The Creeks*, 53; Hawkins, *Letters, Journals, and Writings*, 2:744; Royce, *Indian Land Cessions*, 678–79; Winn, *Triumph of the Ecunnau-Nuxulgee*, 13.

33. Green, *Politics of Indian Removal*, 49–54; Green, *The Creeks*, 55–56; Saunt, *Unworthy Republic*, 3–26.

34. Edmunds, Hoxie, and Salisbury, *The People*, 176–77; Ellisor, *Second Creek War*, 9–46; Ethridge, *Creek Country*, 197; Green, *Politics of Indian Removal*, 49–54; Green, *The Creeks*, 56–57; Royce, *Indian Land Cessions*, 688, 702, 708, 714, 720, 734, Map 5, Georgia; Wilkins and Lomawaima, *Uneven Ground*, 57, 72–73.

35. Ellisor, *Second Creek War*, 15–16; Green, *Politics of Indian Removal*, 70–72; Saunt, *Black, White, and Indian*, 88–89; Zellar, *African Creeks*, 21–22.

36. Ethridge, *Creek Country*, 105–8, 232–38; Green, *Politics of Indian Removal*, 70–72, 77–78; Green, *The Creeks*, 58–60.

37. Green, *Politics of Indian Removal*, 54–56; Green, *The Creeks*, 56–60; Winn, *Triumph of the Ecunnau-Nuxulgee*, 35–84. For a biography of McIntosh, see Griffith, *McIntosh and Weatherford*.

38. Green, *Politics of Indian Removal*, 81–97; Green, *The Creeks*, 60–61; Haveman, *Rivers of Sand*, 11–22; Winn, *Triumph of the Ecunnau-Nuxulgee*, 84–110.

39. Green, *Politics of Indian Removal*, 96–97; Green, *Creek Indians*, 62–63; Saunt, *Unworthy Republic*, 35; Winn, *Triumph of the Ecunnau-Nuxulgee*, 112–15.

40. Green, *Politics of Indian Removal*, 98–125; Green, *The Creeks*, 68 ("they had won"); Haveman, *Rivers of Sand*, 21–25; Saunt, *Unworthy Republic*, 36–37; Winn, *Triumph of the Ecunnau-Nuxulgee*, 178–90.

41. Ellisor, *Second Creek War*, 9–46; Green, *Politics of Creek Removal*, 126–39; Haveman, *Rivers of Sand*, 24–41; Royce, *Indian Land Cessions*, 714–15, 720–21, Map 5, Georgia; Saunt, *Unworthy Republic*, 37–38; Winn, *Triumph of the Ecunnau-Nuxulgee*, 194–228.

42. Ellisor, *Second Creek War*, 9–46; Foreman, *The Five Civilized Tribes*, 211; Haveman, *Rivers of Sand*, 22–41, 59, 66, 74; Saunt, *New Order of Things*, 111–35, 273–90.

43. Ellisor, *Second Creek War*, 9–46; Green, *Politics of Indian Removal*, 141–73; Haveman, *Rivers of Sand*, 58–94; Saunt, *Unworthy Republic*, 38–40.

44. Saunt, *Unworthy Republic*; Winn, *Triumph of the Ecunnau-Nuxulgee*.

45. Saunt, *Unworthy Republic*, 53–99.

46. Saunt, 45, 47, 63–68.

47. Green, *The Creeks*, 69–70; Saunt, *Unworthy Republic*, 70–82; "An act to provide for an exchange of lands," May 28, 1830 ("And be it further" at 412).

48. Saunt, *Unworthy Republic*, 45.

49. Green, *Politics of Indian Removal*, 166–71; Green, *The Creeks*, 71–72; Haveman, *Rivers of Sand*, 94–100; "Treaty with the Creeks, 1832," 368 ("The Creek country").

50. Green, *Politics of Indian Removal*, 174–86; Green, *The Creeks*, 72; Haveman, *Rivers of Sand*, 100–113; Saunt, *Unworthy Republic*, 176, 182, 196–97, 217–21; Winn, *Triumph of the Ecunnau-Nuxulgee*, 334–71.

51. Ellisor, *Second Creek War*; Green, *The Creeks*, 73; Haveman, *Rivers of Sand*, 121–26; 140–48; Saunt, *Unworthy Republic*, 246–47; Winn, *Triumph of the Ecunnau-Nuxulgee*, 437–67.

52. Saunt, *Unworthy Republic*, 243–46, 251 ("exposed the dark impulse" at 251).

53. Haveman, *Rivers of Sand*, 299; Haveman, *Bending Their Way Onward*, 179–210.

54. Haveman, in *Rivers of Sand*, provides the most detailed descriptions of the Creek removal. See also Saunt, *Unworthy Republic*, 115–230. Firsthand accounts of the removal process for the Creeks are in Haveman, *Bending Their Way Onward*. Haveman, who has done the most thorough examination of the Creek removal documents, estimates that upward of twenty-three thousand Creeks were removed; *Rivers of Sand*, 299. Saunt, *Unworthy Republic*, 252, puts the number of Creeks removed at fourteen thousand; Michael Green, *The Creeks*, 83, estimates the Creek population at the time of removal as twenty-five thousand. Although Creeks continued to emigrate from Alabama in small, family-sized detachments into the 1840s and 1850s, government-sponsored removal ended officially in 1837 and 1838. In Alabama, many of those who escaped removal attained federal recognition in 1984 as the Poarch Band of Creek Indians. They live in Atmore, Escambia County, and reside on the only remaining officially recognized Creek lands in the state.

55. Haveman, *Rivers of Sand*, 259–60.

56. Foreman, *The Five Civilized Tribes*, 211; Haveman, *Rivers of Sand*, 271, 297–99, table 1. Green, *The Creeks*, 83, puts the death toll during the deportations at 3,500, with up to 40 percent of the population lost after their removal to Oklahoma.

Chapter 3

1. Burton, *Indian Territory*, 3–4; Calloway, *Scratch of a Pen*, 99; Creel, "A Court of Its Own," 1–2.

2. "An act to provide for an exchange of lands," May 28, 1830; "Treaty with the Creeks, 1833," 418–19; "Terlton Indian Treaty." The number of U.S. documents relating to Indian affairs is enormous, and there are numerous curated compilations of these documents available in print and online; see, for example, Kappler, *Indian Affairs*. We have opted to use the *United States Statutes at Large*.

3. Hedden-Nicely and Leeds, "Familiar Crossroads," 308–9; Smithers, *Cherokee Diaspora*, 106–7; Wilkins and Lomawaima, *Uneven Ground*, 185.

4. Wilkins and Lomawaima, *Uneven Ground*, 64–69.

5. Wilkins and Lomawaima, 64–79 ("federal responsibility" at 65).

6. Edmunds, Hoxie, and Salisbury, *The People*, 242; Foreman, *The Five Civilized Tribes*, 151–54, 164–65, 187–88; "An act to provide for an exchange of lands," May 28, 1830, 412 ("any other tribe"). For a full-length treatment of relationships between the eastern and western tribes, see La Vere, *Contrary Neighbors*.

7. Haveman, *Rivers of Sand*, 285; Creel, "A Court of Its Own," 2; Wilkins and Lomawaima, *Uneven Ground*, 51.

8. Green, *The Creeks*, 85; Zellar, *African Creeks*, 25. Gregory D. Smithers, in *The Cherokee Diaspora*, offers a modern narrative of the Cherokee removal and post-removal experiences.

9. Green, *The Creeks*, 86; Haveman, *Rivers of Sand*, 284.

10. Foreman, *The Five Civilized Tribes*, 148–50, 156–62; Haveman, *Rivers of Sand*, 283–84, 285.

11. Edmunds, Hoxie, and Salisbury, *The People*, 246–47; Foreman, *The Five Civilized Tribes*, 199–200, 186–87; Haveman, *Rivers of Sand*, 274–75, 281; Zellar, *African Creeks*, 25.

12. Edmunds, Hoxie, and Salisbury, *The People*, 246; Green, *The Creeks*, 86–87; Haveman, *Rivers of Sand*, 273–74, 276, 279.

13. Foreman, *The Five Civilized Tribes*, 182–83; Haveman, *Rivers of Sand*, 276.

14. Foreman, *The Five Civilized Tribes*, 182–93; Edmunds, Hoxie, and Salisbury, *The People*, 247. Smithers, in *The Cherokee Diaspora*, makes the same argument for the Cherokees.

15. Edmunds, Hoxie, and Salisbury, *The People*, 245–46; Haveman, *Rivers of Sand*, 279; "Treaty with the Creeks, etc., 1856"; Work, *Seminole Nation*, 9.

16. "Treaty with the Creeks, etc., 1856," 700–4 ("no portion of either" at 700; "secured in" and "all white persons" at 704); Work, *Seminole Nation*, 10–11.

17. Edmunds, Hoxie, and Salisbury, *The People*, 246; Haveman, *Rivers of Sand*, 279, 284–85; Zellar, *African Creeks*, 24. For full-length treatments of the history of African Creeks, see Littlefield, *Africans and Creeks*; Saunt, *Black, White, and Indian*; and Zellar, *African Creeks*.

18. Foreman, *The Five Civilized Tribes*, 184–86; Green, *The Creeks*, 87–89; Zellar, *African Creeks*, 25.

19. Green, *The Creeks*, 88–89; Haveman, *Rivers of Sand*, 280, 282; Zellar, *African Creeks*, 25, 27–28.

20. Foreman, *The Five Civilized Tribes*, 169–70, 173–81, 194–98; Green, *The Creeks*, 88–89; Zellar, *African Creeks*, 28–31.

21. Edmunds, Hoxie, and Salisbury, *The People*, 245; Foreman, *The Five Civilized Tribes*, 206–7, 213–14; Green, *The Creeks*, 89–90; Zellar, *African Creeks*, 26.

22. Saunt, *Black, White, and Indian*, 88–91; Zellar, *African Creeks*, 38–40, 42–43.

23. Edmunds, Hoxie, and Salisbury, *The People*, 269; Green, *The Creeks*, 90; Gibson, *The Chickasaws*, 259–60; Saunt, *Black, White, and Indian*, 90, 92–93.

24. Edmunds, Hoxie, and Salisbury, *The People*, 269; Gibson, *The Chickasaws*, 259–61; Green, *The Creeks*, 90.

25. Edmunds, Hoxie, and Salisbury, *The People*, 269–70; "Treaty with the Creek Nation," July 10, 1861, 291 ("as long as").

26. Edmunds, Hoxie, and Salisbury, *The People*, 270; Green, *The Creeks*, 90–92; Saunt, *Black, White, and Indian*, 95; Zellar, *African Creeks*, 41, 43–45.

27. Edmunds, Hoxie, and Salisbury, *The People*, 270; Green, *The Creeks*, 92; Saunt, *Black, White, and Indian*, 95; Zellar, *African Creeks*, 44–52.

28. Edmunds, Hoxie, and Salisbury, *The People*, 272; Gibson, *The Chickasaws*, 270–73, 279–80; Green, *The Creeks*, 92–93.

29. Gibson, *The Chickasaws*, 276–77; Green, *The Creeks*, 94; Saunt, *Black, White, and Indian*, 112; Zellar, *African Creeks*, 78–81.

30. "Treaty between the United States of America and the Creek Nation of Indians," June 14, 1866, 785–86, 788 ("perpetual peace" at 786; "shall not" at 788); Saunt, *Black, White, and Indian*, 115–16; Zellar, *African Creeks*, 78–81.

31. Edmunds, Hoxie, and Salisbury, *The People*, 274–76; "Treaty between the United States of America and the Creek Nation of Indians," June 14, 1866, 786 ("the west half" and "be forever set apart").

32. "Treaty between the United States of America and the Creek Nation of Indians," June 14, 1866, 786–87.

33. "Treaty between the United States of America and the Creek Nation of Indians," June 14, 1866, 787–88; Zellar, *African Creeks*, 80.

34. Burton, *Indian Territory*, 79–80; Deer and Knapp, "Muscogee Constitutional Jurisprudence," 149–52; Edmunds, Hoxie, and Salisbury, *The People*, 272; Green, *The Creeks*, 94.

35. Burton, *Indian Territory*, 84–85, 92–96; Deer and Knapp, "Muscogee Constitutional Jurisprudence, 151–52; Edmunds, Hoxie, and Salisbury, *The People*, 273, 274; Gibson, *The Chickasaws*, 279–99; Green, *The Creeks*, 96–97; Saunt, *Black, White, and Indian*, 132–48; Zellar, *African Creeks*, 84–113.

36. Edmunds, Hoxie, and Salisbury, *The People*, 277–93, 295–320; Perdue and Green, *North American Indians*, 74–79.

37. Hoxie, *Final Promise*, 10, 14–15.

38. Saunt, *Black, White, and Indian*, 151–53; "An act making appropriations," March 3, 1871.

39. Perdue and Green, *North American Indians*, 89 ("no longer had"); Work, *Seminole Nation*, 13–14.

40. Burton, *Indian Territory*, 109; Gibson, *The Chickasaws*, 283; Work, *Seminole Nation*, 14–15, 17.

41. Burton, *Indian Territory*, 107–11; Gibson, *The Chickasaws*, 284–86; Edmunds, Hoxie, and Salisbury, *The People*, 273–74; Lewis, *Transforming the Appalachian Countryside*, 45–80 ("touch of capital" at 45); Work, *Seminole Nation*, 16.

42. Edmunds, Hoxie, and Salisbury, *The People*, 274; Zellar, *African Creeks*, 113.

43. Burton, *Indian Territory*, 117–21; Deer and Knapp, "Muscogee Constitutional Jurisprudence," 154–58; Gibson, *The Chickasaws*, 286, 288; Zellar, *African Creeks*, 113–14, 119–20.

44. White, "On to Oklahoma," 81–91; Zellar, *African Creeks*, 121.

45. Perdue and Green, *North American Indians*, 89–90; Work, *Seminole Nation*, 20.

46. "An act making appropriations," March 3, 1885, 385 ("another Indian" and "as are all"); Perdue and Green, *North American Indians*, 90; United States Department of Justice Archives, "Major Crimes Act"; Work, *Seminole Nation*, 20–21. The MCA has since been amended numerous times; see chapter 4 of this volume for a brief discussion of the amendments. For a full-length discussion of the *Lone Wolf* case and its repercussions, see Clark, *Lone Wolf v. Hitchcock*.

47. Burton, *Indian Territory*, 203–36; Hoxie, *Final Promise*, 42; Work, *Seminole Nation*, 21 ("a focal point").

48. Edmunds, Hoxie, and Salisbury, *The People*, 325–26; Green, *The Creeks*, 101–2; Hoxie, *Final Promise*, 54–70, 76–77, 189–210; "An act to provide for the allotment of lands," February 8, 1887; Perdue and Green, *North American Indians*, 82–89.

49. Edmunds, Hoxie, and Salisbury, *The People*, 325; Green, *The Creeks*, 102; Hoxie, *Final Promise*, 71, 72–73, 75–76; "An act to provide for the allotment of lands," February 8, 1887; Perdue and Green, *North American Indians*, 90–91; Ringold, "Indian Land Law," 325–26; Work, *Seminole Nation*, 17. The Dawes Act initially stated that only those Indians who had "adopted the habits of civilized life" were to be granted American citizenship; this was later amended in 1901 to include "every Indian in Indian Territory." See "An act to provide for the allotment of lands," February 8, 1887, 390; "An act to amend," March 3, 1901.

50. Hoxie, *Final Promise*, 71 (remarkably "plastic").

51. Gibson, *The Chickasaws*, 300; Green, *The Creeks*, 102; Hoxie, *Final Promise*, 72–73; "An act to provide for the allotment of lands," February 8, 1887, 391; "An act making appropriations," March 3, 1893, 645–46; Work, *Seminole Nation*, 18.

52. Gibson, *The Chickasaws*, 301–2; Green, *The Creeks*, 102; Work, *Seminole Nation*, 30–31, 33; Zellar, *African Creeks*, 195–96, 213–14.

53. Burton, *Indian Territory*, 43–44, 134; Debo, *And Still the Waters Run*, 13, 20; "An act to establish a United States court," March 1, 1889; "An act to ratify and

confirm an agreement," March 1, 1889; "An act to provide a temporary government," May 2, 1890; White, "On to Oklahoma"; Work, *Seminole Nation*, 19–24.

54. Burton, *Indian Territory*, 130–34, 143–70, 202–32; Deer and Knapp, "Muscogee Constitutional Jurisprudence," 160; Work, *Seminole Nation*, 29–35.

55. Burton, *Indian Territory*, 232–35; Deer and Knapp, "Muscogee Constitutional Jurisprudence," 161; Hoxie, *Final Promise*, 150–53; "An act for the protection of the people," June 28, 1898, 497–98; Work, *Seminole Nation*, 36.

56. Debo, *And Still the Waters Run*, 33–34; "An act to ratify and confirm an agreement," March 1, 1901.

57. Debo, *And Still the Waters Run*, 53–58; Deer and Knapp, "Muscogee Constitutional Jurisprudence," 163–64; Edmunds, Hoxie, and Salisbury, *The People*, 358; Green, *The Creeks*, 104–5.

58. Zellar, *African Creeks*, 200–215.

59. "An act for the protection of the people," June 28, 1898, 497–98; Stremlau, *Sustaining the Cherokee Family*, 141–48; Work, *Seminole Nation*, 49, 58–59.

60. Debo, *And Still the Waters Run*, 47, 51; Gibson, *The Chickasaws*, 305–6; Green, *The Creeks*, 105; Saunt, *Black, White, and Indian*, 159–61; Work, *Seminole Nation*, 61; Zellar, *African Creeks*, 200–205, 213–15, 217, 219. The Dawes Act, which applies to all Indian nations, does not mention blood quantum. This method of racial classification was implemented for only the Five Tribes through the Dawes Commission; it was generalized to all Native people with the 1934 Wheeler-Howard Act. For a full-length study of the use of blood quantum among North American Indians, see Ellinghaus, *Blood Will Tell*.

61. Perdue and Green, *North American Indians*, 91; Saunt, *Black, White, and Indian*, 161–62; Work, *Seminole Nation*, 43, 45–46; Zellar, *African Creeks*, 231.

CHAPTER 4

1. Burton, *Indian Territory*, 246–50; Debo, *And Still the Waters Run*, 159–64; Edmunds, Hoxie, and Salisbury, *The People*, 358; Green, *The Creeks*, 106–7.

2. Debo, *And Still the Waters Run*, 133–58; Hoxie, *Final Promise*, 158–59, 186–87 ("Indians on the outskirts" at 187); Perdue and Green, *North American Indians*, 91.

3. Debo, *And Still the Waters Run*, 133–58; Debo, *Road to Disappearance*, 337; Saunt, *Black, White, and Indian*, 164–68; Zellar, *African Creeks*, 221–26.

4. Debo, *Road to Disappearance*, 264, 366, 367; Green, *The Creeks*, 110; Hoxie, *Final Promise*, 159–60; "An act to ratify and confirm a supplemental agreement," June 30, 1902, 501; Perdue and Green, *North American Indians*, 91.

5. Debo, *Road to Disappearance*, 264, 366, 373; Green, *The Creeks*, 111; Hoxie, *Final Promise*, 79; St. Jean, *Remaining Chickasaw*, 56–72.

6. Debo, *Road to Disappearance*, 336, 342, 367; Green, *The Creeks*, 111; Saunt, *Black, White, and Indian*, 163.

7. Hoxie, *Final Promise*, 79; Work, *Seminole Nation*, 58–60.

8. "An act to provide for the final disposition," April 26, 1906, 148 ("in full force"); Work, *Seminole Nation*, 50.

9. "An act to provide for the final disposition," April 26, 1906, 139; Work, *Seminole Nation*, 51.

10. "An act to provide for the final disposition," April 26, 1906, 138, 144–45; Work, *Seminole Nation*, 60–61.

11. Edmunds, Hoxie, and Salisbury, *The People*, 366; "An act to provide for the final disposition," April 26, 1906, 139–40; Debo, *And Still the Waters Run*, 89–91; Work, *Seminole Nation*, 51. The Burke Act, signed a month later in the same year, reiterated and broadened to all Indians the authority of the commissioner of Indian affairs to determine competency and to put into trust the lands of any Native person he pronounced incompetent.

12. "An act to provide for the final disposition," April 26, 1906, 139–40, 141–42, 143–44; Work, *Seminole Nation*, 52.

13. Debo, *And Still the Waters Run*, 79–80, 86–88; Edmunds, Hoxie, and Salisbury, *The People*, 266–67; "An act to provide for the final disposition," April 26, 1906, 141–42, 145; Work, *Seminole Nation*, 53–54.

14. Debo, *And Still the Waters Run*, 81–84, 126–58; Work, *Seminole Nation*, 56–57.

15. Debo, *And Still the Waters Run*, 92–93, 133.

16. Debo, *And Still the Waters Run*, 159–69.

17. Bunn and Bunn, "Constitution of Oklahoma," 123; Bunn and Bunn, "Enabling Act"; Debo, *And Still the Waters Run*, 170, 291–92; Saunt, *Black, White, and Indian*, 194–95.

18. Bunn and Bunn, "Enabling Act"; Work, *Seminole Nation*, 56–57.

19. Debo, *And Still the Waters Run*, 174.

20. Debo, 178–79.

21. Debo, 178–80, 360 ("almost complete control" at 180); Green, *The Creeks*, 111; "An act for the removal of restrictions," May 27, 1908; Ringold, "Indian Land Law," 3330–32; Work, *Seminole Nation*, 63–65; Zellar, *African Creeks*, 254–55.

22. Work, *Seminole Nation*, 57.

23. Debo, *And Still the Waters Run*, 88, 91–125, 196–202 ("a free-for-all" and "unrestricted rivalry" at 88); Green, *The Creeks*, 110–12; Perdue and Green, *North American Indians*, 91–92; Saunt, *Black, White, and Indian*, 161–64; Zellar, *African Creeks*, 220, 234–36, 254–55.

24. Debo, *And Still the Waters Run*, 182–85, 187–88, 233–34, 305–8; Green, *The Creeks*, 111–12; Work, *Seminole Nation*, 65–67; Zellar, *African Creeks*, 255.

25. Debo, *And Still the Waters Run*, 182–83, 187–88, 233–34, 305–17, 357–58; Green, *The Creeks*, 111–12; Work, *Seminole Nation*, 65–70; Zellar, *African Creeks*, 255.

26. Debo, *And Still the Waters Run*, 181, 193–94, 203–29, 305, 318–50 ("the enormous increase" at 181); Work, *Seminole Nation*, 66–74.

27. Debo, *And Still the Waters Run*, 259–60, 295–97; Deer and Knapp, "Muscogee Constitutional Jurisprudence," 164–65; Edmunds, Hoxie, and Salisbury, *The People*, 362–64; Green, *The Creeks*, 114.

28. Green, *The Creeks*, 111 ("to a state").

29. Debo, *And Still the Waters Run*, 126–58, 356–57 ("they don't know" at 128).

30. Saunt, *Black, White, and Indian*, 181–91; Zellar, *African Creeks*, 251–52.

31. Edmunds, Hoxie, and Salisbury, *The People*, 364–65.

32. Edmunds, Hoxie, and Salisbury, 363–65; Perdue and Green, *North American Indians*, 93.

33. Edmunds, Hoxie, and Salisbury, *The People*, 370–72; Green, *The Creeks*, 112–13; Perdue and Green, *North American Indians*, 93; Meriam, *Problem of Indian Administration*.

34. Debo, *And Still the Waters Run*, 353; Edmunds, Hoxie, and Salisbury, *The People*, 374–75; Perdue and Green, *North American Indians*, 94.

35. Debo, *And Still the Waters Run*, 354, 366–68; Edmunds, Hoxie, and Salisbury, *The People*, 375–79; Green, *The Creeks*, 112–13; Perdue and Green, *North American Indians*, 94–95.

36. Debo, *And Still the Waters Run*, 368; Edmunds, Hoxie, and Salisbury, *The People*, 380–82; Green, *The Creeks*, 113; "An act to conserve and develop Indian lands," June 18, 1934; Perdue and Green, *North American Indians*, 95; Work, *Seminole Nation*, 74–76.

37. Debo, *And Still the Waters Run*, 369–74, 376 ("venomously hostile" at 372); Deer and Knapp, "Muscogee Constitutional Jurisprudence," 165; Edmunds, Hoxie, and Salisbury, *The People*, 381–82, 388; Green, *The Creeks*, 113–14; "An act to promote the general welfare of the Indians," June 26, 1936; Perdue and Green, *North American Indians*, 95–97; Work, *Seminole Nation*, 74–76.

38. Debo, *And Still the Waters Run*, 374–78; Edmunds, Hoxie, and Salisbury, *The People*, 388.

39. Deer and Knapp, "Muscogee Constitutional Jurisprudence," 165.

40. Debo, *And Still the Waters Run*, 379–95.

41. Edmunds, Hoxie, and Salisbury, *The People*, 390–91; Hauptman, "Fighting the Nazis"; Perdue and Green, *North American Indians*, 98.

42. Edmunds, Hoxie, and Salisbury, *The People*, 390–95, 398–402; Perdue and Green, *North American Indians*, 98–99. Some dark-skinned Native people from the South were drafted into African American regiments, where they were subjected to the strict segregation of Jim Crow and therefore were absent from the integrated Native and white working and combat spaces.

43. Wilkins and Lomawaima, *Uneven Ground*, 178–79; Work, *Seminole Nation*, 77–83.

44. "An act relative to restrictions," August 4, 1947; Ringold, "Indian Land Laws," 332–33; Wilkins and Lomawaima, *Uneven Ground*, 180, 192, 183, 185; Work, *Seminole Nation*, 79–82. In 2018, Congress amended the Stigler Act and lifted the minimum blood quantum restrictions on inheriting allotments, replacing them with a requirement that an heir be a descendant of someone on the Dawes Rolls. Cleary, "Stigler Act Amendments."

45. Wilkins and Lomawaima, *Uneven Ground*, 206–15; Work, *Seminole Nation*, 79–88.

46. Burton, *Indian Territory*, 217–19, 237–38, 241.

47. Bunn and Bunn, "Enabling Act," 153–54; Burton, *Indian Territory*, 238, 242–43, 251 ("miscellany of" at 238); Federal Judicial Center, "U.S. District Courts."

48. "An act to revise . . . Title 18," 757; Work, *Seminole Nation*, 123–25 ("somewhere along the way" at 125).

49. Canby, *American Indian Law*, 27–28, 59–62, 265–79, 284; Edmunds, Hoxie, and Salisbury, *The People*, 406–15; Perdue and Green, *North American Indians*, 102–3; Wilkins and Lomawaima, *Uneven Ground*, 208–13; Work, *Seminole Nation*, 125–27.

50. Edmunds, Hoxie, and Salisbury, *The People*, 418–19, 436–37; Green, *The Creeks*, 115; "An act to authorize each of the Five Civilized Tribes," October 22, 1970; Perdue and Green, *North American Indians*, 103–4; Work, *Seminole Nation*, 150–54.

51. Robert Miller, personal communication, 2021.

52. Edmunds, Hoxie, and Salisbury, *The People*, 426–34, 436–37; Perdue and Green, *North American Indians*, 105; Work, *Seminole Nation*, 151, 162–68; "An act to provide maximum Indian participation," January 4, 1975.

53. Deer and Knapp, "Muscogee Constitutional Jurisprudence," 168–70; Green, *The Creeks*, 115–16.

54. Deer and Knapp, "Muscogee Constitutional Jurisprudence," 179; Work, *Seminole Nation*, 170–77, 192–93.

55. Edmunds, Hoxie, and Salisbury, *The People*, 444–48; Perdue and Green, *North American Indians*, 108–11.

56. Edmunds, Hoxie, and Salisbury, *The People*, 439–44; Wilkins and Lomawaima, *Uneven Ground*, 227–37; Work, *Seminole Nation*, 178, 188–91, 203–4, 204–28.

CHAPTER 5

1. *United States v. Winans*, 198 U.S. 371, 381 (1905) ("the treaty was").

2. Prucha, *American Indian Treaties*, 446–502; Deloria and DeMallie, *Documents of American Indian Diplomacy*, 3–5.

3. "Treaty with the Delawares, 1778."

4. Prucha, *American Indian Treaties*, 21, 23, 59, 67, 72–73; United States Constitution, art. VI.

5. Prucha *American Indian Treaties*, 212; Miller, "Speaking with Forked Tongues," 552–55; Gov. Lewis Cass to George Graham, July 3, 1817, in Lowrie and Franklin, *American State Papers*, 137.

6. Miller, "Exercising Cultural Self-Determination," 165; Miller, "Speaking with Forked Tongues," 552–55; Harvey, *History of the Shawnee Indians*, 196, 199–200; Lakomaki, *Gathering Together*, 161–62; Warren, *The Shawnees*, 7, 11, 13–14, 29, 49, 57–58.

7. *Washington v. Washington Commercial Passenger Fishing Vessel Association*, 443 U.S. 658, 675 (1979) ("A treaty"); Canby, *American Indian Law*, 119 ("Indian treaties stand"); Prucha, *American Indian Treaties*, 21, 67, 72–73.

8. United States Constitution, art. I (§ 8, cl. 3), art. VI (cl. 2); Miller, "American Indian Influence," 138, 151–54.

9. United States Constitution, art. I (§ 2, cl. 3), amend. XIV (§ 2); "An act to authorize the Secretary of the Interior," June 2, 1924.

10. *Cherokee Nation v. Georgia*, 30 U.S. 1, 16–17 (1831); *Worcester v. Georgia*, 31 U.S. (6 Pet.) 515, 559 (1832) ("The words").

11. Miller, "Treaties," 107, 111–12; *Worcester v. Georgia*, 31 U.S. (6 Pet.) 515, 582 (1832) ("The language used").

12. *Herrera v. Wyoming*, 139 S.Ct. 1686, 1699 (2019) ("Indian treaties"); *Minnesota v. Mille Lacs Band of Chippewa Indians*, 526 U.S. 172, 204 (1999) ("give effect"); *Choctaw Nation v. Oklahoma*, 397 U.S. 620, 630–31 (1970).

13. *United States v. Dion*, 476 U.S. 734, 738–40 (1986); *United States v. Sioux Nation of Indians*, 448 U.S. 371 (1980); *Menominee Tribe of Indians v. United States*, 391 U.S. 404 (1968); *Lone Wolf v. Hitchcock*, 187 U.S. 553, 566 (1903).

14. *Seymour v. Superintendent of Washington State Penitentiary*, 368 U.S. 351 (1962).

15. *Seymour*, 353–57 ("vacated and restored" and "still reserved" at 354).

16. *Mattz v. Arnett*, 412 U.S. 481 (1973).

17. *Mattz*, 494–505 ("not inclined" at 504; "when Congress" at 504–5, quoting *United States v. Celestine*, 215 U.S. 278, 285 [1909]).

18. *DeCoteau v. District County Court for Tenth Judicial District*, 420 U.S. 425 (1975).

19. *DeCoteau*, 449 ("not departing from").

20. *DeCoteau*, 434–37, 441, 445 ("recited and ratified" at 437; "the Indians" at 441; "'the face'" at 445).

21. *DeCoteau*, 444 (citations omitted).

22. *Rosebud Sioux Tribe v. Kneip*, 430 U.S. 584 (1977).

23. *Rosebud Sioux Tribe*, 587–88, 590–603, 605–13 ("clearly evidence" at 587).

24. *Rosebud Sioux Tribe*, 590–93, 603.

25. *Solem v. Bartlett*, 465 U.S. 463, 470 (1984) ("established"); *Cohen's Handbook*, 199. The *Solem* case created the "three-step" inquiry.

26. *Solem*, 470 ("will not be").

27. *Solem*, 470–71 ("Congress clearly" at 470, quoting *Rosebud Sioux Tribe v. Kneip*, 430 U.S. 584, 615 [1977]; "statutory language" at 471 and "[e]xplicit reference" at 470, citing *DeCoteau v. District County Court for Tenth Judicial District*, 420 U.S. 425, 444–45, 447–48 [1975]; "an unconditional commitment" at 470, citing *Seymour v. Superintendent of Washington State Penitentiary*, 368 U.S. 351, 355 [1962]).

28. *Solem*, 470 ("[t]he most probative evidence"), 471 ("explicit language" and "events surrounding").

29. *Solem*, 471 ("contemporaneous understanding" and "particularly the manner").

30. *Solem*, 471 ("a lesser extent" and "who actually moved," citing *Rosebud Sioux Tribe v. Kneip*, 430 U.S. 584, 588n3, 604–5 [1977]; and "the subsequent"); *DeCoteau v. District County Court for Tenth Judicial District*, 420 U.S. 425, 428 (1975).

31. *McGirt v. Oklahoma*, ___U.S.___, 140 S.Ct. 2452, 2468 (2020).

32. *Hagen v. Utah*, 510 U.S. 399, 410–12 (1994) ("traditional approach" at 412).

33. *Hagen*, 410–16 ("all the unallotted lands" at 414).

34. *Hagen*, 416–20.

35. *Hagen*, 420–21.

36. *South Dakota v. Yankton Sioux Tribe, et al.*, 522 U.S. 329, 338, 344 (1998) ("a nearly insurmountable presumption" and "cede, sell" at 338; "cession [and] sum certain" at 344, citing *DeCoteau v. District County Court for Tenth Judicial Circuit*, 420 U.S. 425, 445 [1975]; *Solem v. Bartlett*, 465 U.S. 463, 470 [1984]; *Hagen v. Utah*, 510 U.S. 399, 411 [1994]).

37. *South Dakota*, 351–57 ("The 1894 Act" at 357).

38. *Nebraska v. Parker*, 136 S.Ct. 1072, 1078 (2016).

39. According to Christensen, in "Predicting Supreme Court Behavior," 73–74, Chief Justice Roberts votes for tribes and Native litigants in only 18 percent of the Court's cases, and Justices Thomas and Alito do so in only about 16 percent of the cases. Even two "liberal" justices did not vote for tribes that often: Justice Breyer has voted for tribal positions 39 percent of the time, and Justice Ruth Bader Ginsburg did so 49 percent of the time.

40. *Nebraska v. Parker*, 136 S.Ct. 1072, 1079–80 (2016) ("with the text," "[e]xplicit reference," "the total surrender," "commitment from Congress," "The 1882 Act," and "merely opened" at 1079, quoting *Solem v. Bartlett*, 465 U.S. 463, 470 [1984]; *South Dakota v. Yankton Sioux Tribe, et al.*, 522 U.S. 329, 345 [1998]; *DeCoteau v. District County Court for Tenth Judicial District*, 420 U.S. 425, 448 [1975]).

41. *Nebraska v. Parker*, 136 S.Ct. 1072, 1080 (2016) ("in no way," quoting *Solem v. Bartlett*, 465 U.S. 463, 471 [1984]).

42. *Nebraska*, 1080–81 ("treatment" and "one additional clue" at 1081, quoting *Solem v. Bartlett*, 465 U.S. 463, 471, 472 [1984]).

43. *Nebraska*, 1078, 1081–82 ("After all" at 1082, quoting *South Dakota v. Yankton Sioux Tribe, et al.*, 522 U.S. 329, 356 [1998]).

44. *Nebraska*, 1075, 1081 ("rel[y] solely" at 1081, citing *South Dakota v. Yankton Sioux Tribe, et al.*, 522 U.S. 329, 356 [1998]).

45. Mann, "Justices Call for Reargument."

46. *Patrick Dwayne Murphy v. State of Oklahoma*, 47 P.3d 876, 879 (Okla. Crim. App. 2002); *post-conviction relief granted in part, denied in part* in *Patrick Dwayne Murphy v. State of Oklahoma*, 124 P.3d 1198 (Okla. Crim. App. 2005).

47. *Patrick Dwayne Murphy v. Terry Royal*, 875 F.3d 896, 905–11 (10th Cir. 2017), *cert. granted, Max Julian Wright v. United States*, 138 S.Ct. 2026 (2018), *argued sub nom. Mike Carpenter v. Patrick Dwayne Murphy*, 139 S.Ct. 626, No. 17-1107 (U.S. Nov. 27, 2018), *restored to calendar, Mike Carpenter v. Patrick Dwayne Murphy*, No. 17-1107 (U.S. June 27, 2019).

48. 18 U.S.C. § 1151(c); *Patrick Dwayne Murphy v. State of Oklahoma*, 124 P.3d 1198, 1199–1200, 1202 (Okla. Crim. App. 2005).

49. *Patrick Dwayne Murphy v. State of Oklahoma*, 124 P.3d 1198, 1200, 1207–8 (Okla. Crim. App. 2005) ("refuse[d]" at 1208); *Patrick Dwayne Murphy v. Terry Royal*, 875 F.3d 896, 909 (10th Cir. 2017).

50. *Patrick Dwayne Murphy v. Marty Sirmons*, 497 F.Supp.2d 1257, 1286–92 (E.D. Okla. 2007).

51. *Patrick Dwayne Murphy v. Terry Royal*, 875 F.3d 896, 911 (10th Cir. 2017), *cert. granted, Max Julian Wright v. United States*, 138 S.Ct. 2026 (2018), *argued sub nom. Mike Carpenter v. Patrick Dwayne Murphy*, 139 S.Ct. 626, No. 17-1107 (U.S. November 27, 2018), *restored to calendar, Mike Carpenter v. Patrick Dwayne Murphy*, No. 17-1107 (U.S. June 27, 2019).

52. *Patrick Dwayne Murphy v. Terry Royal*, 875 F.3d 896, 939–48 (10th Cir. 2017).

53. "An act to confer jurisdiction," August 15, 1953; *Cohen's Handbook*, 537–39.

54. Quoted in Strickland, *The Indians*, 76.

55. Pipestem and Rice, "Mythology of the Oklahoma Indians," 278n48; *Opinion of Oklahoma Attorney General*, No. 79-216 (Dec. 31, 1979).

56. *Patrick Dwayne Murphy v. Terry Royal*, 875 F.3d 896, 966–68 (10th Cir. 2017) ("I write" at 966; "In sum" at 968); Bubar, "Who Owns Oklahoma?"; Epps, "Who Owns Oklahoma?"

57. Brief for Petitioner Oklahoma, *Mike Carpenter v. Patrick Dwayne Murphy*, 139 S.Ct. 626, No. 17-1107 (July 23, 2018); Brief for Petitioner, *Tommy Sharp v.*

Patrick Dwayne Murphy, 140 S.Ct. 2412, No. 17-1107 (U.S. July 9, 2020), 2018 WL 3572365 at 2.

58. Brief for Petitioner Oklahoma, *Mike Carpenter v. Patrick Dwayne Murphy*, No. 17-1107 (July 23, 2018); Brief for Petitioner, *Tommy Sharp v. Patrick Dwayne Murphy*, 140 S.Ct. 2412, No. 17-1107 (U.S. July 9, 2020), 2018 WL 3572365 at 3–4; Transcript of Oral Argument, *Carpenter v. Murphy*, No. 14-1406, 23, 75–77 (U.S. argued Nov. 27, 2018).

59. Transcript of Oral Argument, *Carpenter v. Murphy*, No. 14-1406, 2, 75–77 (U.S. argued Nov. 27, 2018); Rubin, "Oklahoma Tribal Border Battle."

60. Transcript of Oral Argument, *Carpenter v. Murphy*, No. 14-1406, 2, 75–77 (U.S. argued Nov. 27, 2018); Rubin, "Oklahoma Tribal Border Battle."

61. Sturtevant, "Is Oklahoma Indian Country?"; Mann, "Argument Analysis."

62. *City of Sherrill v. Oneida Indian Nation*, 544 U.S. 197 (2005).

63. Order Directing the Parties to File Supplemental Briefs, *Mike Carpenter v. Patrick Wayne Murphy*, 139 S.Ct. 626 (2018); Rubin, "Oklahoma Tribal Border Battle"; Mann, "Justices Call for Reargument."

64. *Tommy Sharp v. Patrick Dwayne Murphy*, No. 17-1107 (U.S. July 9, 2020). The *per curiam* decision reads, "The judgment of the United States Court of Appeals for the Tenth Circuit is affirmed for the reasons stated in *McGirt* v. *Oklahoma, ante*, p. ___ [*sic*]."

Chapter 6

1. *McGirt v. Oklahoma*, ___U.S.___, 140 S.Ct. 2452, 2482 (2020).

2. *McGirt*, 2459, 2482, 2501; *McGirt v. Oklahoma*, No. PC-2018-1057, *order issued* (Okla. Crim. App. Feb. 25, 2019).

3. *McGirt v. Oklahoma*, ___U.S.___, 140 S.Ct. 2452, 2459 (2020) ("whether the land").

4. Brief for Oklahoma, *Jimcy McGirt, Petitioner v. State of Oklahoma, Respondent*, No. 18-9526, 43–45 (March 13, 2020); Transcript of Oral Argument, *Jimcy McGirt v. Oklahoma*, No. 18-9526, 4, 12, 19, 23–24, 54, 62, 87–88 (May 11, 2020).

5. Brief for Oklahoma, *Jimcy McGirt, Petitioner v. State of Oklahoma, Respondent*, No. 18-9526 (March 13, 2020); Transcript of Oral Argument, *Jimcy McGirt v. Oklahoma*, No. 18-9526, 4, 12, 19, 23–24, 54, 62, 87–88 (May 11, 2020).

6. *McGirt v. Oklahoma*, ___U.S.___, 140 S.Ct. 2452, 2459, 2453–66, 2482 (2020) ("Because Congress" at 2482; "On the far end" at 2459).

7. *Talton v. Mayes*, 163 U.S. 376 (1896); *Worcester v. Georgia*, 31 U.S. (6 Pet.) 515, 561 (1832); Hedden-Nicely and Leeds, "Familiar Crossroads"; Berger, "*McGirt v. Oklahoma*"; Miller, "Tribal, Federal, and State Laws," 164–65; Work, *Seminole Nation*, 55–57; Oklahoma Constitution, art. 1, § 3 (1907); "An act to enable the people of Oklahoma," June 16, 1906.

8. 18 U.S.C. § 1153(a); *McGirt v. Oklahoma*, ___U.S.___, 140 S.Ct. 2452, 2459–60, 2474 (2020) ("State courts," "key question," and "the land" at 2474).

9. *McGirt v. Oklahoma*, ___U.S.___, 140 S.Ct. 2452, 2459–61 (2020) ("Congress established" at 2460; "guarantied" and "establish[ed] boundary lines" at 2461, quoting preamble of "Treaty with the Creeks, 1833," February 14, 1833, 418).

10. *McGirt v. Oklahoma*, ___U.S.___, 140 S.Ct. 2452, 2461–62 (2020) ("no question" at 2462). A number of references to a Creek reservation are cited at 2461, including "reduced Creek reservation," quoting "Treaty between the United States of America and the Creek Nation of Indians," June 14, 1866, 788 [art. IX]; "Creek Reservation," quoting "Treaty between the United States of America and the Cherokee Nation of Indians," July 19, 1866, 800 [art. IV], and "To authorize the Secretary of the Interior to negotiate with the Creek Indians," March 3, 1873; and "the Creek Reservation," quoting "An act to ratify and confirm agreements with the Sac and Fox," February 13, 1891, 750 [art. I]).

11. *McGirt v. Oklahoma*, ___U.S.___, 140 S.Ct. 2452, 2461–63 (2020) ("the Acts of Congress" at 2461; "that Congress" at 2463); *Solem v. Bartlett*, 465 U.S. 463, 470 (1984) ("only Congress"); *Accord Hagen v. Utah*, 510 U.S. 399, 411–12 (1994); *Mattz v. Arnett*, 412 U.S. 481, 504n22 (1973).

12. "An act to provide for the allotment of lands," February 8, 1887 (codified at 25 U.S.C. §§ 331–34, 339, 341–42, 348–49, 354, 381); *Cohen's Handbook*, 71–79; Royster, "Legacy of Allotment," 1; Miller, "Tribal, Federal, and State Laws."

13. *Mattz v. Arnett*, 412 U.S. 481, 497 (1973) ("allotment . . . is"); *Seymour v. Superintendent of Washington State Penitentiary*, 368 U.S. 351 (1962), 356–57 ("The Act did no more than open the way for non-Indian settlers to own land on the reservation" at 356).

14. *McGirt v. Oklahoma*, ___U.S.___, 140 S.Ct. 2452, 2463 (2020) ("charged" and "'would not'").

15. *McGirt*, 2463, 2464, 2484n2, 2487 ("turned [its] attention" at 2463, citing "An act making appropriations," March 3, 1893, 645–46; "Missing in all this" at 2464, quoting "Report of Commission to the Five Civilized Tribes," 7; "the dissent fails" at 2464n2; "No one here" at 2487).

16. *McGirt*, 2465–68 ("Despite these" at 2466, quoting "An act to provide for the final disposition," April 26, 1906, 148; "in all this history" at 2468).

17. *McGirt*, 2459, 2482.

18. *McGirt*, 2468–81 ("can only be" and "The only role" at 2469; "acknowledge[d] that" at 2470n9, citing *Rosebud Sioux Tribe v. Kneip*, 430 U.S. 584, 588n4 [1977]; *South Dakota v. Yankton Sioux Tribe, et al.*, 522 U.S. 329, 343 [1998]; "Oklahoma does not point" at 2468, quoting and citing *Nebraska v. Parker*, 136 S.Ct. 1072, 1082 [2016], and *DeCoteau v. District County Court for Tenth Judicial District*, 420 U.S. 425, 447 [1975]).

19. *McGirt*, 2468.

20. Gorsuch, "Why Originalism Is the Best Approach"; Gorsuch, *A Republic*; McGinnis, "Which Justices Are Originalists?"

21. *McGirt v. Oklahoma*, ___U.S.___, 140 S.Ct. 2452, 2469 (2020) ("restate[d] the point," "[t]here is no need," and "[t]he only role").

22. *McGirt*, 2478–79 ("In the end" and "[i]f we dared" at 2478; "could unsettle" and "admittedly speculative" at 2479).

23. *McGirt*, 2480 ("dire warnings" and "the magnitude").

24. *McGirt*, 2480, 2481–82 ("By suggesting" and "Yet again" at 2480; "Congress remains free" at 2481).

25. *McGirt*, 2481.

26. *McGirt*, 2481–82 ("[i]n reaching" at 2481; "[M]any of the arguments" at 2482).

27. *McGirt*, 2474.

28. *Solem v. Bartlett*, 465 U.S. 463, 471–72 (1984) ("the . . . reservation" at 471).

29. *McGirt v. Oklahoma*, ___U.S.___, 140 S.Ct. 2452, 2486–87 (2020) ("announce[d]" at 2487; "[did] not even" at 2486).

30. *McGirt*, 2487 ("new approach" and "our traditional approach," quoting *Hagen v. Utah*, 510 U.S. 399, 412 [1994]).

31. *Solem v. Bartlett*, 465 U.S. 463, 470 (1984) ("almost insurmountable presumption"); compare with *McGirt v. Oklahoma*, ___U.S.___, 140 S.Ct. 2452, 2468 (2020).

32. *McGirt*, 2482, 2489 ("relentless series of statutes" at 2489).

33. *McGirt*, 2494–98 ("[t]he available evidence" at 2494).

34. "An act to enable the people of Oklahoma," June 16, 1906, 267–69 (§§ 1–3), 271–73 (§§ 6 and 8).

35. Oklahoma Constitution, art. 1 (§ 3).

36. *McGirt v. Oklahoma*, ___U.S.___, 140 S.Ct. 2452, 2466 (2020) ("Congress expressly recognized," quoting "An act to provide for the final disposition," April 26, 1906, 148).

37. *McGirt*, 2498–2500 ("a century" at 2500).

38. *McGirt*, 2482, 2501 ("the State's ability" at 2501; "decades" and "the Court" at 2482).

39. *McGirt*, 2481–82, 2501, 2501n10, 2502 ("[b]eyond the criminal law" at 2501; "significant uncertainty" and "the State's continuing authority" at 2482; "dire warnings" at 2481).

40. *McGirt*, 2484 ("'determination'" and "rapidly transfor[m]"); Kirsch, "The 3 Richest Americans."

41. *McGirt v. Oklahoma*, ___U.S.___, 140 S.Ct. 2452, 2484 (2020) ("millions," "had no," and "meaningful access").

42. Miller, "Tribal, Federal, and State Laws," 165; Debo, *The Five Civilized Tribes*, 1. Brief of Amici Curiae Historians, Legal Scholars, and Cher-

okee Nation in Support of Petitioner, *Jimcy McGirt, Petitioner v. Oklahoma, Respondent*, No. 18-9526, 9–15, 23–31 (S.Ct. Feb. 11, 2020); Strickland, *The Indians*, 32–38, 40–46, 52–53, 72–73, 82, 113; Debo, *And Still the Waters Run*, viii, 48–51, 86–87, 94–98, 104–6, 117–18, 181, 196–97, 200, 233–34, 313; *McGirt v. Oklahoma*, ___U.S.___, 140 S.Ct. 2452, 2484 (2020); Grann, *Killers of the Flower Moon*; Bonnin, Fabens, and Sniffen, *Oklahoma's Poor Rich Indians*; "Charges against United States Court Officials in Indian Territory," H.R. Doc. No. 528, 58th Cong., 2d Sess. (Feb. 11, 1904). Prucha, in *The Great Father*, 411, 736–38, 744, 901–2, 903–6, cites 1912, 1914, 1923, 1924, 1925, and 1926 reports to the commissioner of Indian affairs to characterize this era. The reports, for example, describe "throngs of whites" invading Indian Territory, and state that the U.S. proposed "civilization" for Indians while Americans were stealing their lands and assets. They also cite "illegal invasions of the Indian Territory." Prucha, again citing the reports, states that allotment led to charges of graft being reported to Congress, that "investigators did indeed turn up questionable dealings," that "the scandal of the probate courts" resulted in the exploitation of "defenseless" minors, and that guardians and the courts cheating Indian wards was widely researched in numerous reports, including the 1926 Board of Indian Commissioners report on "evils in the work of the probate courts" as well as in a 1924 and 1925 report that Indians were "shamelessly and openly robbed in a scientific and ruthless manner." A 1923 federal report showed outrageous guardian and attorneys' fees and court costs.

43. *McGirt v. Oklahoma*, ___U.S.___, 140 S.Ct. 2452, 2473 (2020) ("that the loss," citing Debo, *And Still the Waters Run*, 86–87, 104–6, 117–18, 233–34); Brief of Amici Curiae Historians, Legal Scholars, and Cherokee Nation in Support of Petitioner, *Jimcy McGirt, Petitioner v. Oklahoma, Respondent*, No. 18-9526, 26–30 [S.Ct. Feb. 11, 2020]).

44. *McGirt v. Oklahoma*, ___U.S.___, 140 S.Ct. 2452, 2474, 2481–82 (2020) ("[n]one of" at 2474; "To hold otherwise" at 2482).

45. Prucha, *The Great Father*, 272–79 ("showed tremendous resilience" at 272); Debo, *The Five Civilized Tribes*, 1.

46. Federal Judicial Center, "Gorsuch, Neil M."; Wikipedia, s.v. "Neil Gorsuch," last modified March 10, 2022, 12:07, https://en.wikipedia.org/wiki /Neil_Gorsuch.

47. Duignan, "Neil Gorsuch."

48. Dossett, "Justice Gorsuch," 8–10; Porter, "Judge Neil Gorsuch."

49. Christensen, "Predicting Supreme Court Behavior," 73, 111nn187, 188; Wikipedia, s.v. "Neil Gorsuch."

50. *Washington State Dept. of Licensing v. Cougar Den, Inc.*, ___U.S.___, 139 S.Ct. 1000, 1021 (2019) (Gorsuch, J., concurring).

51. Christensen, "Predicting Supreme Court Behavior," 73–74, 113; Fletcher, "Justice Ginsburg's Indian Law Record."

52. *City of Sherrill v. Oneida Indian Nation,* 544 U.S. 197, 202–4, 211, 214 (2005) ("We . . . hold" at 214).

53. *City of Sherrill,* 200, 202, 214–21, 219–20 ("settled expectations" at 200; "justifiable expectations" at 215); *Rosebud Sioux Tribe v. Kneip,* 430 U.S. 584, 604 (1977); *Hagen v. Utah,* 510 U.S. 399, 421 (1994).

54. Transcript of Oral Argument, *Carpenter v. Murphy,* No. 14-1406, 12–13 (U.S. argued Nov. 27, 2018); Mann, "Argument Analysis."

55. *McGirt v. Oklahoma,* 140 S. Ct. 2452, 2481 (2020) ("reliance interests").

CHAPTER 7

1. Office of the Governor, "Governor Stitt Releases Statement"; Snyder, "Gov. Stitt"; Fox 25 Staff, "McGirt Ruling"; Standard & Poor's Financial Services, "Bulletin"; Office of the Governor, "Oklahoma Commission"; Hilleary, "Native Americans."

2. Jones, "State Lawmakers"; Casteel, "State Files More Petitions"; Scarcella, "Paul, Weiss"; *Oklahoma v. Hathcoat,* No. 21-253, Pet. Cert., 2021 WL 3726207 (Aug. 16, 2021); Westney, "Justices Sink Many Okla. Petitions."

3. Hoskin, "On August 30"; Chickasaw Nation Media Relations Office, "Chickasaw Nation."

4. Miller, "Tribal, Federal, and State Laws," 149–50; Trigger, *Handbook,* 83, 85, 202–6, 344–47, 384, 430; Strickland, *Fire and the Spirits,* 10–39, 103–5, 168–74; Debo, *History of the Indians,* 13–14; Llewellyn and Hoebel, *The Cheyenne Way,* 26–28, 132–46, 157–71, 181–86, 212–38, 310–24.

5. 18 U.S.C. § 1153; "An act to regulate trade and intercourse," July 22, 1790; "An act to provide for the punishment of crimes and offences," March 3, 1817; 18 U.S.C. § 1152; Canby, *American Indian Law,* 202–3; *Cohen's Handbook,* 736–52.

6. *Ex parte Crow Dog,* 109 U.S. 556 (1883); 25 U.S.C. § 1302(a)(7)(B); *Oliphant v. Suquamish Indian Tribe,* 435 U.S. 191, 208n17, 210 (1978); Violence Against Women Act, 108 Stat. 1796 (1994); Violence Against Women Reauthorization Act of 2013, 127 Stat. 54, 120 (2013). On tribal domestic violence, see 25 U.S.C. § 1304.

7. 18 U.S.C. § 13; *Williams v. United States,* 327 U.S. 711, 712, 718 (1946); *United States v. Thunder Hawk,* 127 F.3d 705 (8th Cir. 1997); *Cohen's Handbook,* 759–62; Canby, *American Indian Law,* 170–76, 179–80.

8. *Washington v. Confederated Tribes of Colville Indian Reservation,* 447 U.S. 134, 154 (1980) ("tribal sovereignty"); *United States v. McBratney,* 104 U.S. 621 (1881); *Oklahoma v. Castro-Huerta,* __U.S.__, No. 21-429, 2022 WL 2334307 (June 29, 2022). The oral argument was held April 27, 2022.

9. In Fox 25 Staff, "McGirt Ruling," Governor Stitt claimed that seventy-six thousand Oklahoma convictions are being questioned, and that people are

being let out of prison. Hilleary, "Native Americans"; Nagle and Herrera, "Where Is Oklahoma Getting Its Numbers?"

10. Tomlinson, "Courts 'in Limbo.'"

11. United States Department of Justice, "Eastern District of Oklahoma Federal Grand Jury"; Merrefield, "McGirt v. Oklahoma"; Gowen and Barnes, "'Complete, Dysfunctional Chaos'"; General Order No. 20-29 (Nov. 5, 2020); Smoot, "Commissioners OK Federal Use."

12. Gowen and Barnes, "'Complete, Dysfunctional Chaos'"; Killman, "McGirt Decision"; Smoot, "Commissioners OK Federal Use"; General Order No. 20-29 (Nov. 5, 2020); Raymond, "U.S. Judiciary."

13. Hoskin, "Chief Chat"; Leeds et al., "Policing in Indian Country"; Holloway, "Muscogee Creek Nation." See also remarks by Chrissi Ross Nimmo in Leeds et al., "Policing in Indian Country."

14. *McGirt v. Oklahoma*, ___U.S.___, 140 S.Ct. 2452, 2480–82 (2020); Berry, "13 Chickasha Police Officers"; Cluiss, "Johnston County Deputy Sheriffs."

15. Hedden-Nicely and Leeds, "Familiar Crossroads," 344–47; Casteel, "Biden Administration."

16. Hoskin, "Chief Chat"; Leeds et al., "Policing in Indian Country"; Weaver, "Muscogee (Creek) Nation"; Holloway, "Muscogee Creek Nation."

17. Leeds et al., "Policing in Indian Country"; Gowen and Barnes, "'Complete, Dysfunctional Chaos.'"

18. *United States v. Cooley*, ___U.S.___, 141 S.Ct. 1638, 1645 (2021).

19. Morrow, "Bridging the Jurisdictional Void."

20. *United States v. Cooley*, ___U.S.___, 141 S.Ct. 1638, 1645 (2021); Tomlinson, "Courts 'in Limbo'"; Agoyo, "'Shame on You.'"

21. *Bosse v. Oklahoma*, 484 P.3d 286, 291–92 (Okla. Crim. App. 2021); *United States v. Prentiss*, 273 F.3d 1277, 1280, 1282–83 (10th Cir. 2001); Gowen and Barnes, "'Complete, Dysfunctional Chaos.'"

22. *Seymour v. Superintendent of Washington State Penitentiary*, 368 U.S. 351, 358 (1962); Gowen and Barnes, "'Complete, Dysfunctional Chaos.'"

23. *Washington v. Confederated Tribes of Colville Indian Reservation*, 447 U.S. 134, 152–54 (1980); *Iowa Mutual Insurance Company v. LaPlante*, 480 U.S. 9, 18 (1987) ("presumptively lies").

24. United States Constitution, art. I (§ 8, cl. 3), art. VI; *Worcester v. Georgia*, 31 U.S. (6 Pet.) 515, 556–57 (1832) ("manifestly consider[s]" at 557); *Williams v. Lee*, 358 U.S. 217, 220–22 (1959) ("to make their own laws" at 220); *Santa Clara Pueblo v. Martinez*, 436 U.S. 49, 55–56, 66 (1978) ("to enforce that law" at 56); *United States v. Mazurie*, 419 U.S. 544, 557 (1975) ("attributes of sovereignty"); *Talton v. Mayes*, 163 U.S. 376, 384 (1896); *McClanahan v. Arizona State Tax Commission*, 411 U.S. 164, 170–71 (1973); *New Mexico v. Mescalero Apache Tribe*, 462 U.S. 324, 334 (1983).

25. *Merrion v. Jicarilla Apache Tribe*, 455 U.S. 130, 149 (1982); *Washington v. Confederated Tribes of Colville Indian Reservation*, 447 U.S. 134, 152–54 (1980).

26. *Worcester v. Georgia*, 31 U.S. (6 Pet.) 515, 561 (1832); *McClanahan v. Arizona State Tax Commission*, 411 U.S. 164, 170–71 (1973) ("State laws generally" at 170); *New Mexico v. Mescalero Apache Tribe*, 462 U.S. 324, 334 (1983) ("[s]tate jurisdiction"); *Williams v. Lee*, 358 U.S. 217, 220, 223 (1959) ("consistently guarded" at 223).

27. American Land Title Association, "U.S. Supreme Court Tribal Ruling."

28. American Land Title Association; Canby, *American Indian Law*, 81–83; *Cohen's Handbook*, 239–45; *Montana v. United States*, 450 U.S. 544, 565 (1981).

29. *Montana*, 565; *Knighton v. Cedarville Rancheria*, 922 F.3d 892 (9th Cir. 2019); *Water Wheel Camp Recreational Area, Inc. v. LaRance*, 642 F.3d 802, 818–19 (9th Cir. 2011); *First Specialty Ins. v. Confederated Tribes of the Grand Ronde Comm.*, Case A-05-09-001 (Grand Ronde Ct. App. 2006).

30. *Montana v. United States*, 450 U.S. 544, 566 (1981) ("threatens"); *United States v. Cooley*, ___U.S.___, 141 S.Ct. 1638, 1643 (2021); *Knighton v. Cedarville Rancheria*, 922 F.3d 892 (9th Cir. 2019); *Attorney's Process, Inc. v. Sac & Fox Tribe*, 609 F.3d 927 (8th Cir. 2010); *Skokomish Indian Tribe v. Mosbarger*, 7 NICS App. 90 (Skokomish Ct. App. 2006).

31. Leeds and Beard, "Wealth of Sovereign Choices," 468; Buzzard, Haunschild, and McBride, "*McGirt v. Oklahoma*."

32. *Atkinson Trading Company v. Shirley*, 532 U.S. 645, 653–54 (2001); *Merrion v. Jicarilla Apache Tribe*, 455 U.S. 130, 149 (1982); *Washington v. Confederated Tribes of Colville Indian Reservation*, 447 U.S. 134 (1980); Leeds and Beard, "Wealth of Sovereign Choices"; Jensen, "Taxation and Doing Business." The Navajo Nation had no jurisdiction to tax non-Indian hotel guests on fee lands within the reservation.

33. Oklahoma Tax Commission, "Report of Potential Impact," 2; Forman, "Some Oklahomans."

34. *Oklahoma Tax Commission v. Citizen Band, Potawatomi Indian Tribe of Oklahoma*, 498 U.S. 505 (1991); *Oklahoma Tax Commission v. Sac and Fox Nation*, 508 U.S. 114 (1993); *Oklahoma Tax Commission v. Chickasaw Nation*, 515 U.S. 450 (1995).

35. *Cass County v. Leech Lake Band of Chippewa Indians*, 524 U.S. 103, 113 (1998); *County of Yakima v. Confederated Tribes and Bands of the Yakima Nation*, 502 U.S. 251, 270 (1992); *Washington v. Confederated Tribes of Colville Indian Reservation*, 447 U.S. 134 (1980); *Moe v. Confederated Salish and Kootenai Tribes*, 425 U.S. 463, 480–81 (1976).

36. 25 U.S.C. § 1901 *et seq.* See also remarks by Chrissi Ross Nimmo in Leeds et al., "Policing in Indian Country."

37. 25 U.S.C. § 1911(a); *Mississippi Band of Choctaw Indians v. Holyfield*, 490 U.S. 30, 53–54 (1989).

38. Herrera, "Attorney General."

39. University of Oklahoma College of Law professor emeritus Drew Kershen, quoted in Crum, "Professor: U.S. Supreme Court's Ruling"; personal communication, Rhett Larson, July 6, 2021.

40. *Winters v. United States*, 207 U.S. 564, 576–77 (1908); *Arizona v. California*, 373 U.S. 546 (1963).

41. "State of Oklahoma . . . Water Settlement," 12–18, 60–74. This is also known as the WIIN Act: Choctaw Nation of Oklahoma and the Chickasaw Nation Water Settlement, PL 114-322, S.612—114th Congress (2015–2016); Mills, "McGirt Policy Briefs," 26–27.

42. Canby, *American Indian Law*, 505–8; *United States v. Powers*, 305 U.S. 527 (1939); *United States v. Ahtanum Irrigation District*, 235 F.2d 321, 342 (9th Cir. 1956); *Colville Confederated Tribes v. Boyd Walton, Jr.*, 647 F.2d 42 (9th Cir. 1981).

43. *Wyoming v. United States*, 492 U.S. 406 (1989), affirming by a 4–4 vote *State v. Owl Creek Irrigation District Members*, 753 P.2d 76, 99–100 (Wyo. 1988), *contra Agua Caliente Band v. Coachella Valley Water Dist.*, 849 F.3d 1262, 1271 (9th Cir. 2017), *cert. denied*, 138 S.Ct. 464 (2017).

44. *Choctaw Nation v. Oklahoma*, 397 U.S. 620, 628–31 (1970); Mills, "McGirt Policy Briefs," 25–26; *Cohen's Handbook*, 1018–25.

45. Oklahoma Secretary of State, "Hunting and Fishing Compact between the State of Oklahoma and the Cherokee Nation," art. 1; Oklahoma Secretary of State, "Hunting and Fishing Compact between the State of Oklahoma and the Choctaw Nation," art. II(1)(a)n1; Mills, "McGirt Policy Briefs," 19–20.

46. Casteel, "Seminole Nation's Attempt"; Hoberock and Krehbiel, "Oklahoma Conservative Group"; Wayne et al., "Implications for the Energy Industry."

47. "An act relative to restrictions," August 4, 1947, 734; Mills, "McGirt Policy Briefs," 11–12, 14; Work, *Seminole Nation*, 79–86.

48. "An act relative to restrictions," August 4, 1947, 734; 25 C.F.R. Part 213 (2020); Mills, "McGirt Policy Briefs," 11–12. The Stigler Act amendments of 2018 continue oil and gas leases as valid for Indian landowners of less than one-half blood quantum without state court approval. See Cleary, "Stigler Act Amendments."

49. Department of the Interior, "Loss of State Jurisdiction."

50. Department of the Interior; 30 U.S.C. § 1291(9); Tomlinson, "Federal Notice"; Laco, "Oklahoma Suing."

51. 25 U.S.C. §§ 3001–13; 18 U.S.C. § 1170; *Cohen's Handbook*, 1271–85.

52. 16 U.S.C. § 470bb(4) states, "'Indian lands' means lands of Indian tribes or Indian individuals, which are either held in trust by the United States or subject to a restriction against alienation imposed by the United States." *Cohen's Handbook*, 1285–88.

53. 54 U.S.C. §§ 300101(6), 300319(1), 302701–2; *Cohen's Handbook*, 1288–1300; Miller, "Consultation or Consent," 52–53; Fitzpatrick, "Potential Land and Natural Resources Policy."

54. Miller, "Consultation or Consent," 50–62; *Pit River Tribe v. United States Forest Service*, 469 F.3d 768 (9th Cir. 2006) (federal agencies violated the NHPA consultation requirements by not consulting with tribes over historic sites before extending geothermal leases).

55. *Western Watersheds Project, et al. v. Bureau of Land Management of the U.S. Department of the Interior, et al.*, No. 3:21-cv-00103-MMD-CLB, 6–8 (D. Nevada July 28, 2021).

56. 25 U.S.C. §§ 450–58hh; *Reed v. Salazar*, 744 F.Supp.2d 90 (D. D.C. 2010); Confederated Salish and Kootenai Tribes, "Bison Range Restoration"; *Cohen's Handbook*, § 22.02.

57. Investopedia, s.v. "Administrative Law," by Will Kenton, last modified July 30, 2021, https://www.investopedia.com/terms/a/administrative-law.asp; Wikipedia, s.v. "Regulatory Law," last modified February 3, 2022, https://en.wikipedia.org/wiki/Regulatory_law; *Bryan v. Itasca County*, 426 U.S. 373, 385, 388–90 (1976); *California v. Cabazon Band of Mission Indians*, 480 U.S. 202, 208 (1987); *Segundo v. Rancho Mirage*, 813 F2d 1387, 1392–93 (9th Cir. 1987); *Santa Rosa Band of Indians v. Kings County*, 532 F.2d 655, 667 (9th Cir. 1975); *Bugenig v. Hoopa Valley Tribe*, 5 NICS App. 37, 49 (Hoopa Ct. App. 1998), *aff'd en banc*, *Bugenig v. Hoopa Valley Tribe*, 266 F.3d 1201 (9th Cir. 2001), *cert. denied*, *T.S. v. Independent School District No. 54, Stroud, Oklahoma*, 535 U.S. 927 (2002).

58. *Brendale v. Confederated Tribes and Bands of Yakima Indian Nation*, 492 U.S. 408, 433 (1989) ("Zoning is").

59. *Brendale*, 447–48.

60. *Big Horn County Electric Cooperative v. Adams*, 219 F.3d 944 (9th Cir. 2000); *Big Horn County Electric Cooperative v. Alden Big Man*, 2021 WL 754143 (D. Montana Feb. 26, 2021).

61. *Application of Otter Tail Power Co.*, 451 N.W.2d 95, 106–7 (North Dakota 1990); *North Central Electric Cooperative v. North Dakota Public Service Commission*, 837 N.W.2d 138 (D. North Dakota 2013); *Devils Lake Sioux Indian Tribe v. North Dakota Public Service Commission*, 896 F. Supp. 955, 961 (D. North Dakota 1995).

62. On implications for the Clean Air Act, see *Arizona Public Service Commission v. Environmental Protection Agency*, 211 F.3d 1280 (D.C. Cir. 2000). On implications for the Clean Water Act, see *Montana v. United States EPA*, 137 F.3d 1135, 1140–41 (9th Cir. 1998), and *City of Albuquerque v. Browner*, 97 F.3d 415, 423–24 (10th Cir. 1996).

63. "An act to authorize funds for Federal-aid highways," August 10, 2005, 1937 (§ 10211(a) and (b)); Nolan, "Midnight Rider."

64. Murphy, "EPA Grants Stitt Request"; "EPA Proposes to Withdraw."

65. *Williams v. Lee*, 358 U.S. 217, 223 (1959) ("would infringe"); *Water Wheel Camp Recreational Area, Inc. v. LaRance*, 642 F.3d 802, 818–19 (9th Cir. 2011); *Cohen's Handbook*, 597–607.

66. *Williams v. Lee*, 358 U.S. 217, 220 (1959); *National Farmers Union Insurance Cos. v. Crow Tribe of Indians*, 471 U.S. 845, 856 n21 (1985).

67. *Strate v. A-1 Contractors*, 520 U.S. 438, 456–59 and n14 (1997).

68. *Nevada, et al. v. Hicks, et al.*, 533 U.S. 353, 367 (2001) ("Tribal courts"); *Plains Commerce Bank v. Long Family Land & Cattle Co.*, 554 U.S. 316, 330–32, 336–41 (2008).

69. Oklahoma Statutes, Title 12, § 728 (1992); Muscogee (Creek) Nation Code Annotated, Title 27, § 7-101.

70. *McGirt v. Oklahoma*, ___U.S.___, 140 S.Ct. 2452, 2480–81 (2020); Conference of Western Attorneys General, *American Indian Law Deskbook*, 1037–62; Johnson et al., *Government to Government*, 3; Zelio, *Piecing Together*.

71. Hedden-Nicely and Leeds, "Familiar Crossroads," 318. See remarks by Chrissi Ross Nimmo in Leeds et al., "Policing in Indian Country." Transcript of Oral Argument, *Carpenter v. Murphy*, No. 14-1406 (Nov. 27, 2018); Oklahoma Secretary of State, "Tribal Compacts and Agreements."

72. Killman, "McGirt Decision"; Killman, "AG, Tribes Reach Agreement."

73. A draft of the bill is available on Congressman Tom Cole's website at https://cole.house.gov/sites/cole.house.gov/files/documents/Cherokee_Nation _And_Chickasaw_Nation_Criminal_Jurisdiction_Compacting_Act.pdf (accessed November 18, 2021). The final bill can be viewed at https://www .govinfo.gov/content/pkg/BILLS-117hr3091ih/html/BILLS-117hr3091ih .htm.

74. Casteel, "State Files More Petitions."

75. Douglas, "Gov. Stitt."

CONCLUSION

1. Miller and Dolan, "Indian Law Bombshell," 2102.

2. Miller and Dolan, 2104.

3. Cooper, "Judging Jurisdiction," 46, 49; Legal Tender Cases, *Knox v. Lee*, 79 U.S. 457 (1871), overruling in part *Hepburn v. Griswold*, 75 U.S. 603 (1870); *West Virginia State Board of Education v. Barnette*, 319 U.S. 624 (1943), overruling *Minersville School Dist. v. Gobitis*, 310 U.S. 586 (1940), in Congressional Research Service, "Table of Supreme Court Decisions."

4. See Editorial Board, "Justice Gorsuch"; Liptak, "Tribes' Victory"; Gowen and Barnes, "'Complete, Dysfunctional Chaos'"; *contra* Westney, "Tribal Leaders"; Hill, "Fear-mongering"; Hoskin, "On Aug. 30"; Cooper, "Judging Jurisdiction" ("a threat" at 49).

EPILOGUE

1. See *McGirt v. Oklahoma*, 140 S.Ct. 2452, 2482 & 2502 (2020) (Roberts, C.J., dissenting).

2. See, e.g., Opinion, "The Supreme Court's *McGirt* Dilemma," *Wall Street Journal*, April 28, 2022, at https://www.wsj.com/articles/the-supreme-courts-mcgirt-dilemma-oklahoma-v-castro-huerta-neil-gorsuch-samuel-alito-11651182201; Opinion, "More *McGirt* Fallout: The Case of the White Supremacist Choctaw," *Wall Street Journal*, April 11, 2022, at https://www.wsj.com/articles/the-case-of-the-white-supremacist-choctaw-supreme-court-mcgirt-oklahoma-native-americans-crime-11649260615; Opinion, "More *McGirt* Mayhem in Oklahoma," *Wall Street Journal*, Feb. 21, 2022, at https://www.wsj.com/articles/mcgirt-decision-oklahoma-native-american-reservation-jurisdiction-muscogee-creek-hughes-county-crime-racial-injustice-systemic-racism-11644772881.

3. Michael K. Velchik & Jeffery Y. Zhang, *Restoring Indian Reservation Status: An Empirical Analysis*, 40 Yale. J. Reg. Forthcoming in 2023; at https://papers.ssrn.com/sol3/papers.cfm?abstract_id=4057695 at 2 & 7.

4. *Id.* at 2, 20–32.

5. Sarah Johnston & Dominic Parker, *Causes and Consequences of Policy Uncertainty: Evidence from* McGirt vs. Oklahoma, at https://papers.ssrn.com/sol3/papers.cfm?abstract_id=4124658.

6. *Id.* at 1–4, 14–26.

BIBLIOGRAPHY

Government Documents

"An act for the protection of the people of the Indian Territory, and for other purposes," June 28, 1898. In *United States Statutes at Large*, vol. 30 (1897–1899), chap. 517, 495–519.

"An act for the removal of restrictions from part of the lands of allottees of the Five Civilized Tribes, and for other purposes," May 27, 1908. In *United States Statutes at Large*, vol. 35 (1908–1909), chap. 199, 312–16.

"An act making appropriations for current and contingent expenses, and fulfilling treaty stipulations with Indian tribes, for fiscal year ending June thirtieth, eighteen hundred and ninety-four," March 3, 1893. In *United States Statutes at Large*, vol. 27 (1892–1893), chap. 209, 612–46.

"An act making appropriations for the current and contingent expenses of the Indian Department, and for fulfilling treaty stipulations with various Indian tribes, for the year ending June thirty, eighteen hundred and seventy-two, and for other purposes," March 3, 1871. In *United States Statutes at Large*, vol. 16 (1869–1871), chap. 120, 544–71.

"An act making appropriations for the current and contingent expenses of the Indian Department, and for fulfilling treaty stipulations with various Indian tribes for the year ending June thirtieth, eighteen hundred and eighty-six, and for other purposes," March 3, 1885. In *United States Statutes at Large*, vol. 23 (1884–1885), chap. 341, 362–85.

"An act relative to restrictions applicable to Indians of the Five Civilized Tribes of Oklahoma, and for other purposes," August 4, 1947. Public Law 80-336. In *United States Statutes at Large*, vol. 61 (1947), chap. 458, 731–34.

"An act to amend section six, chapter one hundred and nineteen, United States Statutes at Large numbered twenty-four," March 3, 1901. In *United States Statutes at Large*, vol. 31 (1900–1901), chap. 868, 1447.

"An act to authorize each of the Five Civilized Tribes of Oklahoma to popularly select their principal officer, and for other purposes," October 22, 1970. Public Law 91-495. In *United States Statutes at Large*, vol. 84 (1970–1971), 1091–92.

"An act to authorize funds for Federal-aid highways, highway safety programs, and transit programs, and for other purposes," August 10, 2005. Public Law 109-59. In *United States Statutes at Large*, vol. 119 (2005), 1144–978.

"An act to authorize the Secretary of the Interior to issue certificates of citizenship to Indians," June 2, 1924. Public Law 68-175. In *United States Statutes at Large*, vol. 43 (1923–1925), chap. 233, 253.

"An act to confer jurisdiction on the States of California, Minnesota, Nebraska, Oregon, and Wisconsin, with respect to criminal offenses and civil causes of action committed or arising on Indian reservations within such States, and for other purposes," August 15, 1953. Public Law 83-280. In *United States Statutes at Large*, vol. 67 (1953), chap. 505, 588–90.

"An act to conserve and develop Indian lands and resources; to extend to Indians the right to form business and other organizations; to establish a credit system for Indians; to grant certain rights of home rule to Indians; to provide for vocational education for Indians; and for other purposes," June 18, 1934. In *United States Statutes at Large*, vol. 48 (1933–1934), chap. 576, 984–88.

"An act to control and prevent crime," September 13, 1994. Public Law 103-322. In *United States Statutes at Large*, vol. 108 (1994), 1796–2153.

"An act to enable the people of Oklahoma and of the Indian Territory to form a constitution and State government and be admitted into the Union on an equal footing with the original States; and to enable the people of New Mexico and of Arizona to form a constitution and State government and be admitted into the Union on an equal footing with the original States," June 16, 1906. Public Law 59-234. In *United States Statutes at Large*, vol. 34 (1905–1907), chap. 3335, 267–86.

"An act to establish a United States court in the Indian Territory, and for other purposes," March 1, 1889. In *United States Statutes at Large*, vol. 25 (1888–1889), chap. 333, 783–88.

"An act to promote the general welfare of the Indians of the State of Oklahoma, and for other purposes," June 26, 1936. In *United States Statutes at Large*, vol. 49 (1935–1936), chap. 831, 1967–68.

"An act to provide a temporary government for the Territory of Oklahoma, to enlarge the jurisdiction of the United States Court in the Indian Territory, and for other purposes," May 2, 1890. In *United States Statutes at Large*, vol. 26 (1890–1891), chap. 182, 81–100.

"An act to provide for an exchange of lands with the Indians residing in any of the states or territories, and for their removal west of the river Mississippi," May 28, 1830. In *United States Statutes at Large*, vol. 4 (1824–1835), chap. 148, 411–12.

"An act to provide for the allotment of lands in severalty to Indians on the various reservations, and to extend the protection of the laws of the United States and the Territories over the Indians, and for other purposes," February 8, 1887. In *United States Statutes at Large*, vol. 24 (1886–1887), chap. 119, 388–91.

"An act to provide for the final disposition of the affairs of the Five Civilized Tribes in the Indian Territory, and for other purposes," April 26, 1906. Public Law 59-129. In *United States Statutes at Large*, vol. 34 (1905–1907), chap. 1876, 137–48.

"An act to provide for the punishment of crimes and offences committed within the Indian boundaries," March 3, 1817. In *United States Statutes at Large*, vol. 3 (1813–1823), chap. 92, 383.

"An act to provide maximum Indian participation in the government and education of the Indian people; to provide for the full participation of Indian tribes in programs and services conducted by the Federal Government for Indians and to encourage the development of human resources of the Indian people; to establish a program of assistance to upgrade Indian education; to support the right of Indian citizens to control their own educational activities; and for other purposes," January 4, 1975. Public Law 93-638. In *United States Statutes at Large*, vol. 88 (1974), 2203–17.

"An act to ratify and confirm a supplemental agreement with the Creek tribe of Indians, and for other purposes," June 30, 1902. In *United States Statutes at Large*, vol. 32 (1902–1903), chap. 1323, 500–505.

"An act to ratify and confirm agreements with the Sac and Fox Nation of Indians, and the Iowa tribe of Indians, of Oklahoma Territory, and to make appropriations for carrying out the same," February 13, 1891. In *United States Statutes at Large*, vol. 26 (1890–1891), chap. 165, 749–53.

"An act to ratify and confirm an agreement with the Muscogee (or Creek) Nation of Indians in the Indian Territory, and for other purposes," March 1, 1889. In *United States Statutes at Large*, vol. 25 (1888–1889), chap. 317, 757–59.

"An act to ratify and confirm an agreement with the Muscogee or Creek tribe of Indians, and for other purposes," March 1, 1901. In *United States Statutes at Large*, vol. 31 (1900–1901), chap. 676, 861–73.

"An act to reauthorize the Violence Against Women Act of 1994," March 7, 2013. Public Law 113-4. In *United States Statutes at Large*, vol. 127 (2013), 54–160.

"An act to regulate trade and intercourse with the Indian tribes," July 22, 1790. In *United States Statutes at Large*, vol. 1 (1789–1799), chap. 33, 137–38.

"An act to revise, codify, and enact into positive law, Title 18 of the United States Code, entitled 'Crimes and Criminal Procedure,'" June 23, 1948. In *United States Statutes at Large*, vol. 62 (1948), chap. 645, 683–868.

"Charges against United States Court Officials in Indian Territory." H.R. Doc. No. 528, 58th Cong., 2d Sess. (Feb. 11, 1904).

"Report of Commission to the Five Civilized Tribes." S. Misc. Doc. No. 24, 53d Cong., 3d Sess. (Dec. 10, 1894).

"Terlton Indian Treaty, Creek Nation Muscogee." Land patent, issued August 11, 1852. The Land Patents, serial no. OKNMAA 078779, information last updated July 14, 2021. https://thelandpatents.com/patents/oknmaa-078779.

"To authorize the Secretary of the Interior to negotiate with the Creek Indians for the cession of a portion of their reservation, occupied by friendly Indians," March 3, 1873. In *United States Statutes at Large*, vol. 17 (1871–1873), chap. 322, 626.

"Treaty between the United States of America and the Cherokee Nation of Indians," July 19, 1866. In *United States Statutes at Large*, vol. 14 (1865–1867), 799–807.

"Treaty between the United States of America and the Creek Nation of Indians," June 14, 1866. In *United States Statutes at Large*, vol. 14 (1865–1867), 785–91.

"Treaty with the Creek Nation," July 10, 1861. In *The Statutes at Large of the Provisional Government of the Confederate States of America, from the Institution of the Government, February 8, 1861, to Its Termination, February 18, 1862, Inclusive: Arranged in Chronological Order, Together with the Constitution for the Provisional Government, and the Permanent Constitution of the Confederate States, and the Treaties Concluded by the Confederate States with Indian Tribes*, edited by James M. Matthews, 289–310. Richmond, Va.: R. M. Smith, 1864.

"Treaty with the Creeks, 1832," May 24, 1832. In *United States Statutes at Large*, vol. 7 (1789–1845), 366–68.

"Treaty with the Creeks, 1833," February 14, 1833. In *United States Statutes at Large*, vol. 7 (1789–1845), 417–20.

"Treaty with the Creeks, etc., 1856," August 7, 1856. In *United States Statutes at Large*, vol. 11 (1856–1857), 699–707.

"Treaty with the Delawares, 1778," September 17, 1778. In *United States Statutes at Large*, vol. 7 (1789–1845), 13–15.

Published and Online Sources

Agoyo, Acee. "'Shame on You': Authorities Warn Criminals Not to Make False Claims about Indian Status." Indianz.com, August 12, 2020. https://

www.indianz.com/News/2020/08/12/shame-on-you-authorities-warn
-criminals.asp.

American Land Title Association. "How U.S. Supreme Court Tribal Ruling in Oklahoma Impacts Title Industry, Property Rights." ALTA, September 1, 2020. https://www.alta.org/news/news.cfm?20200901-How-US -Supreme-Court-Tribal-Ruling-in-Oklahoma-Impacts-Title-Industry -Property-Rights.

Anderson, David G., and Kenneth E. Sassaman. *Recent Developments in Southeastern Archaeology: From Colonization to Complexity.* Washington, D.C.: Society for American Archaeology Press, 2012.

Berger, Bethany R. "*McGirt v. Oklahoma* and the Past, Present, and Future of Reservation Boundaries." *University of Pennsylvania Law Review* 169 (2021): 250–92. https://www.pennlawreview.com/2021/11/24/mcgirt-v -oklahoma-and-the-past-present-and-future-reservation-boundaries/.

Berry, Brya. "13 Chickasha Police Officers Can Now Force Tribal Law on Native American Suspects." KFOR (Oklahoma City), June 11, 2021. https://kfor.com/news/local/13-chickasha-police-officers-can-now -force-tribal-law-on-native-american-suspects/.

Biedma, Luys Hernández de. "Relation of the Island of Florida." In *The De Soto Chronicles: The Expedition of Hernando de Soto to North America in 1539– 1543,* 2 vols., edited by Lawrence A. Clayton, Vernon J. Knight Jr., and Edward C. Moore, translated by John E. Worth, 1:221–46. Tuscaloosa: University of Alabama Press, 1993.

Blitz, John H., and Karl G. Lorenz. *The Chattahoochee Chiefdoms.* Tuscaloosa: University of Alabama Press, 2006.

Bonnin, Gertrude, Charles H. Fabens, and Matthew K. Sniffen. *Oklahoma's Poor Rich Indians: An Orgy of Graft and Exploitation of the Five Civilized Tribes—Legalized Robbery.* Philadelphia, Pa.: Office of the Indian Rights Association, 1924.

Boyd, Mark F., ed. and trans. "The Expedition of Marcos Delgado from Apalachee to the Upper Creek Country in 1686." *Florida Historical Quarterly* 16 (1936): 1–32.

Braley, Chad O. *Yuchi Town (1Ru63) Revisited: Analysis of the 1958–1962 Excavations.* Report submitted to Environmental Management Division, Directorate of Public Works, U.S. Army Infantry Center, Fort Benning, Georgia. Athens, Ga.: Southeastern Archaeological Services, 1998.

Braund, Kathryn E. Holland. "The Creek Indians, Blacks, and Slavery." *Journal of Southern History* 57 (1991): 601–36.

———. *Deerskins and Duffels: The Creek Indian Trade with Anglo-America, 1685– 1815.* Lincoln: University of Nebraska Press, 1993.

———, ed. *Tohopeka: Rethinking the Creek War and the War of 1812.* Tuscaloosa: University of Alabama Press, 2012.

Bubar, Joe. "Who Owns Oklahoma? A Supreme Court Ruling Could Return Nearly Half of the State to Native Americans." *New York Times Upfront* 151, no. 8 (January 28, 2019): 10–11.

Bunn, Clinton O., and Wm. C. Bunn, comps. "Constitution of Oklahoma—1907." In *Constitution and Enabling Act of the State of Oklahoma*, 2–139. Ardmore, Okla.: Bunn Brothers, 1907.

———. "Enabling Act of the State of Oklahoma, Approved June 6, 1906." In *Constitution and Enabling Act of the State of Oklahoma*, 141–62. Ardmore, Okla.: Bunn Brothers, 1907.

Burton, Jeffrey. *Indian Territory and the United States, 1866–1906: Courts, Government, and the Movement for Oklahoma Statehood.* Norman: University of Oklahoma Press, 1995.

Buzzard, Greg, Christopher Haunschild, and Mike McBride III. "*McGirt v. Oklahoma*: Impacts on Tribal Taxation." JD Supra, May 12, 2021. https://www.jdsupra.com/legalnews/mcgirt-v-oklahoma-impacts-on-tribal-2545437/.

Calloway, Colin G. *The Indian World of George Washington: The First President, the First Americans, and the Birth of the Nation.* New York: Oxford University Press, 2018.

———. *The Scratch of a Pen: 1763 and the Transformation of North America.* New York: Oxford University Press, 2006.

Canby, William C., Jr. *American Indian Law in a Nutshell.* 6th ed. St. Paul, Minn.: West Academic, 2015.

Casteel, Chris. "Biden Administration Seeking $82 Million for McGirt-Related Costs in Oklahoma." *Tulsa World*, June 13, 2021. https://tulsaworld.com/news/local/biden-administration-seeking-82-million-for-mcgirt-related-costs-in-oklahoma/article_6078924a-cc72-11eb-891d-73adbac90fc4.html.

———. "Seminole Nation's Attempt to Tax Oil Companies Prompts Swift Response from Hunter, Stitt." *The Oklahoman* (Oklahoma City), December 16, 2020. https://www.oklahoman.com/story/news/columns/2020/12/16/seminole-nations-attempt-to-tax-oil-companies-prompts-swift-response-from-hunter-stitt/316814007/.

———. "State Files More Petitions Seeking High Court Reversal of McGirt." *The Oklahoman* (Oklahoma City), August 23, 2001. https://www.oklahoman.com/story/news/local/oklahoma-city/2021/08/23/oklahoma-attorney-general-files-more-petitions-seeking-mcgirt-reversal/8235417002/.

Chickasaw Nation Media Relations Office. "Chickasaw Nation Expands Criminal Justice Capabilities." Press release. Chickasaw Nation, Office of the Governor, March 11, 2022. https://www.chickasaw.net/News/Press-Releases/Release/Chickasaw-Nation-expands-criminal-justice-capabili-57980.aspx.

Christensen, Grant. "Predicting Supreme Court Behavior in Indian Law Cases." *Michigan Journal of Race and Law* 26 (2021): 65–114.

Clark, Blue. *Lone Wolf v. Hitchcock: Treaty Rights and Indian Law at the End of the Nineteenth Century.* Lincoln: University of Nebraska Press, 1999.

Cleary, Conor. "The Stigler Act Amendments of 2018." *Oklahoma Bar Journal* 91 (January 2020): 50–76. https://www.okbar.org/barjournal/jan2020/obj9101cleary/.

Cluiss, Caroline. "Johnston County Deputy Sheriffs Now Federal Officers." KXII (Sherman, Tex.), July 14, 2021. https://www.kxii.com/2021/07/14/johnston-county-deputy-sheriffs-now-federal-officers/.

Cohen's Handbook of Federal Indian Law. 2012 Edition. Edited by Nell Jessup Newton. Albuquerque: LexisNexis, 2012.

Confederated Salish and Kootenai Tribes. "Bison Range Restoration." Accessed November 17, 2021. https://bisonrange.org/.

Conference of Western Attorneys General. *American Indian Law Deskbook.* 2019 Edition. New York: Thomson Reuters, 2019.

Congressional Research Service. "Table of Supreme Court Decisions Overruled by Subsequent Decisions." Constitution Annotated: Analysis and Interpretation of the U.S. Constitution, accessed November 29, 2021. https://constitution.congress.gov/resources/decisions-overruled/.

Cooper, Cynthia L. "Judging Jurisdiction: Federal and Tribal Courts in Oklahoma Grapple with the Aftermath of *McGirt.*" *ABA Journal* 108, no. 2 (April/May 2022): 46–53.

Creel, Von. "A Court of Its Own: The Establishment of the United States Court for the Indian Territory." *Oklahoma City University Law Review* 27 (2002): 231–44.

Cronon, William. *Changes in the Land: Indians, Colonists, and the Ecology of New England.* New York: Hill and Wang, 1983.

Crum, William. "Professor: U.S. Supreme Court's Ruling Affects the Water Future That Is Vital to Oklahoma City." *The Oklahoman* (Oklahoma City), July 13, 2020. https://www.oklahoman.com/article/5666700/professor-u.s.-supreme-courts-ruling-affects-the-water-future-that-is-vital-to-oklahoma-city.

Debo, Angie. *And Still the Waters Run: The Betrayal of the Five Civilized Tribes.* 1940. Reprint, Princeton, N.J.: Princeton University Press, 1973.

———. *The Five Civilized Tribes of Oklahoma: Report on Social and Economic Conditions.* Philadelphia, Pa.: Indian Rights Association, 1951.

———. *A History of the Indians of the United States.* Norman: University of Oklahoma Press, 1970.

———. *The Road to Disappearance: A History of the Creek Indians.* Norman: University of Oklahoma Press, 1941.

Deer, Sarah, and Cecilia Knapp. "Muscogee Constitutional Jurisprudence: Vhakv Em Pvtakv (The Carpet under the Law)." *Tulsa Law Review* 49,

no. 1 (2013): 125–81. https://digitalcommons.law.utulsa.edu/tlr/v0149
/iss1/5.

Deloria, Vine, Jr., and Raymond DeMallie. *Documents of American Indian Diplomacy: Treaties, Agreements, and Conventions, 1775–1979.* Norman: University of Oklahoma Press, 1999.

Department of the Interior. "Loss of State Jurisdiction to Administer the Surface Mining Control and Reclamation Act of 1977 within the Exterior Boundaries of the Muscogee (Creek) Nation Reservation in the State of Oklahoma." *Federal Register* 86, no. 94 (May 18, 2021): 26941. https://www.federalregister.gov/documents/2021/05/18/2021-10400/loss
-of-state-jurisdiction-to-administer-the-surface-mining-control-and
-reclamation-act-of-1977.

DePratter, Chester B., Charles Hudson, and Marvin T. Smith. "Hernando de Soto Expedition: From Chiaha to Mabila." In *Alabama and the Borderlands: From Prehistory to Statehood,* edited by R. Reid Badger and Lawrence A. Clayton, 108–27. Tuscaloosa: University of Alabama Press, 1985.

Dossett, John. "Justice Gorsuch and Federal Indian Law." *Human Rights* 43, no. 1 (2017): 6–10. https://www.americanbar.org/groups/crsj/publications
/human_rights_magazine_home/vol--43/vol--43--no--1/justice
-gorsuch-and-federal-indian-law/.

Douglas, Kaylee. "Gov. Stitt Calls for Tribes to Enter Formal Negotiations with State Following McGirt Ruling." KFOR (Oklahoma City), January 22, 2021, updated January 25, 2021. https://kfor.com/news/local/gov-stitt
-calls-for-tribes-to-enter-formal-negotiations-with-state-following
-mcgirt-ruling/.

Duignan, Brian. "Neil Gorsuch: United States Jurist." *Encyclopedia Britannica,* August 25, 2021, updated November 12, 2021. https://www.britannica
.com/biography/Neil-Gorsuch.

Editorial Board, *Wall Street Journal.* "Justice Gorsuch Tears Up Oklahoma: His 5–4 *McGirt* Opinion Is Causing Havoc in the Sooner State." *Wall Street Journal,* September 8, 2021. https://www.wsj.com/articles/justice
-neil-gorsuch-tears-up-oklahoma-mcgirt-creek-supreme-court-tribal
-11627221756.

Edmunds, R. David, Fredrick E. Hoxie, and Neal Salisbury. *The People: A History of Native America.* New York: Houghton Mifflin, 2007.

Ellinghaus, Katherine. *Blood Will Tell: Native Americans and Assimilation Policy.* Lincoln: University of Nebraska Press, 2017.

Ellisor, John T. *The Second Creek War: Interethnic Conflict and Collusion on a Collapsing Frontier.* Lincoln: University of Nebraska Press, 2010.

Elvas, Gentleman of. "The Account by a Gentleman from Elvas." In *The De Soto Chronicles: The Expedition of Hernando de Soto to North America in 1539–1543,* 2 vols., edited by Lawrence A. Clayton, Vernon J. Knight Jr., and

Edward C. Moore, translated by James Alexander Robertson, 1:19–220. Tuscaloosa: University of Alabama Press, 1993.

"EPA Proposes to Withdraw and Reconsider 2020 Decision on State of Oklahoma's Regulatory Authority within Indian Country." News release. United States Environmental Protection Agency, December 22, 2021. https://www.epa.gov/newsreleases/epa-proposes-withdraw-and-reconsider-2020-decision-state-oklahomas-regulatory

Epps, Garrett. "Who Owns Oklahoma? The Supreme Court Must Decide the Fate of a Murderer—and Whether Roughly Half of Oklahoma Is Rightfully Reservation Land." *The Atlantic*, November 20, 2018. https://www.theatlantic.com/ideas/archive/2018/11/murphy-case-supreme-court-rules-muscogee-land/576238/.

Ethridge, Robbie. *Creek Country: The Creek Indians and Their World*. Chapel Hill: University of North Carolina Press, 2003.

———. *From Chicaza to Chickasaw: The European Invasion and the Transformation of the Mississippian World, 1540–1715*. Chapel Hill: University of North Carolina Press, 2010.

———. "Introduction." In *Mapping the Mississippian Shatter Zone: The Colonial Indian Slave Trade and Regional Instability in the American South*, edited by Robbie Ethridge and Sheri M. Shuck-Hall, 1–62. Lincoln: University of Nebraska Press, 2009.

———. "The Rise and Fall of Mississippian Ancient Towns and Cities, 1000–1700." In *Oxford Research Encyclopedia of American History*, Online Edition, March 28, 2018. https://oxfordre.com/americanhistory/view/10.1093/acrefore/9780199329175.001.0001/acrefore-9780199329175-e-349.

Ethridge, Robbie, and Charles Hudson. "The Early Historic Transformation of the Southeastern Indians." In *Cultural Diversity in the U.S. South: Anthropological Contributions to a Region in Transition*, edited by Carole E. Hill and Patricia D. Beaver, 34–50. Athens: University of Georgia Press, 1998.

Ethridge, Robbie, and Maureen Meyers. "Indian Eras, Mississippian Period: 1000–300 B.P. (A.D. 1000–1700)." In *The New Encyclopedia of Southern Culture*, vol. 3, *History*, edited by Charles Reagan Wilson, 141–45. Chapel Hill: University of North Carolina Press, 2006.

Ethridge, Robbie, Victor Thompson, and Maureen Meyers. "Indian Eras, Archaic Period: 10,000–3000 B.P. (8000–1000 B.C.)." In *The New Encyclopedia of Southern Culture*, vol. 3, *History*, edited by Charles Reagan Wilson, 133–37. Chapel Hill: University of North Carolina Press, 2006.

———. "Indian Eras, Late Archaic Domestication of Plants and the Woodland Period: 3000–1000 B.P. (1000 B.C.–A.D. 1000)." In *The New Encyclopedia of Southern Culture*, vol. 3, *History*, edited by Charles Reagan Wilson, 137–41. Chapel Hill: University of North Carolina Press, 2006.

————. "Indian Eras, Paleoindian Period: 12,000–10,000 B.P. (10,000–8000 B.C.)." In *The New Encyclopedia of Southern Culture*, vol. 3, *History*, edited by Charles Reagan Wilson, 130–33. Chapel Hill: University of North Carolina Press, 2006.

Federal Judicial Center. "Gorsuch, Neil M." FJC, accessed November 22, 2021. https://www.fjc.gov/history/judges/gorsuch-neil-m.

————. "U.S. District Courts for the Districts of Oklahoma: Legislative History." FJC, accessed August 24, 2021. https://www.fjc.gov/history/courts/u.s.-district-courts-districts-oklahoma-legislative-history.

Fitzpatrick, Tana. "Potential Land and Natural Resources Policy Implications of *McGirt v. Oklahoma*." Congressional Research Service, IN11486, August 21, 2020. https://crsreports.congress.gov/product/pdf/IN/IN11486.

Fletcher, Matthew L. M. "Justice Ginsburg's Indian Law Record." Turtle Talk, September 21, 2020. https://turtletalk.blog/2020/09/21/justice-ginsburgs-indian-law-record/.

Foreman, Grant. *The Five Civilized Tribes: Cherokee, Chickasaw, Choctaw, Creek, Seminole*. Norman: University of Oklahoma Press, 1934.

Forman, Carmen. "Some Oklahomans Seek Tax Exemptions in Light of McGirt Decision." *The Oklahoman* (Oklahoma City), April 4, 2021. https://www.oklahoman.com/story/news/politics/2021/04/04/supreme-court-mcgirt-decision-results-tax-protests-oklahoma/4699712001/.

Fox 25 Staff. "McGirt Ruling Leaves Oklahoma in Turmoil over Native American Land." KOKH (Oklahoma City), May 17, 2021. https://okcfox.com/news/local/mcgirt-ruling-leaves-oklahoma-in-turmoil-over-native-american-land.

Frank, Andrew K. *Creeks and Southerners: Biculturalism on the Early American Frontier*. Lincoln: University of Nebraska Press, 2005.

Galloway, Patricia. *Choctaw Genesis, 1500–1700*. Lincoln: University of Nebraska Press, 1995.

Gibson, Arrell M. *The Chickasaws*. Norman: University of Oklahoma Press, 1971.

Gorsuch, Neil M. *A Republic, If You Can Keep It*. New York: Crown Forum, 2019.

————. "Why Originalism Is the Best Approach to the Constitution." *Time*, September 6, 2019. https://time.com/5670400/justice-neil-gorsuch-why-originalism-is-the-best-approach-to-the-constitution/.

Gowen, Annie, and Robert Barnes. "'Complete, Dysfunctional Chaos': Oklahoma Reels after Supreme Court Ruling on Indian Tribes." *Washington Post*, July 24, 2021. https://www.washingtonpost.com/national/complete-dysfunctional-chaos-oklahoma-reels-after-supreme-court-ruling-on-indian-tribes/2021/07/23/99ba0b80-ea75-11eb-8950-d73b3e93ff7f_story.html.

Grann, David. *Killers of the Flower Moon: The Osage Murders and the Birth of the FBI*. New York: Doubleday, 2017.

Grantham, Bill. *Creation Myths and Legends of the Creek Indians.* Gainesville: University Press of Florida, 2002.

Green, Michael D. *The Creeks.* New York: Chelsea House, 1990.

———. *The Politics of Indian Removal: Creek Government and Society in Crisis.* Lincoln: University of Nebraska Press, 1982.

Griffith, Benjamin W., Jr. *McIntosh and Weatherford, Creek Indian Leaders.* Tuscaloosa: University of Alabama Press, 1988.

Hahn, Steven C. "The Cussita Migration Legend: History, Ideology, and the Politics of Mythmaking." In *Light on the Path: The Anthropology and History of the Southeastern Indians,* edited by Thomas J. Pluckhahn and Robbie Ethridge, 57–93. Tuscaloosa: University of Alabama Press, 2006.

———. *Invention of the Creek Nation, 1670–1763.* Lincoln: University of Nebraska Press, 2004.

———. *The Life and Times of Mary Musgrove.* Gainesville: University Press of Florida, 2012.

Hally, David J. "Platform Mound Construction and the Instability of Mississippian Chiefdoms." In *Political Structure and Change in the Prehistoric Southeastern United States,* edited by John Scarry, 92–127. Gainesville: University Press of Florida, 1996.

———. "The Territorial Size of Mississippian Chiefdoms." In *Archaeology of Eastern North America: Papers in Honor of Stephen Williams,* edited by James A. Stoltman, 143–68. Jackson: Mississippi Department of Archives and History, 1993.

Hally, David J., and John F. Chamblee. "The Temporal Distribution and Duration of Mississippian Polities in Alabama, Georgia, Mississippi, and Tennessee." *American Antiquity* 84, no. 3 (2019): 420–27.

Harvey, Henry. *History of the Shawnee Indians, from the Year 1681 to 1854, Inclusive.* Cincinnati: Ephraim Morgan & Sons, 1855.

Hauptman, Laurence M. "Fighting the Nazis: A Creek Indian Wins the Congressional Medal of Honor." *American Indian* 19, no. 1 (Spring 2018). https://www.americanindianmagazine.org/story/creek-indian-wins-medal-of-honor.

Haveman, Christopher D., ed. *Bending Their Way Onward: Creek Indian Removal in Documents.* Lincoln: University of Nebraska Press, 2018.

———. *Rivers of Sand: Creek Indian Emigration, Relocation, and Ethnic Cleansing in the American South.* Lincoln: University of Nebraska Press, 2016.

Hawkins, Benjamin. *The Letters, Journals, and Writings of Benjamin Hawkins.* Edited by C. L. Grant. 2 vols. Savannah, Ga.: Beehive Press, 1980.

Hedden-Nicely, Dylan R., and Stacy L. Leeds. "A Familiar Crossroads: *McGirt v. Oklahoma* and the Future of the Federal Indian Law Canon." *New Mexico Law Review* 51, no. 2 (2021): 300–348. https://digitalrepository.unm.edu/nmlr/vol51/iss2/2.

Herrera, Allison. "Attorney General Recommends Optional State-Tribe Compacting on Criminal Jurisdiction Post-McGirt." KOSU (Stillwater, Okla.), October 21, 2020. https://www.kosu.org/news/2020-10-21/attorney-general-recommends-optional-state-tribe-compacting-on-criminal-jurisdiction-post-mcgirt.

Hill, David. "Fear-mongering by AG, Governor Does Not Work." *The Oklahoman* (Oklahoma City), September 5, 2021. https://www.oklahoman.com/story/opinion/2021/09/05/stitt-ag-fear-mongering-does-not-work/5683600001/.

Hilleary, Cecily. "Native Americans, State Leaders Grapple with Legal Uncertainty in Oklahoma." Voice of America, July 31, 2021. https://www.voanews.com/a/usa_native-americans-state-leaders-grapple-legal-uncertainty-oklahoma/6208933.html.

Hoberock, Barbara, and Randy Krehbiel. "Oklahoma Conservative Group Wants Tribal Reservation Borders Gone." *Tulsa World*, October 10, 2020. https://tulsaworld.com/news/state-and-regional/govt-and-politics/oklahoma-conservative-group-wants-tribal-reservation-boundaries-gone/article_5ff72b0e-0a5f-11eb-9ee3-afcf85c16b89.html.

Holloway, Joseph. "Muscogee Creek Nation Investing Millions in Lighthorse Police Department." News on 6 (Tulsa, Okla.), September 30, 2020. https://www.newson6.com/story/5f746d9210991b0c17a80d5a/-muscogee-creek-nation-investing-millions-in-lighthorse-police-department.

Hoskin, Chuck, Jr. "Chief Chat: Strengthening Cherokee Nation's Self-Determination." *Muskogee Phoenix*, May 15, 2021.

———. "On Aug. 30, the 'Oklahoma Council of Public Affairs' Published a Propaganda Piece Centered on the Cherokee Nation Marshall Service." Facebook, August 30, 2021. https://www.facebook.com/permalink.php?story_fbid=4147694188689661&id=114167895375664.

Hoxie, Fredrick E. *A Final Promise: The Campaign to Assimilate the Indians, 1880–1920*. Lincoln: University of Nebraska Press, 1984.

Hudson, Charles. *Knights of Spain, Warriors of the Sun: Hernando de Soto and the South's Ancient Chiefdoms*. Athens: University of Georgia Press, 1997.

Jenkins, Ned. "Tracing the Origins of the Early Creeks, 1050–1700 CE." In *Mapping the Mississippian Shatter Zone: The Colonial Indian Slave Trade and Regional Instability in the American South*, edited by Robbie Ethridge and Sheri M. Shuck-Hall, 188–249. Lincoln: University of Nebraska Press, 2009.

Jenkins, Ned J., and Craig T. Sheldon. "The Hernando de Soto and Tristán de Luna y Arellano Expeditions in Central Alabama, 1540–1560: Routes, Cultures, and Consequences." In *Modeling Entradas: Sixteenth-Century Assemblages in North America*, edited by Clay Mathers, 162–202. Gainesville: University of Florida Press.

Jensen, Eric. "Taxation and Doing Business in Indian Country." *Maine Law Review* 60 (2008): 1–96.

Johnson, Susan, Jeanne Kaufmann, John Dossett, Sarah Hicks, and Sia Davis. *Government to Government: Models of Cooperation between States and Tribes.* 2nd ed. Washington, D.C.: National Conference of State Legislatures, 2009.

Jones, Storme. "State Lawmakers Greenlight $10 Million for Legal Fight against Tribes." *News 9* (Oklahoma City), May 21, 2021. https://www.news9 .com/story/60a84af034edb30bc83c6ce8/state-lawmakers-greenlight-10 -million-for-legal-fight-against-tribes.

Juricek, John T. *Colonial Georgia and the Creeks: Anglo-Indian Diplomacy on the Southern Frontier, 1733–1763.* Gainesville: University Press of Florida, 2010.

———. *Endgame for Empire: British-Creek Relations in Georgia and Vicinity, 1763– 1776.* Gainesville: University Press of Florida, 2015.

Kappler, Charles J., comp. and ed. *Indian Affairs: Laws and Treaties.* 7 vols. Washington: U.S. Government Printing Office, 1907–71. Digital Collections, Oklahoma State University Library. https://dc.library.okstate.edu/digital /collection/kapplers/.

Killman, Curtis. "AG, Tribes Reach Agreement on Jurisdictional Issues." *Tulsa World*, July 17, 2020. https://tulsaworld.com/news/local/ag-tribes-reach -agreement-on-jurisdictional-issues/article_eb55c534-dcc1-5c10-a6c3 -f3c44bad2cba.html.

———. "McGirt Decision Results in Record Number of Criminal Federal Filings in 2020." *Tulsa World*, January 4, 2021, updated February 7, 2022. https://tulsaworld.com/news/local/crime-and-courts/mcgirt-decision -results-in-record-number-of-criminal-federal-filings-in-2020/article _acb656d6-4bb4-11eb-b090-4bc211e4475a.html.

Kirsch, Noah. "The 3 Richest Americans Hold More Wealth Than Bottom 50% of the Country, Study Finds." *Forbes*, November 9, 2017. https:// www.forbes.com/sites/noahkirsch/2017/11/09/the-3-richest-americans -hold-more-wealth-than-bottom-50-of-country-study-finds/?sh= 2c0d725a3cf8.

Knight, Vernon J., Jr. "The Formation of the Creeks." In *The Forgotten Centuries: Indians and Europeans in the American South, 1521–1704,* edited by Charles Hudson and Carmen Chaves Tesser, 373–92. Athens: University of Georgia Press, 1994.

———. *Tukabatchee: Archaeological Investigations at an Historic Creek Town, Elmore County, Alabama, 1984.* Office of Archaeological Research, Alabama State Museum of Natural History, University of Alabama, with the cooperation of the Alabama Development Office, 1985.

La Vere, David. *Contrary Neighbors: Southern Plains and Removed Indians in Indian Territory.* Norman: University of Oklahoma Press, 2000.

Laco, Kelly. "Oklahoma Suing Biden Admin, Claiming Federal Overreach of Mining Lands." Fox News Channel, July 16, 2021. https://www.foxnews .com/politics/oklahoma-suing-biden-federal-overreach-mining-lands.

Lakomaki, Sami. *Gathering Together: The Shawnee People through Diaspora and Nationhood, 1600–1870.* New Haven, Conn.: Yale University Press, 2014.

Leeds, Stacy, and Lonnie Beard. "A Wealth of Sovereign Choices: Tax Implications of *McGirt v. Oklahoma* and the Promise of Tribal Economic Development." *Tulsa Law Review* 56, no. 3 (2021): 417–69.

Leeds, Stacy, Chrissi Ross Nimmo, Robert Miller, and Alfred Urbina. "Policing in Indian Country: Cooley, McGirt and Beyond!" American Constitutional Society Webinar, sponsored by the Indian Legal Program at the Sandra Day O'Connor College of Law, Arizona State University, Tempe, July 8, 2021 (virtual).

Lewis, Ronald L. *Transforming the Appalachian Countryside: Railroads, Deforestation, and Social Change in West Virginia.* Chapel Hill: University of North Carolina Press, 1998.

Liptak, Adam. "Tribes' Victory in Oklahoma at Risk in Bold Request to the Supreme Court." *New York Times*, August 16, 2021. https://www.nytimes .com/2021/08/16/us/supreme-court-native-americans-oklahoma.html.

Littlefield, Daniel F., Jr. *Africans and Creeks from the Colonial Period to the Civil War.* Westport, Conn.: Greenwood, 1979.

Llewellyn, K. N., and E. Adamson Hoebel. *The Cheyenne Way: Conflict and Case Law in Primitive Jurisprudence.* Norman: University of Oklahoma Press, 1941.

Lowrie, Walter, and Walter S. Franklin, eds. *American State Papers: Indian Affairs.* Vol. 2, *1815–1827.* Washington: Gales and Seaton, 1834. https://memory .loc.gov/ammem/amlaw/lwsplink.html#anchor2.

Mann, Ronald. "Argument Analysis: Justices Dubious about Ramifications of Broad Indian Reservation in Oklahoma." SCOTUSblog, November 27, 2018. https://www.scotusblog.com/2018/11/argument-analysis -justices-dubious-about-ramifications-of-broad-indian-reservation-in -oklahoma/.

———. "Justices Call for Reargument in Dispute about Oklahoma Prosecutions of Native Americans." SCOTUSblog, July 2, 2019. https://www .scotusblog.com/2019/07/justices-call-for-reargument-in-dispute-about -oklahoma-prosecutions-of-native-americans/.

McGinnis, John O. "Which Justices Are Originalists?" Law & Liberty, November 9, 2018. https://lawliberty.org/which-justices-are-originalists/.

Meriam, Lewis. *The Problem of Indian Administration.* Report submitted to the Secretary of the Interior, February 21, 1928. Baltimore: Johns Hopkins Press for the Institute for Government Research, 1928.

Merrefield, Clark. "McGirt v. Oklahoma: The Ongoing Importance of a Landmark Tribal Sovereignty Case." The Journalist's Resource, July 20,

2021. https://journalistsresource.org/criminal-justice/mcgirt-tribal
-sovereignty/.

Miller, Robert J. "American Indian Influence on the United States Constitution and Its Framers." *American Indian Law Review* 18, no. 1 (1993): 133–60.

———. "Consultation or Consent: The United States' Duty to Confer with American Indian Governments." *North Dakota Law Review* 91 (2015): 37–98.

———. "Exercising Cultural Self-Determination: The Makah Indian Tribe Goes Whaling." *American Indian Law Review* 25, no. 2 (2001): 165–273.

———. "The Legal Adoption of Discovery in the United States." In *Discovering Indigenous Lands: The Doctrine of Discovery in the English Colonies*, edited by Robert J. Miller, Jacinta Ruru, Larissa Behrendt, and Tracey Lindberg, 26–65. New York: Oxford University Press, 2010.

———. *Native America, Discovered and Conquered: Thomas Jefferson, Lewis & Clark, and Manifest Destiny.* Westport, Conn.: Praeger, 2006.

———. "Speaking with Forked Tongues: Indian Treaties, Salmon, and the Endangered Species Act." *Oregon Law Review* 70, no. 3 (1991): 543–84.

———. "Treaties between the Eastern Shawnee Tribe and the United States: Contracts between Sovereign Governments." In *The Eastern Shawnee Tribe of Oklahoma: Resilience through Adversity*, edited by Stephen Warren, 107–48. Norman: University of Oklahoma Press, 2017.

———. "Tribal, Federal, and State Laws Impacting the Eastern Shawnee Tribe, 1812 to 1945." In *The Eastern Shawnee Tribe of Oklahoma: Resilience through Adversity*, edited by Stephen Warren, 149–70. Norman: University of Oklahoma Press, 2017.

Miller, Robert J., and Torey Dolan. "The Indian Law Bombshell: *McGirt v. Oklahoma*." *Boston University Law Review* 101, no. 6 (2021): 2049–104.

Mills, Monte. "McGirt Policy Briefs: Regulation of the Environment and Natural Resources." *Faculty Journal Articles & Other Writings* 156 (December 2020): 4–30. https://scholarworks.umt.edu/faculty_barjournals/156.

Morrow, Kevin. "Bridging the Jurisdictional Void: Cross-Deputization Agreements in Indian Country." *North Dakota Law Review* 94 (2019): 65–94. https://law.und.edu/_files/docs/ndlr/pdf/issues/94/1/94ndlr65.pdf.

Murphy, Sean. "EPA Grants Stitt Request for State Oversight on Tribal Lands." AP News, Oklahoma City, October 5, 2020. https://apnews.com/article/us-supreme-court-environment-oklahoma-archive-754444e8b4887f4045c4604248142665.

Nagle, Rebecca, and Allison Herrera. "Where Is Oklahoma Getting Its Numbers From in Its Supreme Court Case?" *The Atlantic*, April 26, 2022. https://www.theatlantic.com/ideas/archive/2022/04/scotus-oklahoma-castro-huerta-inaccurate-prosecution-data/629674/.

Nelson, Ted Clay. "Material Evidence for Early Coalescence: The Hightower Village Site (1TA150) in the Coosa River Valley." PhD diss., University of Alabama, 2020.

Nichols, David. *Engines of Diplomacy: Indian Trading Factories and the Negotiation of American Empire.* Chapel Hill: University of North Carolina Press, 2016.

Nolan, Raymond. "The Midnight Rider: The EPA and Tribal Self-Determination." *American Indian Quarterly* 42 (2018): 329–43.

Office of the Governor, State of Oklahoma. "Governor Stitt Releases Statement Regarding U.S. District Court Ruling on Gaming Compacts." Press release. OK.gov, October 23, 2020. https://oklahoma.gov/governor /newsroom/newsroom/2020/october/governor-stitt-releases-statement -regarding-u-s--district-court-.html.

———. "Oklahoma Commission on Cooperative Sovereignty Presents Report to Governor Stitt." Press release. OK.gov, October 22, 2020. https:// oklahoma.gov/governor/newsroom/newsroom/2020/october/oklahoma -commission-on-cooperative-sovereignty-presents-report-t.html.

Oklahoma Secretary of State. "Hunting and Fishing Compact between the State of Oklahoma and the Cherokee Nation." Signed May 29, 2015; filed June 1, 2015. OK.gov. https://www.sos.ok.gov/documents/filelog /90614.pdf.

———. "Hunting and Fishing Compact between the State of Oklahoma and the Choctaw Nation." Signed August 31, 2016; filed August 31, 2016. OK .gov. https://www.sos.ok.gov/documents/filelog/91317.pdf.

———. "Tribal Compacts and Agreements." Records database. OK.gov. https://www.sos.ok.gov/gov/tribal.aspx.

Oklahoma Tax Commission. "Report of Potential Impact of *McGirt v. Oklahoma.*" Report submitted to the Oklahoma Commission on Cooperative Sovereignty, Office of the Governor of Oklahoma, September 30, 2020. Hall Estill, Attorneys at Law, October 5, 2020. https://www.hallestill .com/uploads/McGirt-Oklahoma-Tax-Commission-Report.pdf.

Perdue, Theda. *"Mixed Blood Indians": Racial Construction in the Early South.* Athens: University of Georgia Press, 2003.

Perdue, Theda, and Michael D. Green. *North American Indians: A Very Short Introduction.* New York: Oxford University Press, 2010.

Pipestem, F. Browning, and G. William Rice. "The Mythology of the Oklahoma Indians: A Survey of the Legal Status of Indian Tribes in Oklahoma." *American Indian Law Review* 6 (1979): 259–328.

Pluckhahn, Thomas J. *Kolomoki: Settlement, Ceremony, and Status in the Deep South, c. 350 to 750 AD.* Tuscaloosa: University of Alabama Press, 2003.

Pluckhahn, Thomas J., and Victor D. Thompson. *New Histories of Village Life at Crystal River.* Gainesville: University Press of Florida, 2018.

Porter, Robert Odawi. "Judge Neil Gorsuch Is Worthy of Indian Country Support." *Indian Country Today* (Phoenix, Ariz.), April 4, 2017, updated

September 12, 2018. https://indiancountrytoday.com/archive/judge -neil-gorsuch-worthy-indian-country-support.

Priestley, Herbert Ingram, ed. and trans. *The Luna Papers: Documents Relating to the Expedition of Don Tristán de Luna y Arellano for the Conquest of La Florida in 1559–1561*. 2 vols. Deland: Florida State Historical Society, 1928.

Prucha, Francis Paul. *American Indian Treaties: The History of a Political Anomaly*. Berkeley: University of California Press, 1994.

———. *Documents of United States Indian Policy*. 3rd ed. Lincoln: University of Nebraska Press, 2000.

———. *The Great Father: The United States Government and the American Indians*. Lincoln: University of Nebraska Press, 1995.

Rangel, Rodrigo. "Account of the Northern Conquest and Discovery of Hernando de Soto." In *The De Soto Chronicles: The Expedition of Hernando de Soto to North America in 1539–1543*, 2 vols., edited by Lawrence A. Clayton, Vernon J. Knight Jr., and Edward C. Moore, translated by John E. Worth, 1:247–306. Tuscaloosa: University of Alabama Press, 1993.

Raymond, Nate. "U.S. Judiciary Seeks More Oklahoma Judges after Supreme Court Ruling." Reuters, September 28, 2021. https://www.reuters.com /legal/government/us-judiciary-seeks-more-oklahoma-judges-after -supreme-court-ruling-2021-09-28/.

Regnier, Amanda L. *Reconstructing Tascalusa's Chiefdom: Pottery Styles and the Social Composition of Late Mississippian Communities along the Alabama River*. Tuscaloosa: University of Alabama Press, 2014.

Ringold, A. F. "Indian Land Law—Some Fundamental Concepts for the Title Examiner." *Tulsa Law Review* 10, no. 3 (1975): 321–39. https:// digitalcommons.law.utulsa.edu/tlr/vol10/iss3/2.

Royce, Charles C., comp. *Indian Land Cessions in the United States*. Extract from *Eighteenth Annual Report of the Bureau of American Ethnology*, pt. 2, 521–997. Washington: Government Printing Office, 1899.

Royster, Judith V. "The Legacy of Allotment." *Arizona State Law Journal* 27 (1994): 1–78.

Rubin, Jordan S. "Oklahoma Tribal Border Battle Set for More Argument Next Term." Bloomberg Law, June 27, 2019. https://news.bloomberglaw.com /us-law-week/oklahoma-tribal-border-battle-set-for-more-argument -next-term.

Saunt, Claudio. *Black, White, and Indian: Race and the Unmaking of an American Family*. New York: Oxford University Press, 2006.

———. *A New Order of Things: Property, Power, and the Transformation of the Creek Indians, 1733–1816*. Cambridge: Cambridge University Press, 1999.

———. *Unworthy Republic: The Dispossession of Native Americans and the Road to Indian Territory*. New York: W. W. Norton and Company, 2020.

Scarcella, Mike. "Paul, Weiss Inked $700k Contract with Oklahoma to Undo Tribal Rights Ruling." Reuters, August 16, 2021. https://www

.reuters.com/legal/government/paul-weiss-inked-700k-contract-with
-oklahoma-undo-tribal-rights-ruling-2021-08-16.

Sharp, Robert V., ed. *Hero, Hawk, and Open Hand: American Indian Art of the Ancient Midwest and South.* New Haven, Conn.: Yale University Press for the Art Institute of Chicago, 2004.

Sheldon, Craig T. "The Present State of Archaeological Survey and Site File Data for the Alabama and Adjacent Regions." In *The Search for Mabila: The Decisive Battle between Hernando de Soto and Chief Tascalusa,* edited by Vernon James Knight Jr., 107–28. Tuscaloosa: University of Alabama Press, 2009.

Shuck-Hall, Sheri M. "Alabama and Coushatta Diaspora and Coalescence in the Mississippian Shatter Zone." In *Mapping the Mississippian Shatter Zone: The Colonial Indian Slave Trade and Regional Instability in the American South,* edited by Robbie Ethridge and Sheri M. Shuck-Hall, 250–71. Lincoln: University of Nebraska Press, 2009.

Smith, Marvin T. *Coosa: The Rise and Fall of a Mississippian Chiefdom.* Gainesville: University Press of Florida, 2000.

Smithers, Gregory D. *The Cherokee Diaspora: An Indigenous History of Migration, Resettlement, and Identity.* New Haven, Conn.: Yale University Press, 2015.

Smoot, D. E. "Commissioners OK Federal Use of County Courthouse." *Muskogee Phoenix,* June 14, 2021. https://www.muskogeephoenix.com/news/commissioners-ok-federal-use-of-county-courthouse/article_fa9f8dda-f35d-5d19-8b61-f2da54dcc6b1.html.

Snyder, Christina. *Slavery in Indian Country: The Changing Face of Captivity in Early America.* Cambridge, Mass.: Harvard University Press, 2012.

Snyder, Dan. "Gov. Stitt: 'Don't think there's ever been a bigger issue' for Oklahoma than McGirt Ruling." KOKH (Oklahoma City), May 17, 2021. https://okcfox.com/news/local/gov-stitt-dont-think-theres-ever-been-a-bigger-issue-for-oklahoma-than-mcgirt-ruling.

St. Jean, Wendy. *Remaining Chickasaw in Indian Territory, 1830s–1907.* Tuscaloosa: University of Alabama Press, 2011.

Standard & Poor's Financial Services. "Bulletin: Oklahoma's State, Local Credit Ratings Unlikely to Be Affected in the Near Term by the SCOTUS Decision on Reservations." Thomas J. Zemetis, Primary Credit Analyst. S&P Global Ratings, July 13, 2020. https://www.spglobal.com/ratings/en/research/articles/200713-bulletin-oklahoma-s-state-local-credit-ratings-unlikely-to-be-affected-in-the-near-term-by-the-scotus-decis-11572905.

"State of Oklahoma, Choctaw Nation of Oklahoma, Chickasaw Nation, City of Oklahoma City Water Settlement, August 2016." Water Unity Oklahoma, accessed November 15, 2021. https://www.waterunityok.com/media/1075/agreement-160808.pdf.

Stremlau, Rose. *Sustaining the Cherokee Family: Kinship and the Allotment of an Indigenous Nation*. Chapel Hill: University of North Carolina Press, 2011.

Strickland, Rennard. *Fire and the Spirits: Cherokee Law from Clan to Court*. Norman: University of Oklahoma Press, 1975.

———. *The Indians in Oklahoma*. Norman: University of Oklahoma Press, 1980.

Sturtevant, Chuck. "Is Oklahoma Indian Country? Law, Reckoning, and Recognition." *Anthropology News*, January 18, 2019. https://anthrobook forum.americananthro.org/index.php/2019/01/18/is-oklahoma-indian -country/.

Swanton, John R. *Social Organization and Social Usages of the Indians of the Creek Confederacy*. Forty-Second Annual Report of the Bureau of American Ethnology. Washington: U.S. Government Printing Office, 1928.

Tomlinson, Joe. "Courts 'in Limbo' as Ottawa County Tribes Await Reservation Rulings." NonDoc Media, June 18, 2021. https://nondoc.com/2021 /06/18/ottawa-county-tribes-await-reservation-rulings/.

———. "Federal Notice on Surface Coal Mining a 'Significant Loss of Power by Oklahoma.'" NonDoc Media, June 8, 2021. https://nondoc.com /2021/06/08/federal-notice-on-surface-coal-mining-a-significant-loss -of-power-by-oklahoma/.

Trigger, Bruce, ed. *Handbook of North American Indians*. Vol. 15, *Northeast*. Washington, D.C.: Smithsonian Institution, 1978.

United States Department of Justice. "Eastern District of Oklahoma Federal Grand Jury Hands Down Record Number of Indictments: Impact of the McGirt Decision Continuing to Grow in the Eastern District." United States Attorney's Office, Eastern District of Oklahoma, April 22, 2021. https://www.justice.gov/usao-edok/pr/eastern-district-oklahoma -federal-grand-jury-hands-down-record-number-indictments.

United States Department of Justice Archives. "The Major Crimes Act—18 U.S.C. § 1153." Criminal Resource Manual, CRM 679. https://www .justice.gov/archives/jm/criminal-resource-manual-679-major-crimes -act-18-usc-1153.

Usner, Daniel. *Indians, Settlers, and Slaves in a Frontier Exchange Economy: The Lower Mississippi Valley before 1783*. Chapel Hill: University of North Carolina Press, 1992.

Warren, Stephen, *The Shawnees and Their Neighbors, 1795–1870*. Urbana: University of Illinois Press, 2005.

Waselkov, Gregory A. *A Conquering Spirit: Fort Mims and the Redstick War of 1813–1814*. Tuscaloosa: University of Alabama Press, 2009.

———. "Seventeenth-Century Trade in the Colonial Southeast." *Southeastern Archaeology* 8 (1989): 120–28.

Waselkov, Gregory A., Linda Derry, and Ned J. Jenkins. "The Archaeology of Mabila's Cultural Landscape." In *The Search for Mabila: The Decisive*

Battle between Hernando de Soto and Chief Tascalusa, edited by Vernon James Knight Jr., 227–44. Tuscaloosa: University of Alabama Press, 2009.

Waselkov, Gregory A., and Marvin T. Smith. "Upper Creek Archaeology." In *Indians of the Greater Southeast: Historical Archaeology and Ethnohistory*, edited by Bonnie G. McEwan, 242–64. Gainesville: University Press of Florida, 2000.

Wayne, Fraser F., John Christian, Chris Heasley, Anna G. Rotman, Brian C. Greene, and James Dolphin. "Implications for the Energy Industry in Light of the U.S. Supreme Court Decision in *McGirt v. Oklahoma*." Kirkland & Ellis, LLC, August 13, 2020. https://www.kirkland.com /publications/blog-post/2020/08/supreme-court-mcgirt-decision.

Weaver, Kristen. "Muscogee (Creek) Nation Receives Grant to Aid Influx of New Criminal Cases." News on 6 (Tulsa, Okla.), September 17, 2020. https://www.newson6.com/story/5f641f670811e473c77fa812/muscogee -creek-nation-receives-grant-to-aid-influx-of-new-criminal-cases.

Wesson, Cameron B. *Households and Hegemony: Early Creek Prestige Goods, Symbolic Capital, and Social Power.* Tuscaloosa: University of Alabama Press, 2008.

———. "Prestige Goods, Symbolic Capital, and Social Power in the Protohistoric Southeast." In *Between Contacts and Colonies: Archaeological Perspectives on the Protohistoric Southeast*, edited by Cameron B. Wesson and Mark A. Rees, 110–25. Lincoln: University of Nebraska Press, 2002.

Westney, Andrew. "Justices Sink Many Okla. Petitions Seeking to Upend McGirt." Law360, January 24, 2022. https://www.law360.com/articles /1457923/justices-sink-many-okla-petitions-seeking-to-upend-mcgirt.

———. "Tribal Leaders Say Okla. Needlessly Stirring Fears over McGirt." Law360, September 8, 2021. https://www.law360.com/articles/1419373 /tribal-leaders-say-okla-needlessly-stirring-fears-over-mcgirt.

White, Mark Andrew. "On to Oklahoma: Reportage, Spectacle, and Statehood." In *Picturing Indian Territory: Portraits of the Land That Became Oklahoma, 1819–1907*, edited by B. Byron Price, 77–124. Norman: University of Oklahoma Press, 2016.

Wilkins, David E., and K. Tsianina Lomawaima. *Uneven Ground: American Indian Sovereignty and Federal Law.* Norman: University of Oklahoma Press, 2001.

Winn, William W. *The Triumph of the Ecunnau-Nuxulgee: Land Speculators, George M. Troup, State Rights, and the Removal of the Creek Indians from Georgia and Alabama, 1825–38.* Macon, Ga.: Mercer University Press, 2015.

Work, L. Susan. *The Seminole Nation of Oklahoma: A Legal History.* Norman: University of Oklahoma Press, 2010.

Worth, John E. "The Lower Creeks: Origins and Early History." In *Indians of the Greater Southeast: Historical Archaeology and Ethnohistory*, edited by Bonnie G. McEwan, 265–98. Gainesville: University Press of Florida, 2000.

Wright, Alice P., and Edward R. Henry, eds. *Early and Middle Woodland Landscapes of the Southeast.* Gainesville: University Press of Florida, 2013.

Zelio, Judy. *Piecing Together the State-Tribal Tax Puzzle.* Denver, Colo.: National Conference of State Legislatures, 2005.

Zellar, Gary. *African Creeks: Estelvste and the Creek Nation.* Norman: University of Oklahoma Press, 2007.

COURT DOCUMENTS

Agua Caliente Band v. Coachella Valley Water Dist., 849 F.3d 1262 (9th Cir. 2017).

Application of Otter Tail Power Co., 451 N.W.2d 95 (North Dakota 1990).

Arizona v. California, 373 U.S. 546 (1963).

Arizona Public Service Commission v. Environmental Protection Agency, 211 F.3d 1280 (D.C. Cir. 2000).

Atkinson Trading Company v. Shirley, 532 U.S. 645 (2001).

Attorney's Process, Inc. v. Sac & Fox Tribe, 609 F.3d 927 (8th Cir. 2010).

Big Horn County Electric Cooperative v. Adams, 219 F.3d 944 (9th Cir. 2000).

Big Horn County Electric Cooperative v. Alden Big Man, 2021 WL 754143 (Dist. of Montana Feb. 26, 2021).

Bosse v. Oklahoma, 484 P.3d 286 (Okla. Crim. App. 2021).

Brendale v. Confederated Tribes and Bands of Yakima Indian Nation, 492 U.S. 408 (1989).

Brief for Oklahoma, *Jimcy McGirt, Petitioner v. State of Oklahoma, Respondent*, No. 18-9526 (March 13, 2020).

Brief for Petitioner Oklahoma, *Mike Carpenter v. Patrick Dwayne Murphy*, No. 17-1107 (July 23, 2018).

Brief for Petitioner, *Tommy Sharp v. Patrick Dwayne Murphy*, 140 S.Ct. 2412, No. 17-1107 (U.S. July 9, 2020), 2018 WL 3572365.

Brief of Amici Curiae Historians, Legal Scholars, and Cherokee Nation in Support of Petitioner, *Jimcy McGirt, Petitioner v. Oklahoma, Respondent*, No. 18-9526 (S.Ct. Feb. 11, 2020).

Bryan v. Itasca County, 426 U.S. 373 (1976).

Bugenig v. Hoopa Valley Tribe, 5 NICS App. 37 (Hoopa Ct. App. 1998).

Bugenig v. Hoopa Valley Tribe, 266 F.3d 1201 (9th Cir. 2001).

Caliente Band v. Coachella Valley Water Dist., 849 F.3d 12621 (9th Cir. 2017).

California v. Cabazon Band of Mission Indians, 480 U.S. 202 (1987).

Mike Carpenter v. Patrick Dwayne Murphy, 139 S.Ct. 626, No. 17-1107 (U.S. Nov. 27, 2018).

Mike Carpenter v. Patrick Dwayne Murphy, No. 17-1107 (U.S. June 27, 2019).

Cass County v. Leech Lake Band of Chippewa Indians, 524 U.S. 103 (1998).

Cherokee Nation v. Georgia, 30 U.S. 1 (1831).

Choctaw Nation v. Oklahoma, 397 U.S. 620 (1970).

City of Albuquerque v. Browner, 97 F.3d 415 (10th Cir. 1996).

City of Sherrill v. Oneida Indian Nation, 544 U.S. 197 (2005).

Colville Confederated Tribes v. Boyd Walton, Jr., 647 F.2d 42 (9th Cir. 1981).

County of Yakima v. Confederated Tribes and Bands of the Yakima Nation, 502 U.S. 251 (1992).

DeCoteau v. District County Court for Tenth Judicial District, 420 U.S. 425 (1975).

Devils Lake Sioux Indian Tribe v. North Dakota Public Service Commission, 896 F. Supp. 955 (D. N.D. 1995).

Ex parte Crow Dog, 109 U.S. 556 (1883).

First Specialty Ins. v. Confederated Tribes of the Grand Ronde Comm., Case A-05-09-001 (Grand Ronde Ct. App. 2006).

General Order No. 20-29. In the Matter of Admission of Out-of-District Attorneys (Nov. 5, 2020). United States District Court for the Eastern District of Oklahoma. https://www.oked.uscourts.gov/sites/oked/files /general-ordes/GO_20-29.pdf.

Hagen v. Utah, 510 U.S. 399 (1994).

Hepburn v. Griswold, 75 U.S. 603 (1870).

Herrera v. Wyoming, 139 S.Ct. 1686 (2019).

Iowa Mutual Insurance Company v. LaPlante, 480 U.S. 9 (1987).

Johnson and Graham's Lessee v. McIntosh, 21 U.S. 543 (1823).

Knighton v. Cedarville Rancheria, 922 F.3d 892 (9th Cir. 2019).

Legal Tender Cases, *Knox v. Lee*, 79 U.S. 457 (1871).

Lone Wolf v. Hitchcock, 187 U.S. 553 (1903).

Mattz v. Arnett, 412 U.S. 481 (1973).

McClanahan v. Arizona State Tax Commission, 411 U.S. 164 (1973).

McGirt v. Oklahoma, ___U.S.___, 140 S.Ct. 2452 (2020).

McGirt v. Oklahoma, No. PC-2018-1057, *order issued* (Okla. Crim. App. Feb. 25, 2019).

Menominee Tribe of Indians v. United States, 391 U.S. 404 (1968).

Merrion v. Jicarilla Apache Tribe, 455 U.S. 130 (1982).

Minersville School District v. Gobitis, 310 U.S. 586 (1940).

Minnesota v. Mille Lacs Band of Chippewa Indians, 526 U.S. 172 (1999).

Mississippi Band of Choctaw Indians v. Holyfield, 490 U.S. 30 (1989).

Moe v. Confederated Salish and Kootenai Tribes, 425 U.S. 463 (1976).

Montana v. United States, 450 U.S. 544 (1981).

Montana v. United States EPA, 137 F.3d 1135 (9th Cir. 1998).

Patrick Dwayne Murphy v. Marty Sirmons, 497 F.Supp.2d 1257 (E.D. Okla. 2007).

Patrick Dwayne Murphy v. State of Oklahoma, 47 P.3d 876 (Okla. Crim. App. 2002).

Patrick Dwayne Murphy v. State of Oklahoma, 124 P.3d 1198 (Okla. Crim. App. 2005).

Patrick Dwayne Murphy v. Terry Royal, 875 F.3d 896 (10th Cir. 2017).

National Farmers Union Insurance Cos. v. Crow Tribe of Indians, 471 U.S. 845 (1985).

Nebraska v. Parker, 136 S.Ct. 1072 (2016).

Nevada, et al. v. Hicks, et al., 533 U.S. 353 (2001).

New Mexico v. Mescalero Apache Tribe, 462 U.S. 324 (1983).

North Central Electric Cooperative v. North Dakota Public Service Commission, 837 N.W.2d 138 (N.D. 2013).

Oklahoma v. Castro-Huerta, __U.S.__, No. 21-429, 2022 WL 2334307 (June 29, 2022).

Oklahoma v. Hathcoat, No. 21-253, Pet. Cert., 2021 WL 3726207 (Aug. 16, 2021).

Oklahoma Tax Commission v. Chickasaw Nation, 515 U.S. 450 (1995).

Oklahoma Tax Commission v. Citizen Band, Potawatomi Indian Tribe of Oklahoma, 498 U.S. 505 (1991).

Oklahoma Tax Commission v. Sac and Fox Nation, 508 U.S. 114 (1993).

Oliphant v. Suquamish Indian Tribe, 435 U.S. 191 (1978).

Opinion of Oklahoma Attorney General, No. 79-216 (Dec. 31, 1979).

Order Directing the Parties to File Supplemental Briefs, *Mike Carpenter v. Patrick Wayne Murphy*, 139 S.Ct. 626 (2018).

Phillip v. U.S. Dist. Court for Middle Dist. of Tennessee, 138 S.Ct. 464 (2017).

Pit River Tribe v. United States Forest Service, 469 F.3d 768 (9th Cir. 2006).

Plains Commerce Bank v. Long Family Land & Cattle Co., 554 U.S. 316 (2008).

Reed v. Salazar, 744 F.Supp.2d 90 (Dist. of D.C. 2010).

Rosebud Sioux Tribe v. Kneip, 430 U.S. 584 (1977).

Santa Clara Pueblo v. Martinez, 436 U.S. 49 (1978).

Santa Rosa Band of Indians v. Kings County, 532 F.2d 655 (9th Cir. 1975).

Segundo v. Rancho Mirage, 813 F.2d 1387 (9th Cir. 1987).

Seymour v. Superintendent of Washington State Penitentiary, 368 U.S. 351 (1962).

Tommy Sharp v. Patrick Dwayne Murphy, 140 S.C. 2412, No. 17-1107 (2020).

Tommy Sharp v. Patrick Dwayne Murphy, 591 U.S.___, No. 17-1107 (U.S. July 9, 2020).

Skokomish Indian Tribe v. Mosbarger, 7 NICS App. 90 (Skokomish Ct. App. 2006).

Solem v. Bartlett, 465 U.S. 463 (1984).

South Dakota v. Yankton Sioux Tribe, et al., 522 U.S. 329 (1998).

State v. Owl Creek Irrigation District Members, 753 P.2d 76 (Wyo. 1988).

Strate v. A-1 Contractors, 520 U.S. 438 (1997).

Talton v. Mayes, 163 U.S. 376 (1896).

Transcript of Oral Argument, *Carpenter v. Murphy*, No. 14-1406 (Nov. 27, 2018).

Transcript of Oral Argument, *Jimcy McGirt v. Oklahoma*, No. 18-9526 (May 11, 2020).

T.S. v. Independent School District No. 54, Stroud, Oklahoma, 535 U.S. 927 (2002).

United States v. Ahtanum Irrigation District, 235 F.2d 321 (9th Cir. 1956).

United States v. Celestine, 215 U.S. 278 (1909).

United States v. Cooley, ___U.S.___, 141 S.Ct. 1638 (2021).

United States v. Dion, 476 U.S. 734 (1986).

United States v. Mazurie, 419 U.S. 544 (1975).

United States v. McBratney, 104 U.S. 621 (1881).

United States v. Powers, 305 U.S. 527 (1939).

United States v. Prentiss, 273 F.3d 1277 (10th Cir. 2001).

United States v. Sioux Nation of Indians, 448 U.S. 371 (1980).

United States v. Thunder Hawk, 127 F.3d 705 (8th Cir. 1997).

United States v. Winans, 198 U.S. 371 (1905).

Washington v. Confederated Tribes of Colville Indian Reservation, 447 U.S. 134 (1980).

Washington v. Washington Commercial Passenger Fishing Vessel Association, 443 U.S. 658 (1979).

Washington State Dept. of Licensing v. Cougar Den, Inc., ___U.S.___, 139 S.Ct. 1000 (2019) (Gorsuch, J., concurring).

Water Wheel Camp Recreational Area, Inc. v. LaRance, 642 F.3d 802 (9th Cir. 2011).

West Virginia State Board of Education v. Barnette, 319 U.S. 624 (1943).

Western Watersheds Project, et al. v. Bureau of Land Management of the U.S. Department of the Interior, et al., No. 3:21–cv–0103–MMD–CLB (Dist. of Nevada July 28, 2021).

Williams v. Lee, 358 U.S. 217 (1959).

Williams v. United States, 327 U.S. 711 (1946).

Winters v. United States, 207 U.S. 564 (1908).

Worcester v. Georgia, 31 U.S. (6 Pet.) 515 (1832).

Max Julian Wright v. United States, 138 S.Ct. 2026 (2018).

Wyoming v. United States, 492 U.S. 406 (1989).

STATUTES AND REGULATIONS

C.F.R. (Code of Federal Regulations)

25 C.F.R. Part 213 (2020). Code of Federal Regulations, Title 25: Indians, Chapter 1: Bureau of Indian Affairs, Department of the Interior, Subchapter I: Energy and Minerals, Part 213: Leasing of Restricted Lands of Members of Five Civilized Tribes, Oklahoma, for Mining.

Muscogee (Creek) Codes

Muscogee (Creek) Nation Code Annotated, Title 27: Judicial Procedures, Section 7-101: Recognition of Foreign Judgments.

Oklahoma Statutes

Oklahoma Statutes, Title 12: Civil Procedure, Chapter 12: Judgement, Section 728: Standards Extending Full Faith and Credit to Records and Proceedings (1992).

U.S.C. (United States Codes)

16 U.S.C. § 470bb. United States Code, Title 16: Conservation, Chapter 1A: Historic Sites, Buildings, Objects, and Antiquities, Subchapter II: National Historic Preservation, Section 470bb: Definitions.

18 U.S.C. § 13. United States Code, Title 18: Crimes and Criminal Procedures, Part I: Crimes, Chapter 13: General Provisions, Section 13: Laws of States Adopted for Areas within Federal Jurisdiction.

18 U.S.C. § 1151. United States Code, Title 18: Crimes and Criminal Procedures, Part I: Crimes, Chapter 53: Indians, Section 1151: Indian Country Defined.

18 U.S.C. § 1152. United States Code, Title 18: Crimes and Criminal Procedures, Part I: Crimes, Chapter 53: Indians, Section 1152: Laws Governing.

18 U.S.C. § 1153. United States Code, Title 18: Crimes and Criminal Procedures, Part I: Crimes, Chapter 53: Indians, Section 1153: Offenses Committed within Indian Country.

18 U.S.C. § 1170. United States Code, Title 18: Crimes and Criminal Procedures, Part I: Crimes, Chapter 53: Indians, Section 1170: Illegal Trafficking in Native American Human Remains and Cultural Items.

25 U.S.C. §§ 331–58. United States Code, Title 25: Indians, Chapter 9: Allotment of Indian Lands, Section 331: Allotments on Reservations; Irrigable and Nonirrigable Lands, through Section 358: Repeal of Statutory Provisions Relating to Survey, Classification, and Allotments Which Provide for Repayment out of Indian Moneys.

25 U.S.C. §§ 381–90. United States Code, Title 25: Indians, Chapter 11: Irrigation of Allotted Lands, Section 381: Irrigation Lands; Regulation of Use of Water, through Section 390: Concessions on Reservoir Sites and Other Lands in Indian Irrigation Projects; Leases for Agricultural, Grazing, and Other Purposes.

25 U.S.C. §§ 450–58hh. United States Code, Title 25: Indians, Chapter 14: Miscellaneous, Subchapter II: Indian Self-Determination and Education Assistance, Section 450: Transferred, through Section 458hh: Transferred.

25 U.S.C. § 1302. United States Code, Title 25: Indians, Chapter 15: Constitutional Rights of Indians, Subchapter I: Generally, Section 1302: Constitutional Rights.

25 U.S.C. § 1304. United States Code, Title 25: Indians, Chapter 15: Constitutional Rights of Indians, Subchapter I: Generally, Section 1304: Tribal Jurisdiction over Crimes of Domestic Violence.

25 U.S.C. § 1901. United States Code, Title 25: Indians, Chapter 21: Indian Child Welfare, Section 1901: Congressional Findings.

25 U.S.C. § 1911. United States Code, Title 25: Indians, Chapter 21: Indian Child Welfare, Subchapter I: Child Custody Proceedings, Section 1911: Indian Tribe Jurisdiction over Indian Child Custody Proceedings.

25 U.S.C. §§ 3001–13. United States Code, Title 25: Indians, Chapter 32: Native American Graves Protection and Repatriation, Section 3001: Definitions, through Section 3013: Enforcement.

30 U.S.C. § 1291. United States Code, Title 30: Mineral Lands and Mining, Chapter 25: Surface Mining Control and Reclamation, Subchapter VII: Administrative and Miscellaneous Provisions, Section 1291: Definitions.

54 U.S.C. §§ 300101, 300319, 302701–2. United States Code, Title 54: National Park Service and Related Programs, Subtitle III: National Preservation Programs, Division A: Historic Preservation, Subdivision 1: General Provisions, Section 300101: Policy, Section 300319: Tribal Land, Section 302701: Program to Assist Indian Tribes in Preserving Historic Property, and Section 302702: Indian Tribe to Assume Functions of State Historic Preservation Officer.

INDEX

Printed in the USA
CPSIA information can be obtained
at www.ICGtesting.com
CBHW031359210524
8884CB00002B/46